Lyrics of Sunshine and Shadow

LYRICS
of
SUNSHINE
and
SHADOW

THE TRAGIC COURTSHIP AND MARRIAGE
OF PAUL LAURENCE DUNBAR AND
ALICE RUTH MOORE

*A History of Love and Violence among the
African American Elite*

Eleanor Alexander

New York University Press

New York and London

NEW YORK UNIVERSITY PRESS
New York and London

Library of Congress Cataloging-in-Publication Data
Alexander, Eleanor (Eleanor C.)
Lyrics of sunshine and shadow : the tragic courtship and marriage of
Paul Laurence Dunbar and Alice Ruth Moore : a history of love and
violence among the African American elite / Eleanor Alexander.
    p.   cm.
Includes bibliographical references and index.
ISBN 0-8147-0696-7 (acid-free paper)
1. Dunbar, Paul Laurence, 1872–1906—Marriage. 2. Dunbar-Nelson,
Alice Moore, 1875–1935—Marriage. 3. Authors' spouses—United
States—Biography. 4. Authors, American—20th century—Biography.
5. Poets, American—19th century—Biography. 6. Married people—
United States—Biography. 7. African American women authors—
Biography. 8. African American authors—Biography. 9. African
Americans—Biography.   I. Title.
PS1557 .A76 2001
811'.4—dc21   2001002493

Manufactured in the United States of America

10 9 8 7 6 5 4 3 2 1

For the family

CONTENTS

All illustrations appear as a group following page 86.

Center, Washington, D.C., and Gloria Harper of Dillard University in Louisiana.

Finally, I extend my deepest appreciation to my buddies. I am ever so grateful for the support I got from Richard Angel, Charles Beard, Dan Cavicchi, Gladys-Marie Fry, Nina Guzzetta, Walter Harper, Lloyd Monroe, Rolanda Rawlings, Mary Jane Rubinski, Dan Strother, and Mel Webb.

We did it!

ACKNOWLEDGMENTS

I did not write this book alone. Colleagues, librarians, archivists, friends, and family all aided in crafting this dialogue. Not one of them, however, is responsible for any errors this volume may contain, or for its shortcomings. Those I crafted all by myself.

My thanks to all who brought this project to fruition. I am especially grateful to the endless support and encouragement of Professors Thadious M. Davis and Nell Irvin Painter. I thank them, too, for their generous gifts of time, knowledge, and expert advice. Sincere thanks as well to Professor Mary Jo Buhle for her enthusiastic advocacy of this project and her close and critical reading of the drafts. To Professors Dorothy Denniston, Anani Dzidzienyo, Michael S. Harper, Rhett Jones, Aishah Rahman, and other members of the Brown University community who gave aid when it was most needed, I say many thanks to you. And I will not forget the support and encouragement of my colleagues at the Georgia Institute of Technology. For their detailed critique of the manuscript, I thank Professors Georgia Persons and Don Flamming. It took time, energy, and thoughtfulness to do what they did, and I am ever mindful of that.

I wish also to acknowledge the role of some very generous colleagues—Professors Catherine Clinton, Sybil Kein, Wilson J. Moses, and Rosalyn Terborg-Penn. For providing knowledge on nineteenth-century health care, I thank these medical doctors: Stephen DeZio, Alicia Monroe, and James R. Ralph. And since research is impossible without the aid of librarians and library staff members, I thank those at the John D. Rockefeller and John Hay Libraries at Brown University, and the amiable employees at the Providence, Rhode Island, Public Library, the Rochambeau Branch. This means you: Anne Louise Attar, Jacqueline Cooper, Bonnie Lilienthal, Timothy J. McGinn, Adam Misturado, Donna Snead, Dhana Whiteing, and Michael Vallone. Thanks also to Marva Best of the Moorland Spingarn Research

INTRODUCTION

On February 1, 1902, T. Thomas Fortune, the mercurial African American editor of the *New York Age* newspaper, slipped a bit of gossip into his letter to Booker T. Washington. Wedged between weighty paragraphs on "race" issues was a juicy tidbit on Fortune's drinking chum, the gifted African American writer Paul Laurence Dunbar (1872–1906):

> Saturday night [January 25, 1902] Dunbar went home and tried to kill his wife. He left Washington on the 12 o'clock train, and [has] not been heard from. . . . He is a high class brute, and I will tell you what led up to it when we meet. His family has left home, on the advice of friends. . . . I am sorry for them, as they are helpless.[1]

Five days later, Fortune inserted in a follow-up letter to the same correspondent: "The whole Dunbar business is disgusting and pathetic."[2]

Revelation of the "disgusting, pathetic" business might have shocked some of the public. Viewed from afar, Alice Ruth Moore Dunbar (1875–1935) and Paul were an ideal pair living charmed lives. They occupied a unique position for African Americans in the stringent class and racial climate existing at the turn of the twentieth century. The Dunbars were a celebrated couple, members of the African American upper crust. They even moved in some upper strata Euro-American circles, where African Americans were seldom tolerated. Their accomplishments, and perhaps Alice's mulatto complexion, accorded them these privileges. Paul is practically forgotten today, but with the death of Frederick Douglass in 1895, young Paul became the nation's second most famous African American, ranking just below Booker T. Washington, noted educator and powerbroker. Paul enjoyed an international reputation as poet, novelist, short-story writer, essayist, lyricist, and spokesperson for "the race." Although the author of exquisite mainstream poetry, he was lauded as the best African American writer of southern plantation literature—that genre of black dialect verse and stories about good times on the old

| 1 |

plantation. It was a distinction he grew to despise. By 1902, when his friend T. Thomas Fortune accused him of trying to kill his wife, Paul was at the peak of his career. His prodigious output, since a first book of poems in 1893, included five other poetry volumes, four novels, and two collections of short stories. Moreover, numerous articles, poems, and stories appeared in newspapers and national magazines, and he wrote three unpublished plays.[3] His avid readers included both blacks and whites. At this point in his life, Paul was a legend in his own mind and time. "They know that I am a poet," he wrote unabashedly of a group of Euro-American fans, "and have made it a point to inform me that my . . . verse has afforded me the right to go down in history as one of America's greatest writers."[4] His racially integrated public clamored for autographs, and the nation abounded with "Dunbareans," Paul's term for the hordes of amateur and professional elocutionists reciting his works at private and public events.[5]

But more than the popular writer's poems were on the lips of his fans; so too was his name. It was a household word. Already admirers were affixing the appellation "Paul Laurence Dunbar" to businesses, organizations, and institutions.[6] Paul's talent and fame also attracted contemporary luminaries. The late Frederick Douglass had befriended him, while William Dean Howells, one of America's foremost literary critics, was credited with discovering the thirty-year-old poet. Paul was, furthermore, the sole African American invited to participate in William McKinley's presidential inauguration in 1901, and he boasted of more than a nodding acquaintance with the White House's occupant in 1902, Theodore Roosevelt.[7] The son of former slaves, Paul had risen from rags to riches. He was brilliant, charming, and a fashion dandy. On the surface, then, life appeared to be just grand for this young poet from Dayton, Ohio. And for his winsome wife, Alice.

They had been married for almost four years in 1902, the year of Paul's brutal attack. Since their marriage in 1898, the public viewed her mainly as Mrs. Paul Laurence Dunbar, in accordance with polite social customs. Although this identity often cloaked her accomplishments, Alice relished the limelight it provided. Known as "that pretty yaller girl,"[8] she was also a "noteworthy representative of the educated, cultured and refined class of colored women in the United States to-day . . . a worthy type of progressive womanhood."[9]

Alice was haughty, regal, talented, and as intellectually gifted as Paul. She was considered a beauty and had the features and skin color that allowed her to pass for white. She did so when she found it convenient. A former teacher and journalist who penned "excellent articles in behalf of race and sex,"[10] Alice, like Paul, was an author and poet: she had published two books.[11] Both were collection of poems and stories dealing primarily with Creole characters in her native city of New Orleans. The public viewed her marriage to Paul as a union of poets. They were thought to be a perfect, idyllic pair. Alice fostered this image, writing: "We worked together, read together, and I flattered myself that I helped him in his work. I was his amanuensis and secretary, and he was good enough to write poem after poem 'for me' he said."[12]

Such an ardent overtone verified what seemed to be a real-life fairy tale. Alice and Paul's romance was a fable perfect for its time. In elite African American communities, the Dunbars were revered role models. Blacks wondered how most white Americans could acknowledge this gifted, educated, cultured couple and continue to maintain that African Americans were shiftless, ignorant, and filthy.[13] Race was an irrefutable factor in African American courtship and marriage, and seemingly the Dunbars were above stereotypes. A journalist wrote: "[T]heir influence is especially significant in eradicating unjust prejudices, as bright, intelligent minds prove the fallacy of racial discrimination. . . . [They represent] the advancement which the entire race is capable of making."[14]

The Dunbars also epitomized romantic love. Nineteenth- century America was enamored with the concept. It was heralded as the one true road to happiness—especially for women. Zealous believers proclaimed love to be the core of the nation's most important social institution—the middle-class family. To members of elite African American society, Alice and Paul were the black Brownings. Friends considered their courtship and marriage "a regular [Robert] Browning [1812–1889] and [Elizabeth] Barrett [1806–1861] affair."[15] Paul embraced the characterization that aligned Alice and himself with the married British poets, writing: "Dear, it is not all foolishness that people talk about this Mr. and Mrs. Browning affair of ours—We have the opportunity of showing our friends and the world a beautiful example of a harmony of hearts joined by a sympathy of minds."[16]

Alice and Paul were indeed like the Brownings. Both Paul and Robert Browning had introduced themselves to their prospective brides through the mail, with a letter complimenting the women's literature. Because of parental objections, the sets of lovers courted covertly, mainly by correspondence. Robert Browning visited Elizabeth Barrett a few times during their clandestine romance. But Alice and Paul exchanged "letters that make one's very heart leap for joy" for almost two years before they actually saw each other.[17] When they finally met, they became engaged, keeping it a secret from Alice's family for close to a year. Then, like the Brownings, Paul and Alice eloped. As if fated to their predecessors' scheme, the new Mrs. Dunbar rhapsodized: "Paul, my precious . . . thus far we have done as our own models. There is but one thing left—for you to write a 'Pippa Passes' [*sic*] and I an 'Aurora Leigh' [*sic*]. Then we can rest content. (Oh conceit!)"[18]

But the Dunbars did not rest content, despite the romanticism surrounding their union. In spite of great expectations and material success, an inebriated Paul physically assaulted Alice on January 25, 1902, and according to his friend T. Thomas Fortune, tried to kill her.[19] Alice confirmed the allegation: "He came home one night in a beastly condition. I went to him to help him to bed—and he behaved . . . disgracefully. He left that night, and I was ill for weeks with peritonitis brought on by his kicks."[20] In pre-penicillin America at the turn of the twentieth century, peritonitis could be a deadly disorder.

This potentially fatal beating was not the first instance of abuse. Psychological, verbal, and physical battering suffused the relationship, even before the storybook elopement of March 6, 1898. Although scholars skirt the issue, letters between the Dunbars clearly show that on a November night in 1897, during their engagement period, Paul, in a drunken state, raped Alice, leaving her with internal injuries requiring medical treatment.[21]

Similarly, scholars overlook evidence demonstrating that Paul had gonorrhea at the time, and in all probability, infected Alice.[22]

The Dunbars' bittersweet romance vacillated between "days [that] were delightful beyond compare . . . [and] a dog and cat existence," wrote Alice.[23] While that brutal night of January 25, 1902, was not the first time that Paul had physically assaulted Alice, she made certain it was the last. She refused to see him again. For two years he wrote her letters of love, contrariness, contriteness, and news. Alice answered only once, and in one word: "No!"[24]

Paul Laurence Dunbar died at 3:30 P.M. on Friday, February 9, 1906, at his home in Dayton, Ohio.[25] He was thirty-three years old. His death came four years after the last time he was with his wife, that January 1902 night when he brutally beat her. While romantics claimed Paul died of a broken heart, the death certificate listed tuberculosis. The day following Paul's death, Alice boarded a streetcar in Wilmington, Delaware, where she lived and worked as a teacher. Only when she opened her newspaper did she learn of her famous husband's death.[26]

This book examines the most private of private history—romantic love, courtship, marriage, and sexuality. For more than two decades, social historians have explored these elements of mainstream middle-class history, but the intimate history of the African American middle-class/elite is basically unexplored.[27] This glimpse of the subject unfolds through the Dunbars' narrative. Their complex drama is much more than the story of one couple's romance. As a lived experience, it is a private history, with causal factors and effects anchored in public history—that is, contemporary social, political, and economic practices. Historians agree that the features of any epoch or event depend on the general structure of its given society and the conditions of life therein. The same applies to an intimate social history. Along with sociopolitical factors, the Dunbars' relationship was shaped by the legacy of slavery and the ideologies of nineteenth-century race, class, romantic love, and gender-role expectations—the prescribed and institutionalized cultural concepts of femininity and masculinity.[28] This book interprets the Dunbars' history through these elements.

The Dunbars did not live, love, and eventually hate in a vacuum. The same external factors shaping their courtship and marriage enveloped the intimate lives of other elite African Americans. There is a generalized nature to courtship and marriage. The term "courtship," for example, refers to a multilevel, multifaceted group of relational patterns between men and women. As a product of its time, the courtship of any couple in a defined culture is suggestive of the greater experience. Moreover, personal experiences, along with the shared resources of race, class, and gender affect relationships. Therefore, the Dunbars' intimate history—with its components of romantic love, courting and marriage rituals, gender inequity, and sexual and physical violence—mirrored elements in the relationships of their contemporaries.

Thus, the scope of this study is not limited to the Dunbars' romance. While I focus on the two poets, their complicated union is a means of analyzing the culture of middle-class African American courtship and marriage at the turn of the twentieth century. I argue that the Dunbars' multifaceted experience is a legitimate lens for viewing the dynamics of intimate liaisons. As a product of its time, their courtship and marriage indicate the prevailing ethos of intimacy. I argue further that the ideologies and practices of race, class, and gender shaped the Dunbars' union; and that separate spheres—the gender-segregated world of men and women—was detrimental to romantic bliss.

Accordingly, this book is a study of converging temporal rhythms. In the foreground is an analysis of the Dunbar drama, examined against a backdrop of the time period. This examination also includes those elements that make the story uniquely the Dunbars', such as their personalities and idiosyncrasies; for, as one historian accurately observes, "Real men and women do not always literally fulfill the terms of their society's prescriptions or [historians'] analytic categories."[29] This historian recognizes the significance of exploring the construction and interpretation of individual identities within a historical context and urges scholars to do so, too, relating their findings to "activities" and "specific cultural representations."[30] In this study, the Dunbars' personalities are investigated because personalities affect the culture of a courtship and marriage. Both the personal and public segments of Alice and Paul's story emanate from rich sources, including almost five hundred letters between the couple. This correspondence charts the relationship from beginning to end. Its volume and detail make the Dunbar courtship and marriage perhaps the best documented [African] American romance of the late nineteenth and early twentieth centuries. The letters, giving insight into the world of elite African American courting rituals, are a distinct contribution to African American history. Several hundred letters between Alice and Paul were compiled in a dissertation.[31] Because of its accessibility, it was used as a major source for this study, along with Dunbar manuscript collections.[32] Alice and Paul's autobiographical poems, essay, novels, and short stories are also valuable sources.

Interacting with the Dunbars' history is the temporal rhythm of contextual data—the concept of romantic love, the courtship and marriage rituals of middle-class African Americans, and the social, cultural, and political factors governing the climate in which intimate relationships developed. Journals, diaries, autobiographies, and love letters of African Americans provide primary source material here, as do advice manuals for "the race," with their prescribed idealized behavior. Also, since elite African Americans in the late nineteenth and early twentieth centuries patterned much of their lifestyle on that of mainstream America, I also use relevant Euro-American etiquette books.

What is the significance of such a study? Romantic love, courtship, and marriage are cultural products of specific eras. Although based on a trajectory of emotions, love and its manifestations can be historically contextualized, since feelings are expressed through prevailing social customs. However, the form and expression of love may vary from one historical period to another because of changing social forces.

This is evident even in terminology. Couples no longer "court," as did Alice, Paul, and their contemporaries. This process of discovery is now understood as either dating or as living together. Both these contemporary terms and their rites would have been foreign, if not improper and immoral, in late nineteenth century middle-class society. So, too, would today's public approval of premarital sex. To study intimacy, then, is to study another means of cultural change over time; it is another framework for interpreting the past. The study of courtship and marriage provides a simultaneous account of private and public life, since public policy provides the atmosphere in which intimacy develops.

For more than two decades, scholars of American social history have increasingly turned their attention to concepts of romantic love. Numerous articles have appeared, focusing on the relationships of white Americans during the nineteenth and early twentieth centuries. The courtships and marriages of the famous—such as Sam Houston or Emma Goldman—as well as the never famous comprise a voluminous, rich literature.[33] But whether famous or not, only one scholarly article on elite African American courtship and marriage appears in the literature.[34]

Two fine books deal with the courting history of white Americans during the late nineteenth century.[35] In many ways, the Dunbar love letters and those of their African American contemporaries reflect the courting customs examined in these studies of Euro-Americans. For example, one historian writes that white couples used "little girl" and "little boy" as terms of endearment in love letters. So Paul Laurence Dunbar would address Alice as "My Little Girl" in his correspondence.[36] Moreover, in her book, one of the authors of the history of mainstream courting challenges the stereotype of sexual prudery. Similarly, the Dunbars wrote about a robust sex life. It would seem, then, that in some areas, middle-class American romantic culture spanned racial barriers. Where the Dunbar drama demonstrates cross-cultural patterns, it is interpreted within the context of white, middle-class courting and marriage rituals.

The intimate history of elite African Americans is new territory. Even scholars cognizant of the richly textured and documented relationship of Paul Laurence Dunbar and Alice Ruth Moore Dunbar have minimized this vital aspect of their lives. The Dunbars' many biographers have handled their love life in varying degrees, ranging from dismissal to inclusion of fragments of the relationship.[37] The focus has been on the Dunbars' literary accomplishments, and this valuable scholarship must continue. But it is fallacious to assume that Alice and Paul valued their public life more than their personal one, especially when both threatened to commit suicide rather than live without the other.[38]

Courtship and marriage were as important to late-nineteenth, early-twentieth century African Americans as it was to that social class whose records have been used to define the history of intimacy in America. The courting season was crucial for the ebony elite. It was a period when two people decided if they could live together for the remainder of their lives, for divorce was loathsome for middle-class African Americans. Accordingly, strict rules of public etiquette and private propriety governed courtship, addressing everything from the role of race in relationships to behavior, appropriateness of love letters, engagement and marriage ceremonies, and the wife's responsibilities for a happy marriage. Middle-class marriage rituals circumscribed proper health, habits, and lifestyle. Most of these rites and rules were gender biased. Because these elements shaped the Dunbars' relationship and those of their contemporaries, I examine them in this study.

The analysis of courtship and marriage in this project uncovers another untapped area of African American history, mainly, sexuality among the elite. Sexuality has been described as erotic impulses expressed through culturally shaped behavior or rhetoric. Thus, the interaction of gendered sex roles and sexuality is revealing historical evidence. Nothing exists in the literature on middle-class African American sexuality during the Dunbars' era. Yet, the existence of African American sex manuals from the period, the Dunbars' graphic discussions of sex, as well as the sexual tension of other elite couples as revealed in love letters offer proof (although it is not needed) that sex and sexuality indeed were of concern to the black upper crust. Moreover, African American guidebooks prescribed a stricter code of sexual conduct than that evidenced in some Euro-American manuals.

No social class of Americans or African Americans was immune to violent relationships. Several months before her marriage, Alice wrote Paul about a black woman of society who had run away because of a beating by her husband. Prophetically, Alice continued: "You'd better not do me such a trick."[39] The physical and sexual assaults that Alice and women of her time endured emanated from a culture that devalued women. Wife beating, for example, was so common that some states passed laws regulating it. A major proponent of the crimes of rape and spousal abuse is institutionalized gender identity, and its natural offshoot: the ideology and practice of patriarchy. Male violence against women cannot be understood outside an analysis of this social system. This form of male privilege, as exhibited in the Dunbars' lives and in the lives of other elite African Americans, is explored in this project. So, too, is the seldom-examined area of the rape of black women at the turn of the twentieth century.

Traditionally, the scholarship on African Americans and rape has concentrated in two areas: the brutal exploitation of slave women and the politically charged black-on-white rape/lynch syndrome.[40] Only recently have historians, especially Darlene Clark Hine, Catherine Clinton, and Laura Edwards, examined the sexual assault of post–Civil War African American women.[41] They have unearthed valuable evidence through public records. Paul's rape of Alice adds another dimension to this fledgling research. It demonstrates how elite African Americans who would not risk the disgrace and scandal of public inquiry experienced the crime.

The final component of courtship and marriage examined in this study is the mythology of romantic love. Starry-eyed lovers often viewed it as the only important factor of a relationship. This fairy-tale romanticism kept Alice and Paul clinging to each other despite overwhelming evidence that they were mismatched. The most compelling nineteenth-century love myths were that love transcends and solves all problems; a woman's love can change a man; love justifies rebellion against family and friends; and one can only be fulfilled through the love of another. These themes and similar ideals are evidenced and examined in the Dunbars' history, as well as in the lives of their friends.

This book does not promise an all-inclusive exploration of late-nineteenth, early-twentieth century African American elite courtship and marriage; such is the task of many scholars. What is intended is a valid initiation of the subject through an exploration of the Dunbars' courtship and marriage and the accompanying social factors.

The book has five chapters and a conclusion. I begin with brief biographies of Paul and Alice, since personal experiences along with shared social resources comprise a relationship.

Chapter One, "The Child Is Father of the Man," examines Paul's life from his birth in 1872 until his first letter to Alice in 1895. This investigation of early family life and education contends that the factors influencing Paul's relationship with Alice were rooted in his youth. These elements included the dynamics of his family life, his great talent, poor self-image, attitudes about women, romantic love, and marriage. The chapter demonstrates that, as the son of former chattel, Paul's socialization was molded by the legacy of slavery and its resulting cultural dynamics, both in terms of his immediate family and the larger racialized African American community. Race and racism, therefore, were fundamental to intimate African American liaisons of that time.

Chapter Two, "To Escape the Reproach of Her Birth and Blood," explores Alice's development prior to her initial contact with Paul. Like him, she was a member of the generation born after slavery, and the ensuing social ethos is manifested in her upbringing. The chapter traces Alice's transformation from the illegitimate daughter of an ex-bondswoman to the educated, cultured society belle who attracted Paul's attention. In so doing, the construction of proper middle-class African American womanhood is explored. The section also looks at the intraracial tensions between dark- and light-skinned African Americans and its role in Alice's racial ambivalence, as well as her dislike of people with Paul's dark complexion.

Chapter Three, "The Wooing," examines the beginning stages of Alice and Paul's relationship against a backdrop of nineteenth-century romantic love and middle-class African American values regarding court-ship and marriage. Much of the Dunbars' story is told in their voices—through letters, poems, and autobiographical data. Since revealing one's soul to a loved one was a major tenet of romantic love, the chapter shows Alice and Paul gradually dropping the facades of initial acquaintance and unveiling more genuine selves. The importance of courtship and mar-riage to the middle class is underscored through an exploration of other courting African Americans and advice manuals. I also examine the role of love letters, the concept of the ideal mate, gender role dynamics in re-lationships, and the etiquette of courtship.

Chapter Four, "One Damned Night of Folly," interrogates the final stages of Alice and Paul's courtship, from their secret engagement in 1897 to elopement in 1898. The chapter is a study in late-nineteenth-century interpretations of romantic love with its inherent gender in-equities and sexual tension. In this rehearsal period for marriage, the en-gaged woman abandoned career goals and surrendered freedom and au-thority to her loved one. She also became her fiancé's moral guardian. This imbalance of power is explored as a factor in Paul's rape of Alice during their engagement, a crime he lightly dismissed as "one damned night of folly." The chapter further investigates this type of gendered re-sponse to sexual abuse in the late nineteenth century, ending with an analysis of social and personal factors that would cause an educated, mid-dle-class woman like Alice to marry her rapist.

Chapter Five, "Parted," uses the backdrop of late-nineteenth-cen-tury marital expectations, gendered marriage customs, and troubled relationships to explore the demise of Alice and Paul's marriage. The ever-increasing divorce rate, with women as the major plaintiffs, is ex-amined. Posited as major factors are gender power inequities, the ide-ology of companionate marriage, and spousal abuse. The chapter ends with Paul's death in 1906 and a summary of Alice's life until her de-mise in 1935.

The book confirms what has been termed the multilevel nature of courtship and marriage. Like the Dunbars' liaison, each relationship is a one-of-a-kind private history lived only by the couple involved. And yet, even highly personal experiences are modified by the prevailing cultural factors, thereby evincing generalized patterns. The Dunbar drama, then, indicates as well as any text of its time the culture of late-nineteenth, early-twentieth-century African American courtship and marriage.

ONE

The Child Is Father
of the Man

Hello, old friend, are you married?
No, I'd just as soon be buried!

> Take your matrimony with you.
> It's to me as thin as tisheu [*sic*]
> —Paul Laurence Dunbar, age 11 (1883)

One day in 1883, eleven-year-old Paul Laurence Dunbar sat down to write yet another poem.[1] Since the age of six, he had been "rhyming," as he described his juvenile craft. His inspiration came from verses in his first-grade McGuffy Reader, especially those by the British Poet Laureate, William Wordsworth.[2] Paul, who in his prime would be designated Poet Laureate of the Negro Race, did not publicize or save his early works.[3] In secret, he scribbled them in his spelling book, showing them to no one. They were not even shared with the person who was, and would remain, most important in his life—his mother, Matilda Dunbar (c. 1845–1934), a former slave.[4]

But today's poem was different. It would be shared, revised, and added to the growing pile of "stuff" by Dick, as his family called him. Also, Matilda now safeguarded these writings of her youngest son, keeping them in cardboard boxes. She had discovered that Paul was gifted when he was about seven years old. Since then, she had encouraged him in his projects and given him favorite-son treatment. Of her three children, Paul would go farthest. Matilda would see to it.

This new poem about marriage was special, written for the recent engagement of Paul's twenty-year-old half-brother, William Murphy (1864–1932). The poem is also prophetic and revealing. Tension hovers over its seemingly humorous lines. Instead of conveying the love and happiness traditionally associated with an approaching wedding, the poem speaks of distrust, if not a disdain for marriage. A psychiatrist who studied Paul's poetry believes the poet exposed himself in his work and laid "bare [his] emotional life."[5] It would seem then, that even at this early age, Paul knew the darker side of marriage. One of his many biographers contends the marriage rhyme merely expresses a typical young boy's "disgust for romance."[6] Her statement should be augmented. Paul's negative portrayal of love and marriage resulted in no small part from witnessing his parents' union. At its best, that relationship was "as thin as tisheu." Matilda and Joshua Dunbar (1823?–1885), both former slaves, had a stormy, violent union.[7] Young Paul perhaps recorded in rhyme what he had internalized about intimacy from his primary role models. His poem confirms the theory that a person's behavior is a consequence of social situations in which the individual lives, and that this person is profoundly influenced by such environments. Paul's later turbulent relationship with Alice Ruth Moore would reflect much of what he learned about love and marriage at his parents' hearth.

More than familial factors contributed to Paul's development and impacted his adult behavior. George Eliot in 1866 accurately assessed the intermingling of public policy and personal experience, writing: "There is no private life that has not been determined by a wider public life."[8] Paul was nurtured not only in a family in conflict, but also in the factionalism of his city and nation. His era was a time of paradoxes. Its glitz and glitter harbored the cultures of Social Darwinism, sexism, and racism. Alcoholism and tuberculosis flourished, as did various strains of social diseases. Class divisions became more pronounced as industrialism and the growth of big business put great wealth in the hands of few. Large numbers of southern and eastern European immigrants were perceived as threats to the Aryan predominance of the majority Euro-American population. These new immigrants often competed with the "new citizens"—recently freed African American slaves—for low-skilled wages and jobs. In such struggles, African Americans usually lost. If hired, they received less pay than other laborers. Paul's father, Joshua Dunbar, was a perpetual member of this group of itinerant, hapless job seekers.

This time period has been designated the nadir for African Americans because of the intense racism associated with skin color throughout

America. Across the nation, people of color were viewed as lazy, improvident, childlike, irresponsible, chicken-stealing, crap-shooting, razor-toting, immoral, criminal beings. As far as most whites were concerned, the end of slavery did not make people of color their equal. They refused to accept the Fourteenth Amendment making African Americans citizens and vesting them with the same rights of citizenship that other Americans had. In the South, legislators passed black codes that severely restricted the freedom of people of color. Using threats, beatings, rape, and murder, terrorist groups such as the Ku Klux Klan and Knights of the White Camellia attempted to force blacks into subordination. James D. Corrothers, one of Paul Laurence Dunbar's friends, provided further insight on the prevailing racial dynamics:

> The North promises what it *cannot* or does not fulfill; the South is not hypocritical in this respect. In the North, an ambitious Negro bumps into the colour [*sic*] line unexpectedly, on the street cars, in hotels, theaters, parks, public buildings and schools . . . at the polls and even in the church of Christ. Yet he may go a week or a year sometimes without meeting any *unusually* humiliating experience. In the South, he is given immediately to understand that he must get definitely on his side of the color line and *stay* there. (Emphasis in original)[9]

Racial strife was no stranger to Paul's small hometown of Dayton, Ohio. During slavery, Ohio had been considered by bondsmen and slave women as part of the promised land. But not during Paul's era.[10] Some late-nineteenth-century African American Daytonians believed they had been "surrounded by strong prejudice . . . since the Civil War . . . [and] that the prejudice [had] been growing stronger every year."[11] Most Euro-American residents viewed the matter differently. One commented that prejudice existed because "the old-fashioned negroes who 'knew their place' were all gone and . . . the new generation was impudent and vicious."[12] Another expressed a racist ideology that may have been the foundation for the discord, remarking: "This is the way I class the nigger among the races—(1) the white man, (2) the Mongolian, (3) the Japanese, (4) the Chinaman, (5) the dog, and (6) last, the nigger."[13]

Class added another important dimension to Paul's formative years, for he grew up in dire poverty. He was also shaped by the gendered activities and attitudes of his environment and the psychological scars his parents and nation carried from slavery. It would have been impossible for Paul to evade the influence of his cultural milieu. Most people are shaped to the form of their culture because of their enormous malleability. They are plastic to the molding force of the society in which they are born. On the pervasive nature of one's environment, one scholar notes:

> Society . . . is not something "out there" . . . but it's also "in here," part of our innermost being. Society . . . shapes our destiny, our thoughts and emotions. The structures of society become the structures of our own consciousness. Society does not stop at the surface of our skin. [It] penetrates us as much as it envelops us.[14]

Can aspects of Paul's complex, contradictory union with Alice be traced to his childhood nurturing? If so, does that mean that we are merely passive organisms, acting and reacting to the pressures of a past socialization pattern? No event, interaction, or action is the product of one variable or process. While social construction begins at birth, it is a nonending procedure that is negotiated and potentially problematic in every episode between two or more individuals. The ever-continuing socialization process, then, affords a choice. The study of a young child furnishes insights into its adult interactive patterns, and conversely the mind of the adult is a model against which child development can be measured.

The aspects of Paul that attracted Alice—his genius, talent, social charm, driving ambition, and fame—surfaced in his childhood and youth, and he acknowledged the impact of these early years on his adult life. When, at the height of his career, a friend asked: "Who has made it possible for you to loom so far and above any of your people? Whose fine nature do you possess? To whom are you indebted for your bright intelect [*sic*]?"[15] Paul answered: "[G]enerally speaking the influences surrounding me during the formative period were not conducive to growth, and any development in myself came from fighting against them."[16]

Paul did not win the fight against all the negative influences. The seeds of alcoholism, gender-role inequities, racial inferiority and ambivalence, abusive behavior, and near-Oedipal devotion to his mother that were planted in his youth flowered. When full grown, they strangled his private and public lives. In the words of one of Paul's contemporaries, the poet had "sow[n] a character [and] reap[ed] a destiny."[17] Paul's early years give credence to the words of William Wordsworth, the British Poet Laureate whom he so admired as a child: "The child is father of the man."[18]

Paul was born seven years after the Civil War, on June 27, 1872, at 311 Howard Street in Dayton, Ohio. His birth occurred during the evening hours, in a back bedroom of a modest home purchased by his maternal great-grandmother, Rebecca Porter (1790?–1869).[19] Paul's mother later recalled the day of her youngest son's birth as extremely hot for early summer in Dayton. She also remembered in detail how her small, sickly baby received his portentous name. According to Matilda, a few days after giving birth her husband, Joshua Dunbar, came to her and asked:

> "Madame, have you named your baby?"
> "No, I haven't."
> "Well, I have a name."
> "What is it?"
> "Paul."
> "What? Paul? That old name?"
> "Madame, that is a fine name! That's a great name! Why don't you know that [Apostle] Paul was a great man? This child will be great some day and do you honor."

Matilda added that her sister, Rebecca Voss, gave Paul his middle name of Laurence.[20]

The days following Paul's birth were happy ones for Matilda and Joshua. Although married roughly only six months at the time of Paul's birth—having wed on Christmas Eve 1871—Joshua was delighted with his newborn son.[21] "Madame, that's my baby," he reportedly said. "[H]e has my hands. Yes, that's my baby—the little rascal!"[22] Believed to be about forty-nine years old—former slaves rarely knew their exact birth date—Joshua was also believed to be a father for the first time. Matilda, at least twenty years younger than her husband, had two sons from a slave marriage. William Travis Murphy (1866–1932) and Robert Small Murphy (1866–c. 1940) were eight and six years old, respectively, when their half-brother, Paul, was born.[23]

The euphoria surrounding Paul's birth did not last. Fear, tension, and heated verbal exchanges endemic to the household returned. Reportedly, over the years young Paul and his half-brothers hid under the bed or left home during the altercations between Matilda and Joshua to get out of harm's way. It was as a child that Paul learned how later to terrorize his wife; for his father was a brutal husband. Matilda recalled her marital woes in an interview:

> I don't think he [Joshua] was right in his mind. He had some of the worst spells—came home ravin'. When he had one of his tantrums, he threatened to kill me. I got afraid of him—and I had a nasty temper. I still think he wasn't right in his head. Poor man! He had been through the [Civil] war and so much; and around the cannon! And he drank! Sometimes he wouldn't go to bed at night. He would walk the floor. May be I would wake up and he would be standing over me, saying, "I'll get you yet!"[24]

The evidence suggests that Matilda was a battered wife. Thinly veiled characters and situations in Paul's autobiographical novel, *The Uncalled* (1898), paint a chilling portrait of life in his childhood home. In the story set in the mythological town of "Dexter, Ohio," which resembles Paul's hometown of Dayton, Ohio, the hero's father has a drinking problem. This is not unlike Joshua and, subsequently, Paul himself. The fictional father "was a brute: sich beatin's as he used to give [his wife] when he was in liquor you never heerd tell of," says one of the story's characters.[25] The wife, Margaret—obviously Matilda—divorces her husband, just as Matilda divorces Joshua. Further evidence that the novel is drawn from real life may be inferred in Paul's statement about his book: "I mean all I say in it and mean it very much."[26]

Like a typically battered woman, Matilda shouldered some responsibility for her husband's abuse, saying she had a nasty temper. Abusive behavior, however, originates from within. Research indicates that the more violence a man experiences growing up, the more likely he is to use violence as an adult. Also, batterers often have low self-esteem and vulnerable self-concepts. Then, too, there is often a relationship between alcohol use and spousal abuse.

Nothing is known about Joshua's childhood except that he lived with cruelty and violence. In all probability he, too, was victimized. He had been a slave, and whippings were commonly received and witnessed during slavery. So were other forms of brutal treatment. Many who grew up under the lash used it in their homes. The pervasive atmosphere of violence, coupled with complex issues of marital discord, often resulted in spousal abuse in slave families.[27]

It continued after freedom. Since no quantitative studies exist, it is impossible to know the extent of wife beating after emancipation. But a tune sung by some African American women from a small rural area suggests it was common in their community. The women sang: "Black men beat me/White men cheat me."[28] Numerous complaints in Freedmen Bureau records indicate the practice was widespread; and Frances Ellen Watkins Harper, the African American reformer and author, found herself "preaching against [black] men ill-treating their wives" during a post–Civil War lecture tour of the South.[29]

In Paul's childhood home, his parents' marital discord climaxed seven months after his birth, when Matilda realized she was again pregnant. Joshua, who had relished his son's birth, was not happy with the second pregnancy. His subsequent reactions toward this child (a daughter with whom he refused to associate) suggest he may have questioned her paternity or had little value for girl children. Matilda, too, was less than enthused about this pregnancy. She basically supported the family as a washerwoman because her husband was a poor provider. Racial prejudice and personal weaknesses prevented Joshua, a skilled plasterer, from working regularly at his trade. Seemingly, he never had steady work. He numbered among the vast majority of skilled former bondsmen who were excluded from well-paying jobs. Usually, Joshua joined the ranks of itinerant African American laborers, hoping to be hired for the day. In 1871, the year before Paul's birth, the average daily wage for unskilled labor was $1.50.[30]

Several Dunbar biographers cite Joshua's marginal employment as the chief source of conflict between him and his wife.[31] It may have been one factor; however, there appears to have been a general reluctance on Joshua's part to take care of his family. He received a monthly Civil War veteran's pension of $25 that—according to Matilda—he rarely contributed for household use.[32]

Afraid of having more children for whom she could not provide and frightened by Joshua's threats, Matilda left her husband, returning with her three sons to her mother's home. There she and her elderly mother, Eliza Burton (1801?–1877)—a Kentucky slave manumitted when her owners believed her too infirm to work—labored as washerwomen.[33] This task netted Matilda pennies a day.

Joshua renounced all familial responsibilities when Matilda left. He refused to support his family financially and even refused to visit his daughter, Elizabeth Florence, born October 29, 1873. While still a young child, Paul was given some responsibility for Elizabeth. It became his task to rock "Mistress" or "Sister," as she was called, or to otherwise pacify her while Matilda earned the family's living. When not at school, Paul's half-brothers, William and Robert—called Buddy and Rob, respectively—did odd jobs in the neighborhood to enlarge the family coffers.

Like her brother Paul, who constantly coughed, wheezed, and struggled for breath, "Sister" was also sickly. The family was so impoverished that they could not afford professional care and medicines. Matilda became the doctor, applying home-made remedies she had learned from plantation slaves. These salves and brews failed Elizabeth. On May 30, 1876, at roughly two and one-half years of age, she died of dropsy, a kidney disorder.

Matilda later recalled that during her daughter's brief life, Joshua made no attempt to see his little girl. She divorced him on January 9, 1876, after roughly four years of marriage. Paul was three years old.

But divorce did not terminate the relationship. Matilda and Joshua reconciled sometime after baby Elizabeth's death. "I got my divorce," Matilda recalled, "and was all settled, [but] he fixed himself up, had his hair all parted and got to be my beau again."[34]

It is this stage of Joshua and Matilda's relationship from which Paul constructed the childhood memories of his family. Many of these recollections were idyllic and were perhaps manufactured by Paul when he became famous. For example, Paul wrote: "Both my father and mother were fond of books and used to read to us as we sat around the fire at night. To this I owe a great deal."[35] But Paul's parents were barely literate. Along with reportedly reading literature and history, Joshua told his child stories of the Civil War and the harshness of slavery that later found their way into Paul's poetry and prose. Matilda did likewise and is generally credited with being Paul's chief inspirational source. But, unlike her husband, she did not dwell on the evils of slavery. While Matilda did not sugarcoat her days of bondage, she re-created a nostalgic slavery for Paul—the days of Aunt Doshys, plantation Christmases, and dances with banjos and fiddles. This lore became the basis of Paul's international fame.

The reconciliation period of Matilda and Joshua also provides clues on their parenting skills. Matilda is depicted as the more loving of the two, with Joshua being stern, strict, and authoritative—just as Paul would be toward his wife, Alice, in his adult years. Joshua reportedly was especially hard on Paul's half-brothers, Buddy and Rob, and all the children lived in fear of beatings. Even from Matilda. "I never had any trouble bringing up my boys," Paul's mother once told an interviewer. "They obeyed me; they knew what they would get if they didn't."[36] Nor did Joshua spare the rod where his son was concerned. In Paul's dialect poem, "At Night," the father, who has a constant cough (Joshua died of tuberculosis), tries to awaken his son as he snores by the fire. When the child does not respond to his father's calls, the latter threatens to beat him until he awakens.[37] Similarly, in another dialect poem, "In the Morning," the parent promises: "Boy, I'll whup you til you drap," because the son, a habitual late sleeper (like Paul), did not rise at six.[38]

The elder Dunbars' harsh treatment of their children was undoubtedly rooted in their slave experiences. The brutality that owners imposed on their chattel influenced the manner in which slaves disciplined their children. One historian notes:

> The ability to beat someone, to hold that kind of physical control over another human, was a sadistic power that blacks learned repeatedly from their interaction with and observation of white authority figures. This expression of control was meant to impress children with their parents' ability to command some power over their offspring's behavior.[39]

It was probably during this period of reconciliation that Paul internalized some of his father's sexism. These lessons were reinforced by the general society, for late nineteenth-century America was gender rigid. Specific behaviors and responsibilities were attributed to men and women, with men as the superior, authoritative, dominant force. Woman's role was that of submissive nurturer; her place was in the home. Man's role was that of provider/protector; his world was commerce and business. As an adult, Paul would be ever mindful of Alice's gendered responsibilities and roles. Immediately upon their engagement, he would become the authority figure in her life, issuing orders and commands. Matilda remembered that Joshua, too, "liked a lady in a lady's place":

> My husband was peculiar. . . . At the [dinner] table [guests] told the funniest stories; I could hardly restrain myself from laughing out loud; but I knew my husband wouldn't like it if I did. Later, when we were alone, he said, "Madame, I owe you thousand thanks; you laughed just enough!"[40]

The duration of this stage of Matilda and Joshua's relationship is unclear. However, it is certain that their union was still volatile. One Dunbar biographer writes that young Paul "constantly witnessed" his parents' "reoccurring arguments."[41] Moreover, Paul and the neighbors observed Joshua's drunken rages and stupor.

Paul developed an ambivalence toward his father, just as he would later toward Alice. Moreover, he alternately praised and damned both of them in his creative writings. To Paul, Joshua was a hero. He served as a Union soldier in the Civil War. Paul praised his father in his poems "Emancipation," "Our Martyred Soldiers," and "Colored Soldiers."[42] Yet, it has already been noted that in Paul's first novel, *The Uncalled,* Joshua is re-created in the character of Tom, the local drunk of a small town in Ohio. Like Matilda, Tom's wife leaves him and later divorces him because he is an alcoholic given to frequent brawling. And like Joshua, the character Tom refuses to support his wife and child. The hero, Freddie—a barely disguised Paul—harbors bitter memories of his father. (Freddie also marries a woman named Alice.) Paul's third novel, *The Fanatics* (1901), depicts his father Joshua as Nigger Ed, the drunken town buffoon.[43] Again like Joshua, the fictional character fights in the Civil War, thereby gaining a measure of respectability.

The evidence suggests that during their reunion, Matilda and Joshua lived together but did not remarry. Actually, as Matilda recalled it, the cause of the final breakup was her refusal to marry Joshua again. In response to his proposal, she replied: "We have been separated so long, we can spend the remainder of our days apart." Matilda further recalled: "That [answer] embittered him. That man turned against me and said some of the awfullest things to me. But something was the matter with him. He wasn't right."[44] Matilda's statement that Joshua "wasn't right" suggests he was mentally ill. Paul, too, would suffer with a mental disorder.

The disagreement ended finally with Joshua packing a carpetbag and storming out of the house, never to see Matilda again. It was the same course of action the mature Paul would take following the final brutal beating of Alice. While Joshua and Matilda never met again, father and son continued their relationship. Once again, however, Joshua refused to support any member of the family. Indeed, it was Matilda's recollection that Joshua had not contributed to his family's income since their initial separation, when Paul was about three years old. But Matilda maintained that Paul loved his father and visited him regularly until Joshua died on August 16, 1885.[45] His son was then thirteen years old. "Paul went to the cemetery," Matilda recalled, "and hunted row after row of graves until he came to his father's grave. He came running to me and said, 'Ma, I have found Pa's grave.' I went with him to it, and as we stood there, tears came to his eyes."[46]

Little is known of Joshua's life prior to his marriage to Matilda. Because of lack of evidence, it is assumed that he had no slave marriage(s), nor children other than Paul and Elizabeth. In a 1930s interview with Matilda, conducted when she was over eighty years old, she seemed to know or remember very little about her husband's background. She believed that he escaped from bondage in Kentucky and went to Canada. Later, he returned to the United States to fight in the Civil War.[47]

Much of the information about Joshua may have been more fiction than fact. Most came from Paul, the creative writer—author of short stories and novels. Joshua loved telling his son stories of the old slave days. A ubiquitous tale involved a fugitive's escape to Canada, armed with cayenne pepper. This hot spice sprinkled on the trail caused pursuing bloodhounds to sneeze, thereby losing the runaway's scent and, ultimately, the path of flight.

Paul's short story, "The Ingrate" (1900) features a slave hero, Josh, who is ridiculed by friends because he has not yet married. But Josh "had no time for marrying or for love; other thoughts had taken possession of him"—escape to Canada.[48] The storybook Josh, a skilled plasterer, is a hired-out slave; that is, he worked for someone other than his owner, with the owner receiving Josh's wages. He is taught by his owner to write and cipher so that employers will not cheat him out of these wages. But the fictional Josh outwits his owner by forging a pass that aids in his escape. He also plays "the old slave trick of filling his tracks with cayenne pepper" as he flees through the woods. When dogs pick up his trail, they come "yelping back, pawing their noses and rubbing their heads against the ground."[49] In Canada, the fictional Josh's manhood is affirmed as he is paid full measure for his work. But bravely and unselfishly, he returns to the United States to fight in the Civil War. Like Paul's father, the fictional Josh joins a Massachusetts regiment and is quickly promoted to sergeant.

Some Dunbar biographers present this fictional story of Josh, complete with yelping dogs, as the facts of Joshua Dunbar's life. However, the tale seems too conventional to be completely true. Also, some of the "facts" differ from the scant data on Joshua. For example, Paul's father seems to have been illiterate, since he signed his marriage license with an "X."[50]

What is actually known of Joshua Dunbar's early life comes from military records. These documents show that he was born a slave in Garret County, Kentucky, and that his birth year may have been 1823. On June 3, 1863, Joshua enlisted for three years in Company F, 55th Regiment, Massachusetts Volunteer Infantry. It was the second regiment of all African American troops formed during the Civil War.[51] At that time, he cited Troy, Ohio, as his city of residence and plasterer as his occupation. Joshua's army career was short lived. Ten days after enlistment, army officials relieved him of active duty. Later, on October 28, 1863, he was honorably discharged because of an unspecified physical disability.[52] In view of his unconventional behavior during his years with Matilda, one wonders if "unspecified physical disability" may not have been a euphemism for mental illness.

Nevertheless, Joshua Dunbar was determined to be a soldier. He found a new outfit—Company F, 5th Regiment, Massachusetts Volunteer Cavalry—and enlisted for three years. By January 9, 1864, he had become a sergeant. On October 3, 1865, he was, once again, honorably discharged, this time in Clarksville, Texas.[53]

If not a heroic soldier, Joshua was certainly a brave one. African American soldiers in the Union Army faced greater danger than their Euro-American counterparts. It was well known that Confederates were especially brutal with captured black troops. Seldom were they taken as prisoners of war. The Fort Pillow, Tennessee, Massacre (1864) was proof.

Large numbers of captured African American soldiers were indiscriminately slaughtered, burned, or buried alive.

Paul wrote about the bravery of Joshua and other African American Union troops in his poem "The Colored Soldiers." In one of its stanzas, he remembers his father's precarious employment situation and addresses the discrimination these veterans faced by asking the ageless question, "If they were good enough to die for their country, why are they now treated unfairly?"

> They were comrades then and brothers,
>   Are they more or less today?
> They were good to stop a bullet
>   And to front the fearful fray.
> They were citizens and soldiers.
>   When rebellion raised its head;
> And those traits that made them worthy,
>   Ah! those virtues are not dead.[54]

After his army discharge at Clarksville, Texas, Joshua migrated to Dayton, where the best evidence indicates he met Matilda in or after 1866. By that time, she had already experienced one unhappy, unstable marriage, during which her slave husband had deserted her.[55] In fact, it was this abandonment that led her to Dayton, where she had family, in the spring of 1866. Her mother and grandmother lived and labored in the city as washerwomen. Matilda—declaring herself a widow—arrived destitute, with one small son and five months pregnant with her second one, Robert Small Murphy. When she and Joshua met in Dayton, Matilda was well acquainted with hard times and bad marriages.

Bad times and unhappiness had characterized her life since childhood. Because she was a slave at the time, Matilda's experiences speak to the savagery of bondage and the effect it could have on human development and relationships. When coupled with her tenuous interactions with Joshua, a paradigm unfolds that aids in explaining her relationship with Paul. Matilda lavished attention on her favorite son, and even in his adulthood, she held on to him with a tight-fisted grip. This reciprocal mother-son interdependence contributed to some of the marital friction between Paul and Alice. For as Alice would lament: "[Matilda] was with us always. . . . [S]he resented me generally, because he had always been hers solely."[56]

Matilda Jane, the daughter of Willis and Eliza Porter Burton, was born in Fayette County, Kentucky, around 1845, "on the farm of old Squire David Glass—[an] irritable and hard to get along with man," she later recalled.[57] Matilda had at least six siblings. Her youth, a brief period of stability "when I was a small child," was the happiest period of her life. "But it was so short," she said in a 1930s interview. "My father belonged to a different master. . . . He came home every Saturday. . . . We children would all run clapping our hands over our heads and shouting 'Here comes Pappy, here comes Pappy!'"[58] Matilda saw her father for the last time while still quite young. "Squire" Glass sold his farm, thereby scattering the families of his slaves. By the age of seven, Matilda was separated from her mother and was hired out. Before she was sixteen, she had been sold twice.[59] Regardless of the owner, Matilda worked as a hired-out slave until emancipation, when she was about nineteen years old. "I had a number of places," Matilda recollected. "Some of the people I worked for were not good to me."[60] She was also homesick for her mother, found adjusting to some work situations difficult, and developed a sense of insecurity with the constant shift of environments.

Somewhere between the ages of fifteen and seventeen, while at "Marse Jack Venable's" place, Matilda married a slave handyman named R. Weeks Murphy, Wilson Murphy, or Willis Murphy.[61] On February 12, 1864, she gave birth to her first child, William Travis Murphy, who would later be called Buddy by his siblings. Shortly after becoming a mother, Matilda and her son were sent back to her owner. Her husband could not accompany her nor join her later. To do so without his owner's permission would have made him a runaway slave and a fugitive from justice. The separation from her husband remained one of Matilda's most bitter memories of slavery.

This memory of the loss of yet another loved one may have in later years contributed to Matilda's tenacious proclivities toward Paul. It is known that soon after the forced separation from her husband she began exhibiting a strong, protective mother love. When, for example, a Mrs. Cary to whom Matilda was hired cursed her for spending so much time with her sick baby, William, at the expense of her slave duties, Matilda "took her leave . . . [and] when I drove out, that was the last time I saw the Carys."[62] Moreover, on learning that her owner's will accorded freedom only if she went to live with a colony of freed slaves in Liberia, Africa, Matilda chose emigration, even though she did not know where Liberia was and did not want to go there. Her reason? Fear that her child would be sold away from her. "[I] walked a great distance, carrying . . . baby, who was about three months old," said Matilda of that time. "[Then I] borrowed a horse and rode seven miles to the court house to sign to go to Africa! But freedom was declared before it was time for me to go."[63]

Freedom brought Matilda and her slave husband together again, but only briefly. Most Dunbar biographers maintain that Matilda was widowed during the Civil War. They write that sometime near the end of the war, her husband joined the liberating Union Army and never returned. There appears to be no military record of Matilda's slave husband under any of his presumed names; but he may have been a camp follower, like many slaves. By Matilda's testimony, she, her husband, and baby William were reunited at the end of slavery. When she was roughly five months pregnant with their second child, her husband abandoned them. The relationship had been troubled. Like many freed persons—and freed men in particular—Matilda's husband could not get a job that paid well enough to support a family. Years later she remembered:

> I hadn't money to live on and he didn't do his duty by me. . . . When he didn't get work and I didn't have support, I told him that I was going to . . . my mother's [in Dayton, Ohio] which I did. . . . He did not try to help me. He left, and said he was going to join the regular army. That was the last I knew of him.[64]

In Dayton, at 311 Howard Street—home of her mother and grandmother—Matilda give birth to her second son, Robert Small Murphy, on August 1, 1866. He was known affectionately as Rob. Matilda supported her family by doing domestic work for members of Dayton's Euro-American community. Of this period, she has been quoted as saying: "I was alone. I was poor and had troubles to spare."[65] Perhaps this was the time that she met Joshua Dunbar, a five-feet, ten-inch Civil War sergeant with a pension and a sometimes courtly manner.[66] Any happiness in Matilda's life stemmed from the fact that she was no longer a slave. "But I was free," she said. "Nobody could take my babies away from me. I was free to work for them my own self."[67] From the time that Paul was four years old until he was in his early twenties, Matilda worked mainly for him and with him to make him the Poet Laureate of the Negro Race.

"Once when Paul was in high school," recalled the elderly Matilda after her famous son's death, "I went to get some money for washing I had done and . . . a man said to me, 'Mrs. Dunbar, what are you educating Paul for? What are you going to make out of him?' I didn't answer," she continued. "I hope he found out what I educated Paul for."[68] Dunbar scholars characterized Matilda as the self-sacrificing, hard-working, devoted mother. One source heralds her as "one of that noble legion of black mothers who after the Civil War dedicated their lives to . . . the education of their children."[69] Another depicts her as the "typical negro mammy, used to hard work, which she does uncomplainingly. She is faithful to every duty, kind, gentle, devout."[70] Some Dunbar biographers come close to canonizing Matilda.

Matilda was, as Paul described her, "very unusual." She labored at grueling, low-paying jobs and made sacrifices for her sons. In this respect, she was not unlike many freedwomen. A large number of this hard-working group were widowed or abandoned. In southern rural areas, they share cropped or worked as tenant farmers. In cities they labored mainly as domestic servants and washerwomen. Economically, few were better off than when enslaved. Often, employers refused to pay their meager wages. Some were beaten if they were late to work or failed to perform to the employer's satisfaction. Many were sexually exploited by male employers or their sons.[71]

Matilda Dunbar was a member of this determined group whose backs were bent but not broken. Undoubtedly, at some point, she too sighed and said, "I have done a mountain of washing and ironing in my life."[72] But she was not the self-sacrificing saint of the Dunbar biographies. Matilda was ambitious for herself and her boys—especially Paul. She practically educated herself after arriving in Dayton by attending the "colored" night school for six weeks, then learning from and with her sons. Matilda also worked constantly. In addition to her arduous task of washerwoman, she did pick-up work as cook and seamstress.[73] Any extra pennies were spent on books for Paul, especially short stories and poetry by Mark Twain and Henry Wadsworth Longfellow.

All three boys had household chores and outside paying jobs. Before school, they helped with the housework. After school, Buddy and Rob worked in the more affluent neighborhoods, cutting grass, sweeping floors, and holding the reins of shoppers' horses as they went about their activities. Paul had his first job while still in grade school. Although frail and often short of breath, he worked as a Dayton city lamplighter for about a year. Paul carried a wooden ladder that he placed against each post, climbed to the top of the column, and lighted the gas jet.

Even with every family member working, their combined financial efforts were insufficient. Matilda and her boys moved constantly from one inexpensive form of housing to another. When Buddy and Rob dropped out of school to work full time as janitors, the family became more solvent. But by the time Paul was thirteen, both half-brothers, now adults, lived and worked away from home. Although acquaintances suggested that Paul should now quit school and work to support his mother, Matilda would not consider the prospect. She and Paul struggled on.

Perhaps Matilda was not completely selfless and self-sacrificing. Social relations are based on reciprocity. We give, but we also expect to receive eventually. Matilda did receive, emotionally and materially. Correspondence between her and her son after he became famous shows she continuously requested and received money from him. Matilda confirmed this in an interview, saying: "Paul was indulgent, and if I wanted anything, he gave me money to buy it."[74] That she expected to be rewarded for her hard years of toil is demonstrated in an incident with her son, Rob. While visiting him in Chicago, Matilda asked him for twenty dollars. Rob, at that time only marginally employed, told Matilda he was bereft of funds. "In fact," Rob wrote his famous half-brother, "I had just 60 [cents] in the world. She began to scream and rage and call me all sort of bad names." Matilda's antics drew a crowd of curious neighbors. "[W]hen she saw she had enough people for her purpose," Rob continued, "she commenced to scream out personal parts of [my wife's] history. I then told her to leave the house. . . . She sprang on me like a tiger, hitting me in the face and clawing me."[75]

Regardless of motive, Matilda's early devotion to Paul was genuine. It forged a lifelong interdependence between them. In her relationship with him, she found the security that had previously eluded her as a slave and wife. Matilda rarely left Paul's side. She lived with him during his marriage to Alice and was at his bedside when he died. Indeed, one Dunbar biographer believes that Matilda exhibited a "love deeper than motherhood" for Paul.[76]

It was returned full measure. By the time Paul was thirteen years old, he was the catalyst in her life, and she in his. Joshua, Paul's father, was dead, and Matilda's other sons, Buddy and Rob, had moved to Cincinnati in search of better economic opportunities. Paul and Matilda had only each other, and contemporaries noted that they were almost inseparable. In fact, in 1893, when it became necessary for the two to separate for the first time in order for Paul to take a temporary job at the World's Columbian Exposition in Chicago, the parting overwhelmed twenty-one-year-old Paul. Reportedly, "he leaned on the mantelpiece and sobbed like a child, saying, 'Oh, ma[,] I don't want to go.'"[77]

Upon arrival in Chicago, he initiated a regular correspondence with his mother. His letters had the same character and tone as would his letters to Alice during their courtship by mail. Once, Matilda sent him flowers from the family garden, to which he responded: "It was thoughtful of you to send them, Ma, knowing how I longed to see those bushes in bloom. But that's just like my own little Mom."[78] Within four years, he would similarly have endearing names for Alice, such as "my Little Girl," and "my Little Wife-to-Be."[79] Historians of mainstream courting rituals note that the word "little" was frequently used as a term of affection in love letters.

Paul was unhappy away from Matilda. Just as he would express a desire for Alice to be near him during their long-distance romance, so he wanted Matilda with him in Chicago. Paul promised in a letter: "Ma, you shall come out here if you want to come—just as soon as I can bring you."[80] Later, he wrote: "I want you to come out here very much, but I don't know how to manage it. What do you think of renting a furnished room here where I am staying and you do your own cooking here in this woman's kitchen."[81] In another letter he added tenderly, "Your little home will only cost me seven dollars a month and you will have it to yourself."[82]

Matilda joined her son in Chicago, where he worked at the World's Fair for his childhood idol, Frederick Douglass. But Matilda and Paul soon faced another traumatic separation. With the closing of the exposition, Paul returned to Dayton, leaving his mother in Chicago visiting

Buddy and Rob. This time Paul's anguish was so real that he wrote the Negro dialect poem, "Lonesome." In it, a weeping son speaks of the unhappiness and depression that cloaks him, "Sence mother's gone a-visitin' to spend a month er two." The final stanza reads:

> The sparrers ac's more fearsome like an won't hop quite so near
> The cricket's chirp is sadder, an' the sky ain't ha'f so clear;
> When ev'nin' comes, I set an' smoke tell my eyes begin to swim,
> An' things aroun' commence to look all blurred an' faint an' dim.
> Well, I guess I'll have to own up 'at I'm feelin' purty blue
> Sence mother's gone a-visitin' to spen' a month er two.[83]

Dunbar friends and relatives commented on this intense relationship. Amelia Douglass, daughter-in-law of Frederick Douglass, told Matilda: "[N]ever has there been so tender an affection between mother and son as exists between Paul and you."[84] Alice remembered that prior to her engagement, Paul wore Matilda's wedding band.[85] Moreover, a psychiatrist who analyzed Paul through his poetry and prose declared Matilda—rather than Alice—Paul's one great love.[86]

There is evidence supporting that theory; for example, some of the dedication pages in Paul's books. Tributes to Matilda are laudatory, while inscriptions to Alice simply acknowledge her. The dedication in Paul's first book, a collection of poetry called *Oak and Ivy* (1893), reads:

> To Her
> who has ever been
> my guide, teacher, and inspiration
> My Mother
> this little volume is
> affectionately inscribed[87]

Majors and Minors (1895), Paul's second book, and similarly a collection of poems, has this tribute:

> As my first faint pipings were inscribed to her, I deem
> it fitting as a further recognition of my love
> and obligation, that I should
> also dedicate these later
> songs to
> MY MOTHER[88]

By contrast, the inscription in his novel, *The Uncalled* (1898), published after his marriage, says only:

Dedicated

TO MY WIFE[89]

And a volume of poetry, *Lyrics of the Hearthside* (1899), reads:

TO

ALICE[90]

The nature of the bond between mother and son perhaps began with the death of Paul's sister, Elizabeth Florence. Matilda never stopped mourning her. As the elderly mother of the deceased famous writer, she told her interviewer, "As a baby [Elizabeth] was brighter than Paul. If only my little girl had lived!"[91]

With her daughter's death, Matilda determined that Paul, although frail and often in poor health, would not die. During the long Dayton winters, she kept him in the house with her and refused to let him engage in strenuous activities. Moreover, Matilda safeguarded Paul because she knew he was special. Early on, Joshua realized that his son was gifted and repeatedly told Matilda so. The mature Paul recalled: "My father used to tell her that I was not an ordinary boy, and one of my regrets is that he did not live to realize any of his hopes in regards to me."[92]

Shortly after her daughter's death, when Paul was about four years old, Matilda—with her limited knowledge—taught Paul to read. Although she believed, as did many former slaves, that education was the key to opportunity, she had not taught her other sons, Buddy and Rob. They learned in grade school when they were six or seven years old. At that age, Paul was writing childish poems, or "rhyming," as he called it. By the time he was seven, writes one Dunbar biographer, Matilda "felt that her son was destined for greatness and she worked exceedingly hard to do everything possible to ensure his success."[93] She outfitted his bedroom with a desk and several bookcases, and never let anyone—including relatives—enter young Paul's room.

Matilda was committed to Paul's education, although it was an economic hardship. In Dayton, Ohio, public education was free, but not compulsory. Many poor families chose not to send their children to school because they needed the pennies their labor could bring. Most

African Americans who attended school quit at the end of the seventh grade, if not sooner, and entered the workforce, as did many Euro-American students. There were, in fact, so few eighth graders that Dayton had only one intermediate school. Smaller numbers of children attended high school, and the graduating classes rarely had more than thirty students.

William Murphy, Paul's older half-brother, completed the ninth grade, and Rob the eighth grade, before the need or desire for money drove them from the classroom. They secured menial jobs at the Beckel House, a local hotel. However, Matilda made Paul's education her top priority. Neither lack of funds nor any other factor—great or small—would interfere with it. If, for example, Paul had not performed his household chores and was doing his "lessons," Matilda delegated those chores to her other sons. (Not surprisingly, Paul was often conveniently at his "lessons.") This practice prevailed even after Buddy and Rob quit school and worked full time. In 1887, Rob married and moved to Chicago. When he tried to convince Matilda that this city offered African Americans better opportunities and that she and Paul should move there, too, fifteen-year-old Paul refused to go. He reasoned that he had good teachers and was in a good school, and maybe that would not be the case in Chicago. As had now become the custom, Matilda yielded to Paul's wishes, and mother and son remained in Dayton.

Paul's preferential treatment paid dividends. With the exception of mathematics, he was an outstanding student, in his subjects, excelling in writing and other verbal skills. For example, at his school, Central High, Paul ended the quarter of June 20, 1890, with the impressive grades of 100 (Literature), 92 (Psychology), 86 (Greek), and 100 (Humanities/English). Other grades were 83 (Latin), 81 (Chemistry), and 85.6 (Physics).

Paul's literary talents also blossomed and gained him recognition. Early in his academic life, his teachers encouraged him to write, and by age twelve he had completed his first short story. Within a year, Paul presented, in a public forum, an original poem, the lugubrious "An Easter Ode," which began: "To the cold dark grave they go/ Silently and sad and slow."[94] The five-stanza poem later appeared in *Oak and Ivy* (1893), his first book.

While at Central High, the developing poet published frequently in the school newspaper, *High School Times*. Moreover, he constantly submitted prose and poetry for publication to both local and national sources. Finally, on June 8, 1888, just weeks before Paul's seventeenth birthday, he had his first major publication. The *Dayton Herald* newspaper published a poem honoring his father, Joshua, called "Our Martyred Soldiers."[95] Thereafter, local and regional news sources, as well as African American journals, printed Paul's materials regularly.

There were other indicators of Paul's talents and ambitions. At Central High, where he was the only African American in his graduating class, he received two literary awards, served as editor in chief of the school newspaper, and was elected to the Philomaethean Literary Society, one of the school's most prestigious organizations. Paul also wrote the song for his graduating class, the class of 1891.[96] Outside of school, Paul was equally precocious. He formed the Philodramians, a local drama club, for which he wrote the plays and Matilda sewed the costumes. In 1890, he started a weekly African American newspaper, the *Dayton Tattler*, with himself as editor and practically the only staff writer. Retailing for five cents a copy, the short-lived *Tattler* was another forum for Paul's prose and poetry. It showcased his reportorial skills, for he had his eye on a journalism career.[97] During this period of development and recognition, he wrote no literature in the Negro dialect that would make him famous.

By Paul's graduation day, June 16, 1891, there were few Daytonians who did not know about "that Dunbar boy."[98] That late spring evening at the Dayton Opera House, site of the commencement activities, Paul and Matilda must have thought that they were on the brink of achieving their dreams. And why not? He was not unknown. His talents were proven; and in the race-conscious world where it counted, his formal education equaled that of his white peers. In short, Paul measured up to the prevailing standard of excellence. A Euro-American Daytonian said of him:

> He was bred in the public schools with children of well-to-do white people. He came under the instruction of the same teachers in High School. He . . . read Shakespeare, the newspapers, the magazines and the American classics. *In bringing-up he was as far from the ordinary negro [sic] boy as is the ordinary white boy.* (Emphasis added)[99]

As Paul's graduating class of thirty-four women and nine men rose and sang the lyrics of the class song he had written, Paul must have felt certain of his immediate success. His goal was to become a journalist; failing that, he would take a good clerking position in a major business house.

But Paul's dreams were not immediately realized. Success eluded him for many years, and despair took its place. Upon graduating from high school, he unexpectedly ran straight into the color line, which relegated his job possibilities to menial work or little better. Reverberations of the experience affected his professional and personal life. Alice Dunbar once said of her late husband that there was a great deal of bitterness in him which he had to suppress. Much of this acrimony stemmed from Paul's belief that only his color kept him from being the most outstanding man in America during his time.

Dunbar's genius, Matilda's nurturing, and both parents' insistence on his being "exceptional" created a positive self-image and an atmosphere in which to excel. But at the same time, these factors also created such an inflated ego that Paul could never fully come to terms with his denigration by whites. Nor could he ever acknowledge or accept his personal flaws. The racism drenching his personal life permeated his professional life as well. In fact, one Dunbar scholar believed that racial prejudice "was one of the most powerful forces [in his life] . . . and vicariously contributed to the flowering of [Paul's] genius."[100]

Bigotry also made Paul a phenomenally successful poet. Initially to his surprise, and later to his rancorous chagrin, it was the plantation-dialect pieces—the poems and short stories that evoked a nostalgic form of slavery—that his public, especially Euro-American audiences, demanded. Paul's plays, novels, and other forms of writing that deviated from the formula were rejected and criticized. In this period of time—from 1891, when Paul graduated from high school, to 1895, when he initiated contact with Alice, Paul became saddled with a style of writing that he grew to despise. Unquestionably, in his public life, racism was an integral element.

By all indications, Paul's first realization of racism occurred when he went job hunting as a much-lauded graduate of Central High. Following commencement, he dressed again in his new graduation suit that today, more than a century later, can be seen at the Dunbar House Museum in Dayton.[101] His first stop was the *Dayton Herald* newspaper offices. After all, he reasoned, the paper had published his poems for years; surely he could be hired as a journalist. Paul was aware of racial discrimination in Dayton, despite the city's abolitionist heritage, but he did not feel that he personally would have a problem securing the type of employment he desired. At the *Herald,* the newspaper editor was familiar with Paul's reputation and work. Still, he told the optimistic job seeker that "there was no place on the . . . staff for a Negro. Other reporters might not like it."[102]

For months, Paul searched for work comparable to that accorded his male Euro-American classmates. Eventually, he accepted a position that his colleagues would not have considered—nor been offered—as elevator boy at a downtown office building called the Calahan. Paul worked eleven hours a day, six days per week, for a weekly wage of four dollars. It was a living, but barely so. Rent for the inferior housing in the African American section of Dayton ranged from four to seven dollars monthly. Pork chops were ten cents a pound; five pounds of potatoes, a dime; and cornmeal cost two cents per pound.[103] Still, these were neither the wages nor the employment expected by a stellar high school graduate.

Paul captured his job-hunting experience in "One Man's Fortunes," a short story of a college-educated African American who cannot get a decent job in his Midwestern hometown.[104] Bitterly, the hero writes one of his old school mates:

> Nothing so breaks a man's spirit as defeat, constant, unaltering, hopeless defeat. That's what I've experienced. . . . We have been taught that merit wins. But I have learned that the adages, as well as the books and the formulas were made by and for others than us of the black race.[105]

Clearly, the racism Paul had encountered shocked him. Although the only African American in his high school class, he had been popular and was treated well. However, Paul did recall that he had not gone to his junior class picnic. "He had known that he would have been accepted by his white [male] friends," writes one Dunbar biographer, "but his date would not have been accepted by the girls. At that time, he had thought of it as a girl problem—not a race problem."[106]

As an elevator operator, the intelligent, ambitious Paul continued to educate himself. A regular patron of the Calahan Building where he worked noted that from 1891 to 1892, "the elevator boy was always reading. This is not in itself remarkable. The yellow literature of the day finds its widest field among the employed boys in . . . offices. But this elevator boy was reading Tennyson and Shakespeare, and he was black."[107]

Paul continued sending his literature for publication, often writing in his cramped elevator cage. It was during this period of his life that he wrote his first Negro-dialect piece. He wanted to be more marketable and decided to use the poetic style of the popular Hoosier dialect poet, James Whitcomb Riley, as a model. Paul discovered that Riley's characters were humorous, pleasant, everyday folks, who often tried to make the best out of a bad situation. Although he had written a Hoosier-dialect poem while at Central High that had been well received, Paul decided to impose Riley's paradigm on another literary genre greatly favored by the Euro-American public—the plantation school of writing.[108] In this tradition, African Americans are at best childish buffoons. They are loyal to their "masters," the old plantation, and the southern way of life. While being simple minded and humorous, African Americans, and especially men, could also be rapists, slashers, thieves, and murderers. Both genders had a quaint and jocular form of speech. Paul's chum, James Weldon Johnson, an author and future luminary of the National Association for the Advancement of Colored People (NAACP), defended his friend's dialect work, writing:

> He . . . cut away much that was coarse and "niggerish," and added a deeper tenderness, a higher polish, a more delicate finish . . . nevertheless, practically all his work in dialect fitted into the traditional mold. Not even he [was] able to discard those stereotyped properties of minstrel-stage dialect: the watermelon and possum. He did, however, disdain the use of that other ancient "prop," the razor.[109]

Johnson concluded that any poet writing in dialect, no matter how sincere he might be, was dominated by his audience. Paul's public of mainly Euro-Americans would accept and enjoy only certain conceptions of African American life.

Possibly, Paul's first effort at plantation poetry was "A Banjo Song," in which a slave's "fam'ly an' all de othahs," forget their troubles and pains by listening to "de music o' dat banjo."[110] The *Chicago News Record,* a mainstream newspaper, bought the poem immediately for two dollars, half of Paul's weekly pay!

With the rapid acceptance of "A Banjo Song," Paul poured out a steady stream of nostalgic plantation pieces. He wanted to be published and there were bills to be paid. Also, he mistakenly believed that the publishers who accepted his dialect work would be equally anxious for what he preferred to write—poetry and prose in standard English.

Paul published his first poetry collection in 1893, while still—in his words—chained to his elevator. It was privately printed and sold by subscription; in fact, he peddled copies to his elevator passengers. The volume consisted of poems from his youth and high school days that his mother, Matilda, had preserved in cardboard boxes. His locally and regionally published works were also included. The book's title, *Oak and Ivy,* and its format indicate Paul's desired literary thrust. The first and larger section, the "Oak," holds solemn poems in standard English, while the smaller section, the "Ivy," consists of light dialect pieces. But much to Paul's surprise, the ivy strangled the oak; for the poems in the dialect section garnered the most favorable comment.

It was the same with Paul's second poetry collection, *Majors and Minors* (1895). Once again, the larger "Majors" section contained what Paul considered his serious work, the poems in standard English. And once more the smaller "Minors" section of dialect poems overshadowed the standard pieces. In fact, it was the plantation poems in this book that made Paul nationally famous at age twenty-four and, in a sense, sealed his professional and private fate.

William Dean Howells, the foremost literary critic of American letters in late-nineteenth-century America, reviewed *Majors and Minors* in the prestigious mainstream magazine, *Harper's Weekly,* the June 27, 1896, issue. In so doing, Howells anointed Paul, made him an instant celebrity, and created a demand for his dialect work. That same June 27 was Paul's twenty-fourth birthday.

Howells's review has been both applauded and damned. One of Paul's contemporaries, a Euro-American Daytonian, thought it was a "godsend for a colored boy," writing: "To have been so praised would be a boon to a white man of cultured lineage and college training; to this son of a slave mother, this hewer of wood, and drawer of water, this furnace tender, and elevator boy, it was nothing less than the supreme touch of inspiration and joy."[111]

Howells's review and the above comment from a woman who claimed to be one of Paul's biggest fans reflect the racist tendencies of the times. Moreover, Howells's article especially touched on two of Paul's major insecurities, his physical appearance, and the notion that he was only good at writing plantation dialect.

The critic began in an avuncular manner: "There has come to me from the hand of a friend, very unofficially, a little book of verse, dateless, placeless, and without a publisher, which greatly interests me." He then emphasized that Paul was obviously an African American, judging from the volume's enclosed photograph. His point was to inform the audience that Paul's intellect was so very unusual because he appeared to be of "pure African blood." The thinking at the time was that if any African American succeeded, such as the mulattoes Frederick Douglass and Booker T. Washington, it was because of the blood of their white fathers. Howells continued:

> [T]he face which confronted me when I opened the volume was the face of a young Negro, with the race traits strangely accented: the black skin, the woolly hair, the thick out-rolling lips, and the mild, soft eyes of the pure African type. One cannot be very sure of the age of these people, but I should have thought that the poet was about twenty years old; and would have been worth, apart from his literary gift, twelve or fifteen hundred dollars under the [slave auctioneer's] hammer.[112]

Howells proceeded to analyze *Majors and Minors*. He dismissed the standard English pieces, although they demonstrated "honest thinking and true feelings." That was unique for a black person. But Howells lauded what he called Paul's "darky" poems and thereby instantly created a lifelong market for his dialect work. "It is when we come to Mr. Dunbar's [plantation verse] that we feel ourselves in the presence of a man with a . . fresh authority to do the kind of things he is doing," Howells intoned. Then he rhapsodized:

> I wish I could give the whole of the longest of these pieces . . . but I must content myself with a passage or two. They will impart some sense of the jolly rush of its movement, its livid picturesqueness, its broad characterization; and will perhaps suffice to show what vistas into the simple, sensuous, joyful nature of his race, Mr. Dunbar opens.[113]

Still, Howells was not finished. He compared Paul to Robert Burns, the much honored eighteenth-century farmer-turned-poet, who often wrote with a Scottish burr:

> I shall not do this unknown but not ungifted poet the injury of compar-
> ing him with Burns; yet I do not think that one can read his Negro pieces
> without feeling that they are of like impulse and inspiration with the work
> of Burns when he was most Burns, when he was most Scotch, when he was
> most peasant.[114]

Howells's final statement insured Paul's literary direction. He concluded, "When Burns was least himself, he wrote literary English, and
Mr. Dunbar writes literary English when he is least himself."[115]

Paul was both ecstatic and bitter about the critic's piece. Howells's
concentration on the race issue rekindled self-doubt and feelings of inferiority. As early as 1892, when he began to garner a regional following,
Paul had wondered: Why? "I hope," he confided to a friend, "there is
something worthy in my writing and not merely the novelty of a black
face associated with the power to rhyme that has attracted attention."[116]
For all his supposed good intentions, that thought permeated Howells's
review.

Paul swallowed his acrimony toward the critic, as well as his pride, and
donned the mask of supplicant. In his thank you letter, which came
"from the bottom of my heart," he described himself as a "poor in-
significant, helpless boy" who was suddenly knighted.[117] Subsequently,
when the critic and poet met and Howells loaned Paul his coat because
the night air had suddenly chilled, Paul declared himself an "ass in the
lion's skin."[118] Only to close friends would Paul criticize his benefactor,
commenting, "Mr. Howells has done me irrevocable harm in the dictum
he laid down regarding my dialect verse."[119]

Paul further took umbrage with Howells's preoccupation with his
ethnicity and looks. He was uncomfortable with the racialized self and
had an intense inferiority complex. While one Dunbar scholar believes
that, as a child, Paul suffered very little from the effects of race prejudice,
another argues that the young poet felt subordinate to his Euro-American classmates.[120] Moreover, the first biography of Paul, written the year
following his death, describes him as being "bashful, timid, retiring" as
a child.[121] These are not the characteristics of a well-adjusted youngster.

Many late-nineteenth-century African Americans felt racially inferior, especially those who looked like Paul. His complexion was dark brown, his nose broad, his lips were not thin. Beauty in America was the polar opposite: white skin, narrow nose, thin lips, and "silky" hair. People of color were taught that they had been enslaved because God had cursed them. Dark skin was a sign of the curse, and it made them inferior to whites. Color became a justification for slavery. Racist Christians espoused those carefully selected biblical passages that proved God intended blacks to serve whites. When emancipation brought freedom from bondage, it did not free African Americans from the stigma of color implications.

Paul's internalization of this racial ethos resulted in racial self-hatred. Early creative writings show him to be a racially confused young man, a man consumed with inferiority. During his prolific scholastic writing career, he wrote no stories or poems about African Americans. Even his fiction in his short-lived newspaper, the *Dayton Tattler,* had no African American characters. He acknowledged this audience only with his local gossip items and in editorials in which he often chastised people of color.

Paul's youthful love poems were for and about Euro-American women. "My Best Girl," written while in high school, describes a "lovely young damsel [with] brilliant red hair."[122] Moreover, he sent several love poems to one of his classmates, who much to his indignation shared them with other class members. This ridicule may have been one reason why the adult Paul shifted his love interest to African American women with light skin tones: they approached the nation's standard of loveliness. And in this instance, because of gender hierarchy within the race, black would triumph over white. Even these women would be marked as inferior to a (dark-skinned) man. Paul's complexion and color complex would make all his relations with mulatto women ultimately tense and uneasy.

The young poet believed what most Euro-Americans believed, mainly that "anything with 'Negro' automatically consigned it to an inferior category."[123] He tried to minimize his ethnicity, viewing himself as "first of all a man, then an American, and incidentally a Negro." Moreover, Paul once bitterly described himself as a "black white man," and he wanted to show the majority population that he and other African Americans were "more human than African."[124] Paul further subscribed to the prevailing notion that a dark skin was an odious skin. "Ma," he wrote Matilda from Chicago on receiving a prestigious party invitation, "your ugly black boy has been chosen."[125] That he possessed an unfavorable self-image is further evidenced in his poem, "The Crisis" (ca. 1895). Paul describes himself in the opening line as "a man of low degree . . . sore oppressed."[126]

Although Paul was consumed with racial self-hatred, one Dunbar scholar writes that he never tried to deny his blackness. How could he? He was unmistakably a man of color. Yet he denigrated his looks. How ironic, then, that he rode to fame on his racialized poetry and his skin color. Literary critics and promoters made race Paul's stock in trade. Press releases and book reviews hailed him as a gifted poet who was "pure black—having no admixture of white blood."[127] The race hucksters claimed that this marketing device deflated the ideology that black people were intellectually incompetent, as Howells had intimated in his review. Also, hawking Paul as a "pure African" addressed another part of the myth. If by chance some mulatto or biracial person attained greatness, then that greatness came from his or her "white blood." Some of Paul's staunchest white allies subscribed to this countermyth. Dr. H. A. Tobey, who would prod Paul to super stardom, house him, and allow him to eat at his table, remarked on his first glimpse of the poet: "Thank God, he's black. Whatever genius he may have cannot be attributed to the white blood he may have in his veins."[128]

Most late-nineteenth-century Euro-Americans were extremely race conscious. The open fascination with Paul's skin color was indicative of this overt racism. He is "as black as the shades of night," wrote one supporter; "as black as the core of Cheops's pyramid," said another.[129] Reportedly, one of his mainstream friends said, "[Paul] is as *black* as they come" (emphasis in the original). "No," responded the poet, "'they' come at least two shades blacker than I am."[130]

By today's standards, Paul would be considered an attractive man. One friend described him as "exceedingly dark, graceful . . . with pleasing features and a smooth face."[131] His pal, James Weldon Johnson, said Paul's "black, intelligent face was grave, almost sad, except when he smiled or laughed." But, added Johnson: "There was on him the mark of distinction. He had an innate courtliness of manner, his speech was unaffectedly polished and brilliant, and he carried himself with that dignity of humility which never fails to produce a sense of the presence of greatness."[132] Then, too, added Johnson, Paul often acted as head-strong, as impulsive, and as irresponsible as a boy of six.

Dunbar stood five feet, nine and one-half inches tall (one-half inch shorter than his father, Joshua), had a thin frame, and high, broad chest. When in good health, which was seldom, he weighed between 125 and 135 pounds.[133] "One of his salient characteristics," recalled Alice, "was his beautiful voice. Deep, resonant, mellow and beautifully handled."[134] James Weldon Johnson concurred: "[Paul's] voice was a perfect musical instrument, and he knew how to use it with extreme effect."[135] He was also witty and ingratiating; but by his own admission, he was timid and shy with strangers.

Paul's temerity sprang from his youth. While his father had recognized his son's genius and Paul's mother had enveloped him in an intense love as she groomed him for greatness, a hostile racist environment had denigrated his talents and self-worth. Moreover, Paul's home life had been one of poverty, violence, alcoholism, and desertion. This socialization would affect his livelihood and lifestyle. And his relationship with Alice Ruth Moore.

It did so right from the beginning. Because the nation's color-consciousness had invaded his psyche, Paul was immediately attracted to Alice, a white-skinned African American with European features. In April 1895, while leafing through the current issue of the Boston *Monthly Review* magazine, twenty-two-year-old Paul saw one of Alice's poems and her photograph. He read the poem and liked it; but he loved the photograph. Since Paul had an eye for pretty mulatto women—as well as good literature—he decided to write Miss Moore.

TWO

To Escape the Reproach of
Her Birth and Blood

Even before they met, an infatuated Paul Laurence Dunbar would write Alice Ruth Moore (1875–1935) that he loved her and had loved her since seeing her photograph in the April 1895 issue of the Boston *Monthly Review* magazine.[1] His ardor sprang from what he saw in that picture. Clearly, judging by her clothing and demeanor, she was middle class. And by the prevailing standards for African American beauty, Alice was practically perfect. Paul saw in the photograph "a glorious face and dear upturned nose."[2] There were also long, thick auburn tresses and alabaster skin, "with the African strain slightly apparent," wrote Alice of people of her hue.[3] She looked just like a white woman; she was a beauty.

Plenty of men admired Alice's charms. "They say she is a sugah-lady, Jesus!" exclaimed one who knew her strictly by reputation.[4] Another believed that any man making her acquaintance, "would surely have been undone, for . . . Alice Ruth Moore has *glorious* eyes" (emphasis in the original).[5] At a Chicago stag party, yet another of Alice's unknown admirers recited a poem that he dedicated to her loveliness; and in the nation's capital, two friends—Napoleon Bonaparte Marshall, "a colored Harvard boy," and Frank Stewart—"rhapsodized over" her.[6]

Alice agreed with her admirers. Unlike Paul, who hated his looks, she was more than pleased with herself. When she peered in the mirror, she saw a Roman goddess, a "tall, broad-shouldered Juno."[7] Her ivory toned-skin and European features allowed her to pass for white, which she did, without difficulty or challenge, when she wished to attend cultural events labeled "for whites only."[8] In fact, this writer mistook Alice for a Euro-American. "Who is this white woman?" I asked on viewing an oil portrait of her in an African American's home. "That's my Aunt Alice," replied her niece, Pauline Alice Young.[9]

Alice relished the privileges her fair skin brought her. At nineteen years of age, she was a popular flirt, not unlike a similar character in one of her short stories who never "lacked partners or admirers. Dear no!"[10] Paul knew about her reputation as a "pretty, bright butterfly, a flirt" before instigating their relationship.[11] Subsequently, he would ask, "Are you flirting very desperately with anyone at present?"[12] Two months before Alice and Paul eloped, she still had a reputation for being a coquette, much to Paul's dismay.

Alice captured this frivolous side in one of her least successful poems. A frustrated beau tells his coquettish friend:

> Of your sweet smiles, you laugh at me,
> And treat me like a lump of dirt,
> Until I wish that I were dead,
> *For I am jealous, and you're a flirt.*
> . . . .
> You do not seem to know or care,
> How often you've my feelings hurt,
> While flying round with other boys,
> *For I am jealous, and you're a flirt.*
> (Emphasis in the original)[13]

Alice's diary confirms her immense popularity. Jimmie Vance and Jimmie Lewis adored her in 1892, she wrote.[14] That same year, when "Bis Pinchback went away and life was all black," she recalled in another entry, "exactly a month later, November 5, began my romance with Nelson Mitchell."[15] Falling in love (which Alice did often) and getting married were "natural" to women, she maintained, although she was one of the New Women who believed in careers and independence for her sex.[16] In spite of feminist leanings, however, Alice adhered to the traditional ideals of romantic love and the accompanying rituals that elite African Americans espoused. These gender-based ideals had a patriarchal slant. They were embraced almost as consistently by elite African Americans as by mainstream middle-class Americans. This idealism focused on the subordinate place of women in society and the dominant position of men.

Paul's first letter to Alice, dated April 17, 1895, was received at her home, 1924 Palmyra Street, in Uptown, a desirable section of New Orleans. Alice described the neighborhood in one of her short stories as "semi-fashionable . . . far up-town from the old-time French quarter . . . [t]he sort of neighborhood where millionaires live before their fortunes are made and fashionable high-priced private schools flourish. . . . The small cottages are occupied by aspiring teachers."[17] Alice, an aspiring teacher, shared a cottage with her mother, Patsy, a former slave; and an older sister, Mary Leila, called Leila by the family, who too was a teacher. Living also with the Moores was Alice's maternal grandmother, Mary Wright, a Virginia native and former slave. Because the daughters were educated and cultured school marms, they were part of the African American elite, members of the "best colored society."[18]

Alice's world of African American society was an overwhelmingly mulatto group. Traditionally, they were privileged over their darker race members by the majority culture. Yellow Negroes, as they were often called, were more acceptable to whites since they came closer to the American standard of whiteness. This color caste existed intraracially as well, for many people of color believed the theory that mulatto or biracial African Americans were superior to darker-skinned members. This was a legacy of bondage, when mulatto slaves, sometimes the children of owners, held the more preferred positions of house slaves or trained artisans. They received better treatment than field hands, the majority of whom were dark skinned. The small colony of free people of color existing during the slave era was largely mulatto. Although this group faced discrimination and was considered inferior to whites, it inhabited an unofficial third caste in which its members were considered superior to slaves and even to darker-skinned free blacks. With freedom, mulattoes received yet more respect and better opportunities in the African American world.

This elite group consisted of teachers, preachers, doctors, lawyers, journalists, and successful entrepreneurs. A self-ordained group, these men and women engaged in uplifting the usually darker-skinned, less fortunate African Americans, even though many also distanced themselves from this group.[19] The reason for this attitude, wrote Alice's contemporary, educator Anna Julia Cooper, was that the two groups had little or nothing in common. Elites constituted a "quiet, self-respecting, dignified class of easy life and manners . . . [and] cultivated taste and habits." They shared nothing with their less fortunate brothers and sisters, beyond "the accident of complexion—[and] a symphony of [racial] wrongs."[20]

The upper class of blacks expected their women to exhibit certain graces. "Do you recite? Do you sing? Don't you dance divinely?" Paul asked Alice by letter.[21] Such accomplishments were required for maintaining one's social status and ultimately entering a racially desegregated world. Alice's friend, Azalia Hackley, in her etiquette book, *The Colored Girl Beautiful* (1916), advised young women to be "eternally feminine . . . [and] study piano, elocution or singing [in preparation] for the day when opportunity will open the long-closed social door."[22] Paul's inquiries, then, were more than idle chatter. They gauged Alice's degree of ritualized attainments and social acceptability. His questions may have also been an attempt to assess Alice's marriageability, since Paul enclosed a love poem in his very first letter.[23] Looks, refined manners, social position, money, and accomplishments were the best assets for young middle-class women—whether black or white—in the marriage market.[24] In spite of New Woman ideals emphasizing career and independence, marriage was still considered to be woman's best profession.

Alice had what was expected of a proper lady, and more. "Yes, I recite," she replied to Paul's inquiry, "but not often[.] I dance, I won't vouch for the divine part of it, but I've done it so much that I am finding it rather a bore now-a-days. I don't draw by a little[.] I don't paint; I only sing in choruses . . . I play the mandolin, I am studying the violincello."[25] This list of talents merely hinted at her abilities and achievements. She was also a fine needlewoman, excelling at fancy work—embroidery, lace making, and the like. Alice acted in theatrical productions at her African American Methodist Episcopal church, was president of its Whittier Club, and played her mandolin in a New Orleans orchestra. A college graduate, she had a desirable profession for women of color, teaching school. When not employed in the classroom, she sometimes worked as a bookkeeper-stenographer for a local African American business. Not surprisingly, Paul's correspondent was also a club woman, one of those middle-class African Americans engaged in the many guises of racial uplift. She was a charter member of the local Phyliss Wheatley Club, organized in 1894. Following the trend, this group affiliated itself with the Woman's Era Club, a national black women's organization. Alice served as Newspaper and Current Events chairperson for the New Orleans branch, and she was the New Orleans correspondent and local sales agent for the *Woman's Era,* the popular monthly newspaper issued by the parent club.[26] This latter responsibility allowed her to expand her social connections, since the newspaper had "a circulation . . . particularly among the women of the refined and educated classes."[27] Still, somewhere in this hectic schedule, Alice found time to write a weekly "Women's Column" for a local African American newspaper, the *Journal of the Lodge.*[28]

Among all of her activities, however, Alice liked writing best—that is, writing poems and short stories. She told her correspondent Paul that her "voluminous duties, so to speak," left little time "for that which I love above all," which is writing.[29] Often she began or ended her *Woman's Era* column with one of her poems, and they frequently appeared in other national African American newspapers. Short stories in her first book, *Violets and Other Tales* (1895), in press when she began corresponding with Paul, would later be described by him as "pieces of exquisite art."[30] This collection of poems, short stories, and essays introduced Alice's favorite literary subject matter—New Orleans and its Creole life.

Young Alice was so very accomplished not only because it was a middle-class gender directive, but also because of family expectations. Like many African Americans in the post–Civil War period, the Moores were determined social climbers. Moreover, Alice was expected to excel because she (like Paul) was the family genius.

There were other noted aspects of her persona. Alice was in many ways the ideal sophisticate: elegant, fashionable, with a high regard for social niceties and reputations. Some contemporaries found her to be regal and proud; others, talented and beautiful.[31] Friends thought she was kind, with a lovable disposition and an impulsive nature. Alice loved grand opera. It was her "one weakness, extravagance and passion," she said.[32] But she also peppered her letters and conversations with the then popular New York Bowery slang. By admission, Alice was class-conscious, haughty, and an "aesthetic." She and her sister, Leila, resembled the two snobby siblings in Alice's short story "In Our Neighborhood," who "put on airs . . . holdin' up their heads like nobody's good enough to speak to."[33] Furthermore, Alice admitted to being ambitious, stubborn, and unyielding. In this respect, she was not unlike Paul.

Paul declared Alice his dream girl. Six months after initiating their correspondence, although they had still not met, he confessed, "Dear Miss Moore . . . I love you and have loved you since the first time I saw your picture. . . . You are the sudden realization of an ideal! I love you. I love you."[34]

What Paul loved was his fantasy of Alice; for to fall in love with a photograph is to love a delusion. He was also intoxicated with the portrait she painted of herself. Alice was not all that she seemed to be. True, her talents and beauty were genuine, and she was graceful and poised. The latter resulted from strict adherence to the prevailing class and gender directives for elite ladies. But Alice was also molded by virulent nineteenth-century racism. Her internalization of attitudes regarding African Americans manifested itself in racial pride as well as in confused identity and racial self-loathing. She did not want to be a Negro—the popular label for Americans of African descent. As a result, she spun fantasies about her family and true identity. Paul would use both fabrications as weapons, when his idealistic love of Alice dissipated in the face of reality.

Little is known about Alice's early years, with evidence suggesting that she obfuscated this record. But Alice, a prolific writer, left no clear data on her life prior to her emergence in New Orleans's African American society, though some coded clues surface in her fiction. Her records give the impression that she, like the Greek goddess Athena, emerged full blown into her world.

Alice's reluctance to document her background is curious since she had access to sources about it. During her youth in New Orleans, she lived with her mother and grandmother. When Alice's marriage to Paul ended, her mother, Patsy, moved in with her daughter and stayed there until she died. Surely at some point, the family reflected on Alice's childhood days and discussed family history. If this was so, Alice did not document the information.

She did this on purpose, for she knew the importance of the historical record and of her role in history. She saved hundreds of items regarding her relationship with Paul, including intimate letters brimming with shame or pain. Furthermore, she entered in her personal journal:

"Put in most of the day at the office making up [this] diary. Seemed an awful thing to do just to spend that time, *but my diary is going to be a valuable thing one of these days*" (emphasis added).[35]

The conspicuous lack of evidence regarding her early years suggests that Alice found her family history and childhood more painful and embarrassing than any of the indignities she suffered with Paul. She preserved that period of life with him in letters, short stories, and poem: clearly, she wanted it exposed. However, it seems equally obvious that such candor did not extend to revealing her childhood.

Perhaps it was not unusual for prominent African American women of the era to shroud a childhood that did not enhance their adult image. While the American myth allowed men to be diamonds in the rough and go from rags to riches, no such fable existed for middle-class and elite women, either black or white. Gender directives required gentility and stainless reputations always. It may also be that because mulatto women had greater social mobility—especially through marriage—they had stronger motives for covering "embarrassing" backgrounds. Novelist Nella Larsen (1891–1964), a once prominent author, so muddied her humble origins that even today, despite exhaustive research, she remains the mystery woman of the Harlem Renaissance. Larsen, like Alice, married one of the outstanding African American men of her day.[36]

Alice shared her shameful background with Paul. Once aware of her sensitivity to the subject, it became a tool of abuse. In a letter dated simply "Thursday" (probably written in September 1898), Alice, a recent bride, wrote her husband:

> Sometimes I have told you things. . . . Then when a time comes, when you are half-irritated, wholly nervous, you cast them in my face in derision, and hurt me so. . . . I don't throw bits of your personal history in your face, or deride you about your family. . . . Dearest—dearest—I hate to write this— How often, oh how painfully often, when scarce meaning you have thrust my parentage in my face.[37]

Alice's "parentage" and "bits of personal history" plagued her throughout her adult years. While Paul celebrated his origins—his proverbial rise from rags to riches—Alice for the most part remained mum about her beginnings. What was her history that "hurt her so" and threatened her all-important social status? The evidence suggests that just as she could not reconcile herself to being a much-maligned Negro, so Alice could not reconcile her origins and childhood to her acquired identity as an adult.

Benjamin Brawley, a pioneer in African American history, wrote that the history of a poet is determined by the history of the poet's people in the United States.[38] This theory may be applied to the childhood history of Alice, a noted poet of her day. Her early years reflect the tenor of the times: the poverty of the defeated South after the Civil War, the poverty of its freed people, the efforts of former chattel and their offspring to become economically independent, and the turmoil surrounding their socioeconomic strivings in an era of overt white supremacy.

New Orleans in 1875, the year of Alice's birth, was still reeling from the consequences of being on the wrong side of the war. Once one of the nation's richest centers, with seemingly unlimited economic opportunities for Euro-Americans, the city in the late 1870s was poor. Its once busy harbor saw few docking ships, while business and commerce in general were lackadaisical. The city was dirty and poorly lit. It had no adequate sewage system, nor a regulated method of garbage disposal. Debris rotting in the streets was a common sight. Canals and ditches were dumping sites. Moreover, the water supply was unsafe, and disease and illness were rampant.

Many Southern cities shared New Orleans's economic and civic problems. Throughout the South, African Americans, especially recently freed slaves, were blamed for societal ills. In New Orleans—the South's largest city and home of the nation's largest black population— African Americans were the inevitable scapegoats. One historian explains:

> The white man had hoped for so much in his "war for independence." [H]e had lost so much . . . his self-respect and property at Appomattox; and the burden of defeat and humiliation hung so heavily on him, that he was forced to grasp at any straw that promised some relief for the pain. The Negro, the property the white man went to war to preserve, was the ubiquitous reminder of his . . . humiliation and defeat.[39]

In fact, one returning Confederate soldier probably spoke for many when he declared: "[T]hose black scondrels [*sic*] . . . we will have no mercy on them[,] we will kill them like dogs. I [was] never down on a nigger as I am now."[40]

Figuratively speaking, the method of "killing" African Americans in New Orleans and in the South in general was the suppression of political and social rights granted by the federal government during Reconstruction. This white fight for hegemony reified the concepts of innate white supremacy and black inferiority. It resulted in the iron-clad system of segregation. "Jim Crow," writes Arthe Anthony, a New Orleans scholar, "grew to the point that no black person, nor any white person for that matter, could ever be confused about the nature of Southern race relations."[41]

Alice Ruth Moore was born in this socially charged atmosphere at 8 A.M., July 19, 1875, in a house on Second Street in New Orleans.[42] Circumstances surrounding her birth hint at those bits of personal history that Paul scorned. Her birth neighborhood was not as fashionable as the New Orleans address at which she received her first letter from him. A few boardinghouses and inexpensive lodgings dotted the vicinity.[43]

Alice is believed to be the second child or second daughter of Patsy Wright, a former mulatto slave and native of Opalousas, Louisiana. Alice's birth certificate identifies her father, Monroe Moore, as also a native of the state. Nothing else is known about him. Because of his daughter's near white skin and Euro-American features, Monroe Moore may have been a white man. Or he may have been an extremely fair-skinned mulatto.

Alice's father may have been a laborer named Monroe Moore. According to *Soards' New Orleans City Directory*, a worker by that name lived in New Orleans in 1874, the year before Alice's birth.[44] This Monroe Moore was a white man; the city directory identified African Americans by the word "colored" next to their name, yet no such designation followed Moore's name. He disappeared from the annual city directories after 1874, suggesting that he left New Orleans. The last public New Orleans record of Monroe Moore is his designation as father on Alice's 1875 birth certificate. He was not a presence in Alice's life, never appearing in her personal records, not even as the name of a character in her short stories.

Alice's birth certificate, census records, and New Orleans city directories provide additional clues to her early history. The birth certificate reads: "Alice Moore, lawful issue . . . with Monroe Moore [and] Patsy Moore, born Wright."[45] However, other public documents dispute some of this information. For example, in 1876 and 1877—the two years immediately following Alice's birth—New Orleans city directories listed a Miss Patsy Wright, not a Mrs. Patsy Wright Moore, as indicated on Alice's birth certificate. Patsy Wright lived at 42 N. Robertson.[46] In 1880, a *Mrs.* Patsy Wright (again, not Mrs. Patsy Wright Moore), of 45 Pyrtania Street, is cited.[47] That same year, the federal census shows Patsy Wright, mulatto, age 30, as head of a household that includes two daughters, Mary *Wright* [known as Leila], age 10; and Alice *Wright* (later to be known as Alice Ruth Moore), age 5. Patsy Wright supported her family as a washerwoman. Her marital status is unclear, though she was either widowed or divorced.[48]

It appears, then, that Patsy's marital status on Alice's birth certificate is false. She seems never to have married anyone, since Wright is her mother's surname. The late historian John Blassingame wrote that black mothers often lied to the 1880 census enumerators about their marital status because they did not wish to report their children as illegitimate.[49] Perhaps, also, as Patsy assimilated middle-class values and her daughters grew older, she declared herself married to give herself and the children more respectability.

Mrs. Patsy Wright is listed just once more in the New Orleans city directory. In 1883, her address was still 45 Prytania Street,[50] but she disappears for several years to emerge in 1887 as Patsy Moore, a live-in servant residing at 47 Prytania.[51] Why and when Patsy took the surname Moore is not certain, but it is reasonable to assume she simultaneously conferred it on her daughters. After 1887, Patsy once again disappears from the city directories until 1892.[52] When she reappears, her socioeconomic situation has improved immensely, for her family has entered the middle class, however precariously. Patsy Moore had moved to 56-1/2 Palmyra Street, in "the small house where geraniums grew in the front yard and morning glories climbed over the fence," wrote Alice later of that address in one of her short stories.[53] Her mother shared the house with Alice's sister, Leila, a teacher at the "colored" Robertson School, according to the city directory. Alice is not listed as a resident, perhaps because she was away at school.[54] More importantly, however, is Patsy's new measure of respectability: she is cited as the widow of John Moore.

It is interesting that Patsy's "deceased husband" is John Moore rather than Monroe Moore, the designated father on Alice's birth certificate.

John Moore seems not to have been a randomly selected name. He is the father of Alice's older sister, Mary Leila, according to her birth certificate.[55] Also, Alice's mother and Leila's father were natives of Opalousas, Louisiana. Patsy's name appears on her older daughter's birth record as Patsy Wright, not Patsy Moore, as she later designated herself on Alice's birth certificate. It seems then, that another part of Alice's secret and painful history is that she and her sister were not only born out of wedlock, and out of the middle class; they also, seemingly, had different fathers. And it further appears that the two fathers, John and Monroe Moore, may have been related since both were natives of Louisiana. Moreover, Leila, like Alice, was fair skinned enough to pass for white and sometimes did.[56] But more definitive evidence may be gleaned from the coded clues in one of Alice's short stories about two brothers, one of whom has a common-law wife.

In the story, "Tony's Wife," a common-law couple operate a run-down grocery store on Prytania Street, a street on which Alice and her family lived for several years in various houses. Tony, the owner, loafs and verbally abuses his nameless "wife," factotum of all hard and dirty work. Her work situation, then, is not unlike that of Patsy, who labored long and hard with little monetary reward as washerwoman and servant. Tony, the "husband," falls terminally ill. Although his "wife" nurses him and begs him to marry her, Tony refuses. On his death, his brother—whose name is not so coincidentally John—inherits the business. The nameless wife is turned out into the cold.[57]

Like "Tony's wife," it is possible that Patsy, too, shared a common-law relationship. It is known, for example, that she was living in New Orleans by 1869, the year of daughter Leila's birth, which had occurred in an inexpensive boarding house located at 236 Carondolet Street—home of Patsy's mother, Mary Wright, also a washerwoman.[58] Although Mary Wright still lived at that address in 1875, the year of Alice's birth, Alice was born elsewhere, suggesting that Patsy had some other form of support at that time and/or no longer lived with her mother. In other words, Patsy had a home of her own, possibly as the common-law wife of Alice's father, Monroe Moore; recall that Patsy identified herself on Alice's birth certificate as "Patsy Moore, born Wright."

One other element of Patsy's history points to the probability that she was a common-law wife. Patsy had told Alice that, upon freedom, her former owner established businesses for some of his ex-chattel, inferring that she was a recipient of one.[59] But one Louisiana scholar believes this to be an apocryphal tale, noting that Patsy appeared to have been illiterate at that time and therefore an unlikely entrepreneur.[60]

This theory is credible, as no evidence indicates that Patsy knew the "three R's" shortly after freedom. In fact, as her daughters became literate, they wrote her letters for her and may have read her correspondence to her as well. However, some of Alice's biographers have speculated that Patsy worked as a seamstress, a genteel and respectable occupation. The inference is that she was set up in the sewing business by her former owner. Again, no solid evidence supports this theory.

It is true that Patsy had some sewing skills, as she made her daughters' clothes. Generally, after the Civil War, freed women flocked to sewing classes, operated by Yankee missionaries and teachers, in preparation for the promised middle-class lifestyle. Skill with the needle was expected of middle-class women, and even Alice joined a sewing school while working as a teacher in New York.[61] But acquiring sewing skills does not make one a professional seamstress. Still, Alice's biographers believe that this was Patsy's occupation, even though evidence indicates she was not. Alice spoke of a time in 1892 when she promenaded "the streets of New Orleans, all clad in [a] new frock . . . a dark blue chambray, which Mama had made, fondly believing it a Russian blouse, until Maime Dessauer punctured our pride by saying it was not a Russian blouse."[62] Fashion sewing was a highly competitive business for genteel ladies in the nineteenth century. Someone not cognizant of current trends nor sufficiently skilled to replicate them would not have survived as a professional seamstress. Moreover, New Orleans city directories traditionally contained long lists of seamstresses in each issue, and Patsy's name was never among them. Nor was there any designated occupation for her in the directories except for the notation of "servant" in the 1887 edition. If Patsy were a seamstress, she probably did piece-work sewing, a prevalent, low-paying source of income for poor, working-class women. In Alice's short story, "Little Miss Sophie," the pitiful New Orleans mulatto heroine earned a meager living in this manner,[63] so Miss Sophie may reflect some of Patsy Moore's history. The star of this tale was poverty stricken because her white lover abandoned her and married a woman of his own race.

It seems unlikely, then, that Patsy had her own business. If she were engaged in such an enterprise, it was someone's else's establishment, and she, like the story character in "Tony's Wife," did the hard and dirty work. Moreover, since it is not known how Patsy supported herself since her arrival in New Orleans between 1869 and 1880, when she worked as a washerwoman, it is probable that at some point she was a common-law wife. This type of arrangement was common after the Civil War, according to the late historian John Blassingame, because slavery had fostered and encouraged perfunctory intimate unions. Moreover, Louisiana's state legislature tacitly approved common-law relationships by not passing laws to regulate marital relations among freed slaves immediately after the war. Since no public act or ceremony legitimized marriage; since there were twice as many black women (ages 15–45) as black men in the same age group in New Orleans in 1870; and since there was an unwillingness of many people of color to marry darker African Americans, "[It] was rather a common thing . . . that a man could establish almost any relationship that pleased him."[64] Blassingame adds that it took some members of the freed community many years to realize that one did not mate casually with an attractive party only to desert him or her when someone even more pleasing came along.

Alice's early years help to explain her later desire for a specific elite identity, a high-status lifestyle, and a propensity for social niceties. There was no stable father figure in her life; and unlike Paul, whose relationship with his mother, Matilda, has been compared to a love affair, Alice's relationship with Patsy appears to have been strained. A little more than two weeks after the storybook elopement of Alice and Paul, when he had again verbally assaulted her, Alice wrote: "Those who love me have always spoken tenderly to me. . . . Sister holds a higher place in my affections now than [M]ama because she never spoke a harsh word to me in her life." On another occasion, Alice mentioned that she got "such devotion from [S]ister."[65]

Alice's warm feelings for Leila contrasted sharply with those she held for her mother. "Am afraid I am a cold creature towards her at best," she says of Patsy in her diary. Other entries evidence a mother who always made fusses and stirred up strife in the family; a mother who was insulting, who nagged and criticized and was the personification of gloom.[66] Alice's alienation may also have stemmed from the fact that her mother was a strict disciplinarian, which some of Alice's short stories suggest. Her fictional children are beaten when errands are not performed well; they are soundly cuffed for playing in the mud, and slapped when they intrude into adult conversations.[67] If indeed Alice's art emulated her life, Patsy's forms of punishment were not unusual. Slave mothers, brought up by the lash, were strong believers in the corporal punishment that had been administered to them. Their felt need to be exceedingly harsh with offspring often created an emotional distance between mother and child.

One other factor may have contributed to the strained mother-daughter relationship: Patsy may have been separated from her girls for some time. When she worked as a live-in servant (ca. 1887)—a low-status, low-paying job—Patsy undoubtedly placed her girls in the care of her mother, Mary Wright, of whom Alice was very fond.[68] Because of the brutality commonly afflicted female servants by employers—verbal assaults, beatings, sexual exploitation—servants went to great lengths to keep their daughters out of service and away from the homes of their employers. This was especially true if the servant had been sexually compromised at some point in her life. It is not certain how long Alice's mother worked as a servant, though public records indicate she held such a position in 1887. In that year, Leila was seventeen and Alice twelve. It seems unlikely that their mother would have exposed them to the very real possibilities of psychological and physical harm by having them live with her in her employer's home.

How did Alice leave these humble circumstances of her early years and become a belle in the sometimes pretentious world of African American high society? How did she become an educated, refined, cultured "lady"?

Next to the family, the school is the greatest institution of socialization in American society. Educational systems teach children not only essential knowledge and skill for responsible participation in that society, but also the sanctioned middle-class attitudes and habits of its members. Inculcation of these ideals was a major goal of pedagogy at the turn of the twentieth century. Immigrant children and children of slaves were believed to be in particular need of middle-class ideals. An education focusing on middle-class values thus spawned the African American elite.

The social aspirations of former slaves for their offspring centered on education. Although most families were like Alice's—minimumly paid and poverty stricken—members often pooled meager resources to finance the education of at least one child. Still, even though unusual sacrifices were made, three-fourths of the African American children in New Orleans during Alice's youth in 1880 did not have an opportunity to attend school.[69] Moreover, local governments hampered the full education of African American students as well—there were no public high schools for African Americans in the South until 1924.[70] According to local custom, black children were not entitled to the same education as their Euro-American counterparts. Besides, most southern whites believed that people of color were destined for menial work only, and they did not need a high school education for that.

Alice and Leila were among the privileged few to receive good educations. Unlike Paul, whose ex-slave mother Matilda taught him to read before he entered school, Alice was still illiterate when she began her education at a segregated public school in New Orleans.[71] This suggests, too, that her mother was unlettered and could not teach her daughters.

A clue to these early years may be found in Alice's short story "Brass Ankles Speaks," a blend of fact and fiction. A poor girl, "white enough to pass for white," lives in a "far Southern city where complexion determine[d] one's social status."[72] This fictional being, Alice's mirror image, spends six miserable years in the local school system—miserable because of the hatred meted out by dark-skinned school mates because of her complexion. The character's family sends her away to a private school, which, was also Alice's fate. Following her initial years of public education, she entered the grammar department of Southern University in Baton Rouge, Louisiana.

Southern University, charted in 1881, was one of several academies of higher learning established for African Americans in the South after the Civil War. These institutions offered training at all levels, from grammar school to a university degree. The heroine in "Brass Ankles" loved her new school "because here I found boys and girls like myself, fair [and] light brown." Moreover, her fictitious family could afford the tuition. While it was reasonable, it was still expensive enough to keep "out many a proletariat."[73] The average cost per student at these newly established schools was five to ten dollars per month for room, board, and tuition. Those who could not pay worked ten hours a day in exchange for two hours of schooling at night.[74] Booker T. Washington was educated at Hampton Institute through this rigorous form of work-study.

Alice's regimen at Southern probably emulated that of students at Atlanta University, a highly rated American Missionary Association school established in 1865. The individualism and ease characterizing twenty-first-century institutions was nonexistent in these late nineteenth-century bastions of learning. Students rose at six, and when the breakfast bell rang at seven, they marched swiftly and quietly to the dining hall under the watchful eye of a professor. On reaching the dining hall, a participant wrote:

> We stand an instant behind our chairs, and then seat ourselves simultaneously. . . . [O]ne professor, and perhaps two, presides at each table. . . . [T]he fare is exceedingly plain: meat, usually beef . . . hominy and johnny-cake without butter, and coffee. At noon we have rice *in lieu* of potato; and the teachers have a cup of coffee; for supper there is bread, which only occasionally is new, syrup or canned fruit, or sometimes a custard and a little butter, and tea for the teachers. . . . All through Prof. Francis touches softly a bell; we stand behind our chairs a moment, then at a nod the young men pass out two by two, but the young ladies remain and clear away the tables; and it is done with great order and dispatch. . . . At nine in the morning we assemble for devotional exercises. . . . Friday, the school week closes by a prayer-meeting for thirty minutes.[75]

This regimen undoubtedly instilled in graduates the discipline characteristic of the growing African American elite. Along with rigorous academic training, these schools aimed to instill middle-class virtues and values in former slaves and their children.

Alice, on graduating from Southern University's high school division at age fourteen in 1889, entered another of the premier institutions for African Americans in the South. Straight University, chartered in 1869 and described as the "strongest institution for higher education among Negroes in New Orleans," had the professed goal of becoming the "Harvard of the South."[76] The curriculum was challenging; and each week, students gave public demonstrations of their acquired knowledge.

Alice's metamorphosis into the cultured society belle was further enhanced by her years at Straight. There she rubbed shoulders with African American Creole society, the self-designated elite of black aristocracy. A perusal of the school's catalogues for 1894–1895 and 1897–1898 shows a large number of students with the French and Spanish surnames indicative of Creole families.[77] Moreover, the city's wealthiest African Americans, all of whom were Creoles of color, patronized the institution. Alice undoubtedly immersed herself in this culture while at Straight. Later, she would declare herself a French Creole and write extensively about the lifestyle in her short stories.

Professors and administrators continued Alice's education in middle-class values. According to a Straight University catalog, females were trained "in the manners of a refined Christian home [and had] the constant inculcation of principles of good breeding, by precept and example."[78] This training emphasized gender-role directives. Usually at these schools, female students worked for one hour in the housekeeping department and were expected to iron their clothes. Males put in their daily work hour on the school farm.[79]

Alice's intellect and talents were cultivated at Straight, as well as her breeding and gender training. A contemporary found her to be a "quick, apt scholar . . . [she] developed such a talent for composition that she was encouraged to devote special attention to English literature and the classics."[80] She submitted her first manuscript for publication while a student at Straight, although the title and fate of this work are unknown. Like Paul Laurence Dunbar, Alice too had aspirations of being a great writer. However, like most African American women fortunate enough to attend college, she trained to be a teacher, the profession deemed most desirable for females. It was preferable for many reasons: teaching was one of the better-paying jobs for women of color, one of the few in which their duties would be commensurate with their education; teaching was also part of racial uplift and an acceptable means for women to extend their "natural proclivities" for training and nurturing into the public sector; finally, teachers had prestige and status in African American communities.[81]

It is understandable, then, why the vast majority of educated African American women were school marms. In 1890, in Washington, D.C., capital of the black aristocracy—and Alice's home after her marriage—81.6 percent of African American school teachers were female.[82]

Alice joined the ranks in New Orleans, on May 25, 1892, at age seventeen, when she graduated from Straight University's Normal Department.[83] Once again, like Paul, she was the class poet. Unlike him, however, at age seventeen, Alice had already earned a university degree. Despite his intellectual gifts, Paul never attended college. Also, because of illness, he did not graduate from high school until he was nineteen. These distinctions would not be easily tolerated by Paul, a self-absorbed genius and proponent of male superiority.

Alice continued writing after graduating from Straight. She won third prize in two short-story contests in 1893; and in 1895, when just twenty years old, she published her first book, *Violets and Other Tales*. This collection of short stories, poems, and essays was written in the popular sentimental Victorian mode. Eighteen years later, Alice called the book "sheer slop"; but it was widely and favorably reviewed in contemporary African American newspapers when first published.[84] Literary critics seldom focused on the book's merit and stressed instead what was paramount to all elite African Americans, mainly, how well the person and product represented the race. By that standard, *Violets and Other Tales* was first-rate. A typical review declared the book "evidence of great intelligence among persons of African birth." The talented authoress was one of the "able colored women of this country . . . deserving recognition."[85]

With the publication of her book in 1895, Alice became a full-fledged and stellar member of the African American upper crust. She was educated and cultured; she performed useful "race" work as a teacher at the "colored" Marigny School in New Orleans.[86] By rising in status from the illegitimate daughter of a washerwoman, Alice had not only fulfilled personal and familial ambitions, she had also adhered to a gender-directed maxim. The nineteenth-century Euro-American girl was told that self-improvement was her task and that she could change her condition for the better, whether economic or social. Similarly, poor women of color were exhorted to rise above their lowly station in life by acquiring education, good character, good breeding, and high morals. Such a woman would be rewarded, wrote Alice's friend, Azalia Hackley, in *The Colored Girl Beautiful,* by being "somebody." She would "grow in . . . influence and reputation, until people [would] forget her ancestry and any objectionable relations, as well as [her] former environment."[87]

By the time Alice received her first letter from Paul that spring in 1895, she had become a recognized "somebody" in the African American community. Her regal bearing and lifestyle suggested that, like the

New Orleans mulatto heroine in George Washington Cable's popular book, *Madame Delphine* (1881), Alice, too, had "escape[d] the reproach of her birth and blood."[88] But neither the fictitious Delphine nor Alice overcame what they considered life's greatest calamity: despite social transformation, both remained African Americans. It mattered not to white America that Alice looked like a white woman and did not want to be treated like a black one. The proverbial one drop of African blood— the proclaimed if hard-to-define standard for detecting a person of color—meant that she was an African American, too.

Alice, however, did not accept that racial definition; nor did she consider herself a Negro, the prevailing term for a person of African descent. In her article, "People of Color in Louisiana," she offered proof that she was not, by providing a definition of Negro—one that excluded her. "By common consent," wrote Alice, "[Negro] came to mean in Louisiana, prior to 1865, slave; and after the [Civil] war, *those whose complexions were noticeably dark*. . . . The [mulatto] people were always a class apart, separated from and superior to the Negroes, ennobled were it only by one drop of white blood in their veins" (emphasis added).[89]

Clearly, Alice did not view herself as a Negro even though she lived in an exclusively African American world. Her statement about the relative positions of mulattoes and Negroes in Louisiana society suggests that she, too, saw herself as superior to "those whose complexions were noticeably dark." Alice, however, lived in a nation in which Americans—for political reasons—were classified as black or white. This racial rigidity governed the distribution of material goods, in which whiteness was rewarded and blackness devalued. Alice's Euro-American features accorded both pleasure and pain. Her beauty rested on skin privilege, as did much of her social mobility, but skin privilege was not all positive. The racial ambiguities of being black but being able to pass for white, and of having a white skin but having to live as a black, produced a racially conflicted Alice. Throughout her life she demonstrated a racial ambivalence that manifested itself in feelings of racial inferiority, as well as a strong dislike for dark-skinned African Americans like Paul Laurence Dunbar.

Given that Alice both attempted to deny her African heritage by defining herself as other than a Negro (and by ranking mulattoes above dark-skinned coloreds), and that she disliked African Americans of the darker hue, her relationship with Paul seems problematic from the beginning. Publicity surrounding his genius touted him as a man of "pure African descent." Moreover, one of his major benefactors described him as being as "black as the shades of night."[90]

Alice's racial prejudice raises several questions about her romance with Paul. Was it possible for her to sublimate her bigotry during their relationship? How important were race and skin color as factors in the Dunbars' stormy courtship and marriage?

Exactly when Paul became aware of Alice's racism and its implications is uncertain. She juggled her racial feelings as well as a skilled circus performer plying the juggler's trade. In public, for the most part, she professed to be African American; her articles in black newspapers affirmed women of color. As a self-proclaimed "race woman," she was proud to be African American, and a champion of "the race." She was a doyenne of black society, engaging in social activities to benefit "the race." But despite public declarations, Alice's mind's eye did not want to see herself as a Negro. How could she be, Alice may have rationalized, when by her definition a Negro had "a noticeably dark complexion" and she did not? She may also have asked herself, as a devotee of art, why the popular naturalist painter John James Audubon, who lived for a time in New Orleans, was considered white while she was not. After all, both had white skin, Euro-American features, and mulatto mothers.[91]

The racial ambivalence Alice expressed was not uncommon among African Americans. During this period of overt white supremacy, many mulattoes delighted in their Euro-American features and deprecated the African heritage. This preference for white over black was so prevalent that the book *The Colored Girl Beautiful,* written by a mulatto, gave advice on how to "eliminate or minimize racial spots." Because "others" (i.e., whites, if not other blacks), ridiculed African Americans about these offensive spots—hair, nose, lips—they must be changed, the author concluded. This must happen in order for blacks to meet the approval of the dominant culture.[92] In a similar vein, African American club woman and job broker Fannie Barrier Williams equated superior job skills with the applicant's color, or more specifically, the lack of color. One of her outstanding female African American applicants "did not show much color"; another had "only a slight trace of African blood."[93]

In his classic book the *Black Bourgeoisie,* sociologist E. Franklin Frazier wrote that African Americans who wish to escape their racial identity exhibit "most strikingly [an] inferiority complex." This lack of self-esteem, he continued, is greater in the middle class, "which has striven more than any other element to make itself over in the image of whites."[94] While Frazier focused on the middle class, he realized that devaluation of the black self knew no class lines. Throughout two centuries of slavery, Euro-Americans had attempted to convince Africans and their descendants of their inferiority by using all forms of propaganda, including biblical passages and pulpit sermons. A legal system of racial segregation further stigmatized blacks as unfit for citizenship and social privilege. Moreover, while American popular culture held that all African Americans were bestial and incapable of thought, those with dark skin were seen as particularly ugly, depraved, and stupid. Accordingly, white supremacy became, and remains, endemic among both black and white Americans.

The racial climate surrounding Alice and Paul—she of the white skin, with some attendant privileges; he of the black skin, deemed most odious—contributed to their feelings of inferiority. Both internalized racist attitudes and assumptions about people of color, and both acted on them. Their personal pain often surfaced in a hatred for African American "others," that is, those with a different skin tone. Paul loved Alice's whiteness; but he also hated it. His dialect poem, "Dely," suggests that he preferred "pure" people of color to mulattoes, who are dubious characters because of their "mixed blood":

> Dely's brown as brown kin be,
>   She ain't no mullater;
> She's pure cullud—don' you see
>   Dat's jus what's de mattah?
> Dat's de why I love huh so,
>   D'ain't no mix about huh,
> Soon's you see huh face you know
>   D'ain't no chanst to doubt huh.[95]

Alice vented much of her racial confusion in a prejudice against dark-skinned people. Her barely veiled character in the short story "Brass Ankles Speaks" believes this bigotry is a justifiable means of retaliation, since dark blacks are so mean to white blacks! The ivory-skinned narrator accuses "dark brethren" of initiating an intraracial hatred. "As in Haiti, as in Africa," she intones, "the bitterness and prejudice [has] always come from the blacks to the yellows. . . . [T]he darker brethren DO NOT LIKE THEM . . . [and the yellows] are forced to draw together in a common cause against their blood brothers who visit upon them hatred and persecution" (emphasis in original).[96]

Several real-life incidents indicate that Alice's fictional counterpart spoke for her creator. While working as a school teacher in Brooklyn during her engagement to Paul, Alice had a running battle with a faculty member that evidenced her racist attitudes. Recall that by her definition, a Negro was anyone with a dark brown face, and that mulattoes were superior to them. Also recall that Alice considered Negroes as "others," and that her fictional double in the story "Brass Ankles Speaks" viewed "others" as the enemy.

The Euro-American department head at Alice's school was being replaced by Miss Lyons, an African American. On receiving this news, Alice was appalled. She informed Paul, "I hate to work under Negro women, never did it and my heart [sinks] at the prospect."[97] Later, when the "new head of dept, a Negro woman," assumed her post, Alice confided sarcastically: "[Y]ou can imagine how cheerful things are. I've asked for a transfer and if I don't get it, I'll give her one good 'sassing.'"[98] Shortly thereafter, Alice "teased our new nigger head of dept crazy."[99]

Alice defended her racism by telling Paul that Miss Lyons was part of an African American faction at school that despised her, presumably because of Alice's fair skin. However, the Lyons incident was one mere sally in her war on Negroes. "I leave school Thursday . . . and go to a [new] school where there are neither colored teachers or pupils," Alice wrote Paul. "I can always get along with white people." She then reminded Paul of her current social situation: "I made my friends exclusively with the white teachers [here], ate with them [and] went to and fro with them."[100]

Alice's dislike of dark-skinned people was not limited to her opponents in intrafaculty warfare. A male acquaintance who displeased her was an "inkspot," whom she secretly called "Inky"; a female crony in a group of "blonde and high brown" mulatto women "looked like a fly in a flour barrel."[101] Furthermore, in her mature years, Alice would endorse a bleaching cream in several African American newspapers.[102]

Alice's prejudices, though widespread, were not universal among elite African Americans. The educator Nannie Helen Burroughs, in her essay "Not Color but Character," chastised women who bleached their skin, saying they wanted to be white.[103] In Alice's hometown of New Orleans, many people of African descent—regardless of skin tone—celebrated that heritage. Some referred to themselves as "colored," "Negro," "African," "Africo-American," and even sometimes proudly, rather than disparagingly, as "black." Many joined a campaign to capitalize "Negro," contending that the prevalent lower case "n" fastened on the word was a sign of inferiority devised by white printers. Moreover, P. B. S. Pinchback, acting governor of the state during Reconstruction—and a mulatto—proclaimed that Negroes were "proud . . . and perfectly content to stand where God placed us in the human scale; and would not lighten or dark the tinge of our skins, nor change the color nor current of our blood."[104] Others stalwartly refuted a popular notion that people of color were inferior because they had been enslaved, and because their progenitors were "savages." An article in the African American newspaper *New Orleans Tribune* (1879) argued that

> [w]hites could not point to the condition of the Negro, or his enslavement to prove his inferiority. Whites had been enslaved before the African had: the Britons had enslaved the Saxons and Normans, and the Romans had made slaves of them all. At some point in their history, all Americans had been savages, so what right did whites have to point to the savagery of Africans as proof of the Negro's inferiority?[105]

Alice's displeasure with her racial self contributed to the construction of a new ethnic identity. She decided to become a Creole. Her all-important physical appearance—which some called exotic—and the fact that she was a native of New Orleans gave many the impression that her ancestors were Creoles of color, and more likely free Creoles of color. She encouraged this speculation. Many inhabitants of New Orleans insisted that Creoles were "pure whites," with French or Spanish ancestors and no African ancestry. Nevertheless, there existed a small, tight-knit group of mainly French-speaking mulattoes, calling themselves *gens de couleur,* or Creoles of color. According to the popular nineteenth-century author George Washington Cable, they too, traced their origins to New Orleans's French and Spanish colonial periods, when the sexual liaisons of "merry gallants of a French colonial service . . . [and] comely Ethiopians culled from the less negroidal types of African[s]" produced a distinctive group of colored Franco-Americans.[106]

Becoming a Creole meshed with Alice's distorted conception of African Americans, since she considered herself neither black nor white. By her definition, a New Orleans Creole was a mixed-race, unraced person of Spanish or French descent. She wrote:

> It appears to a Caucasian a Creole is a native of the lower parishes of Louisiana, in whose veins some traces of Spanish . . . or French blood runs. . . . [But] a person of color will retort with his definition that a Creole is a native of Louisiana in whose blood runs mixed strains of everything un-American, with the African strain slightly apparent.[107]

But these Creoles are not what Alice called "true Creoles." The genuine article was much more exotic, much more distinctive, and definitely unraced. The "true Creole," continued Alice, "is like the famous gumbo of the state, a little of everything, making a whole delightfullly flavored, quite distinctive, and wholly unique."[108] Since the latter definition excluded race—the differential factor in the debate—Alice obviously viewed a "true Creole" as an unraced being. To her, "essential Creole attitudes" produced Creoles, and these attitudes negated racial distinctions.[109] It would appear that Alice had found the perfect identity. Since she was not legally white and did not consider herself black, she perceived herself as an aracial, mixed-race Creole. This identity allowed her to circumvent the racial label conferred on her by American society: it enabled her "to escape the reproach of her birth and blood."

Perhaps what Alice attempted to do—that is, to reject the black self—was to be expected in the United States. In this country, the ideal self had been made synonymous with being white. Much of black identity had been enunciated by whites, many of whom did not conceive of blacks as human beings. Accordingly, many people of color rejected their African heritage and searched for elements from which to fashion a new identity.

Alice's solution to a comforting racial identity was the construction of a Creole self—in fact, of two Creole selves: a public one and a private one. Publicly, she professed to be a Creole of color, although no evidence supports her claim. Undoubtedly, she assumed this identity partly because some considered Creoles of color the most elite of

African American society in her hometown of New Orleans. By proclaiming this heritage, she bowed to the social status quo by admitting she was somewhat of a Negro, even though (or perhaps, because) many Creoles of color refused to consider themselves of African descent. Privately, Alice escaped racial labels altogether.

Alice's self-constructions may seem unusual today, but they reflected a common mode of survival in the turbulence of late-nineteenth-century America. Jean Toomer (1894–1967), whose book *Cane* (1923) has been hailed as one of the three best novels written by an African American, anguished, as did Alice, over the precariousness of racial identity. He was descended from a noted family of near-white blacks. His grandfather was the mulatto Louisiana governor, P. B. S. Pinchback. Despite his well-known family of color, Toomer renounced his African heritage and chose to live as a white man.[110]

This type of inner racial turmoil is tied to the tremendous political, social, and economic obstacles of African Americans at the turn of the twentieth century. Instead of reaping the harvest of promises made by the government after the Civil War, African Americans were treated almost as human jetsam by their nation. While their socioeconomic problems were unparalleled, perhaps the greatest problems that people of color faced were psychological. Many, like Alice, wondered who they were or, rather, who they could hope to be; and who was it advisable for them to be in order to engage in the struggle of life with some prospect of survival? Alice believed it was best for her to be a Creole.

Like racist Euro-American elements, the *gens de couleur* had their racist theories about African Americans, too. Many did not consider themselves Negroes. Some Creoles viewed people of noticeable African descent as inferior and consequently separated themselves from these "others." Creoles of color avoided the jobs generally associated with blacks, such as common laborers and domestic or personal servants. These Creoles further differentiated themselves by creating a separate culture. They conversed in French or a local patois, practiced Catholicism, and often educated their offspring in private schools for Creoles. *Gens de couleur* maintained exclusive clubs and other social organizations and published bilingual newspapers in French and English. Prior to the Civil War, the elite Creole community encompassed families of wealth, business and professional persons, writers and poets. They generally had

French or Spanish surnames, relished pedigree and family background to the point of clannishness, and sought to protect their culture from the perceived dangers of external forces.

Creoles of color were the self-acknowledged "best element" of African American society, though, like Alice, many showed little or no signs of color or Negroid features. *Gens de couleur* were the result of generations of miscegenation and inbreeding. In a sense, they were cultural products, for the whiteness of skin and Euro-Americans features were objectified and prized. So value laden was skin color that skin tones were named and graded with "each term [representing] one degree's further transfiguration toward the Caucasian standard of physical perfection," wrote Alice about people of color in Louisiana.[111] The most commonly recognized degrees of whiteness among these people of African descent were

mulatto: child of white and black
quadroon: offspring of white and mulatto
octoroon: progeny of a white and quadroon
tierceron: child of mulatto and quadroon
griffe: offspring of a black and mulatto
marabon: progeny of mulatto and griffe
sacatron: child of black and griffe[112]

Regardless of skin tone, however, Creoles of color were loosely referred to as mulattoes, although by the gradation system, a mulatto actually was an offspring of a black and white sexual union. These free Creoles occupied a special third caste status in antebellum New Orleans, ranking below Euro-Americans in the social order but still several cuts above African Americans, whether slave or free. Nevertheless, Creoles of color were still second-class citizens, although they refused to accept that reality.

Slavery's end and Reconstruction eliminated the special status of the free *gens de couleur*. They were then viewed simply as Negroes by the Euro-American community. Postbellum Creoles responded to their new lack of status by putting more emphasis on what set them apart from other people of color—especially light skin and free ancestors. Moreover, like Alice, many still refused to consider themselves Negroes and were often hostile to the freed slave population and their descendants. Creole isolation from African Americans intensified, as did the continued evolution of a world of their own. Once again, like Alice—herself the descendant of slaves—Creoles of color had a muddled sense of reality. Regardless of their constructed cultural identity, they were still Negroes in American society.

That Alice wished to be perceived as a French Creole of color suggests that she had found an ideological home, even though it did not mesh with her genealogy. It further suggests that she desired a specific and elite cultural identity. As a mulatto, she had the option of considering herself another member of a vast New Orleans mixed-race people in the general populace that was physically indistinguishable from whites. In fact, a Union soldier in occupied New Orleans reported: "It is hard telling who is white here."[113] Most of these native-born mulattoes in New Orleans, and in other cities—North and South—were English-speaking. They had little to distinguish themselves from mulattoes in other areas. Creoles of color, however, were a unique community with a specific identity affirmed through their exclusivity, heritage, and culture. Alice, with her demonstrated need to be above the masses, embraced this lifestyle.

So she became a Creole. Reportedly, she spoke six Louisiana patois, sprinkled her letters with French words and phrases, and was skilled enough in the language to say in a self-deprecating manner that she produced some "very vile . . . translation[s]."[114] However, nothing identifies Alice as Creole, nor does she forthrightly claim this heritage in any of her public or personal papers. It is possible that she had Creole ancestry, since the ethnicity of her father, Monroe Moore, in unknown. But even if he were Creole, it is not certain that he descended from free *gens de couleur*. It is certain, however, that Alice's maternal ancestors were not free. Patsy Wright, Alice's mother, was a former slave, as was Patsy's mother, Mary Wright.

One of Alice's biographers lends credence to the theory that Alice simply adopted a Creole identity. This scholar contends that Alice's Creole stories "and general perspective [demonstrate] she was an outsider looking in."[115] One member of the Creole community explained how such pretenders were sometimes handled, commenting: "There were people who wanted to say they were Creoles, and free people of color who lived uptown, but you just didn't mix with those people."[116] Moreover, at least one of Alice's contemporaries questioned her Creole identity, writing that Alice "did not have so much of the French Culture background."[117]

Although publicly she portrayed herself as a Creole of color, secretly Alice spurned that racialized element of her identity. In her mind's eye, she was—in her words—a "true Creole," a mixed-race person who was neither black nor white, an unraced being, someone who had no place in the racial scheme of the times. Alice's alter ego, the aracial self, surfaces in her short stories that abound with "true Creoles." While it is generally held that these "colorless" characters are white, it now seems evident that Alice considered the French and patois-speaking heroes and heroines, with their French names and "essential Creole attitudes," an aracial group. Alice confirmed this preference for nonracial fictional (and perhaps human) beings, telling her correspondent, Paul Laurence Dunbar, that when she began a story, "I always think of my folk characters as simple human beings, not as types or a race . . . and I seem to be on more friendly terms with them."[118] Her statement mirrored Alice's racial attitudes, as she also seemed "to be on more finely terms with," that is, to prefer the society of those African Americans most devoid of African features.

Despite her stated philosophy of creative literature, Alice *did* conceptualize racial and ethnic characters. They are easily detectable in the two books she published in the late nineteenth century. There are, for example, some "Negro stevedores," minor characters with "glossy black skins" (p. 120), in Alice's second book, *The Goodness of St. Rocque and Other Stories* (1899). Not surprisingly, their "glossy black skins" reiterated Alice's contention that only Negroes have "noticeably dark complexions." Also, these stevedores, people of a definite working-class identity, are the only distinctively African-American characters in her late-nineteenth-century books.

Alice's Euro-American characters are just as obvious as her African Americans. In the *Goodness of St. Rocque*, there is Mercer, "big, blonde and brawny . . . 'un Americain'" (p. 198). However, white characters are generally delineated by nationality rather than race: A little "Jew girl" (p. 19), a "specimen of Italian humanity" (p. 22), a "little ugly . . German" (p. 23), "a daughter of Erin" (p. 29). All these characters contradict Alice's declaration that she did not think of her story folks as "types or race." Moreover, concentration on ethnicity proves that Alice not only pointed out her Euro-American characters, but she also specified them by "types."[119]

She did the same with Creoles of color. The reader knows that the characters are indeed people of color because Alice employs euphemisms to reference their slight African strains. A woman with "flabby yellow cheeks" (p. 79) and the "dusky-eyed fiancee," little Miss Sophie (p. 147), are Creoles of color in Alice's first book, *Violets and Other Tales* (1895).[120] Her second, *The Goodness of St. Rocque*, has a few more. They are a "wizened yellow woman" (p. 8); a girl with a "dusky face" (p.90); Louisettte, with "small brown hands" (p. 156); and Sister Josepha, with trembling "small brown hands" (p. 156).

This leaves the remainder of Alice's Creole characters, the vast majority of heroines, heroes, and bit players in *The Goodness of St. Rocque*. "M'sieu Fortier," "Mr. Baptiste," "Odalie," "Tante Louise," and others too numerous to mention are not white Creoles as scholars have suggested; rather, they are Alice's unraced beings, the "true Creoles" representing her alter ego. By the same token, it is reasonable to assume that other colorless, raceless characters who are not designated Creoles are also unraced beings, rather than Euro-Americans. Just as "essential Creole attitudes" comprise the unraced "true Creole," essential middle-class attitudes indicate this group of Alice's raceless people. The Hart family, in her short story "In Our Neighborhood," is an example. Interestingly, the sisters in the story mirror Alice and her older sibling, Leila.

It seems almost impossible that Alice's conflicted racial feelings and multiple identities did not affect her relationship with Paul Laurence Dunbar. The racial confusion enveloping her gave her a distorted sense of reality. She conceded to being a mulatto, someone superior to those people with dark skins—someone like Paul. But he, too, hated his African self, equating black with ugly, and had an ambivalent relationship with mulattoes besides. Paul loved Alice's whiteness but expressed doubt about mulatto women because of their race "mixture" in his poem "Dely." Mulattoes also angered him because he believed Euro-Americans treated them better than darker-skinned people of color. He once wrote bitterly: "The only sympathy that I have ever seen on the part of the white man was not for the negro himself, but for some portion of white blood that the colored man had got tangled up in his veins."[121]

Paul's and Alice's intraracial prejudices and racial self-hatred must have affected their relationship, as did also their childhood experiences. Paul grew up in a violent home, and neither he nor Alice had parents who were in loving, stable relationships. Yet the two poet-lovers saw no obstacles to their romance. Like the legions of starry-eyed couples of their era, they would be seduced by the nectar of romantic love and the myth that love cures all.

THREE

The Wooing

A youth went faring up and down,
    Alack and well-a-day.
He fared him to a market town,
    Alack and well-a-day.
And there he met a maiden fair,
    With hazel eyes and auburn hair;
His heart went from him then and there,
    Alack and well-a-day.
            —Paul Laurence Dunbar,
              "The Wooing" (1896)

"The Wooing" is a whimsical summary of the courtship of Paul and Alice.[1] It proceeded as sketched in his poem. Paul saw a photograph of Alice—his maiden fair—with hazel eyes and auburn hair. He fell in love with this image, and the love was unrequited. Paul persevered and "the twain were wed/ Alack and well-a-day."[2]

Written during the early stages of the relationship, the five-stanza lyrical account reeks of romance and levity. There is no indication of the poignant, dramatic relationship that would ensue. Yet, as in reality, the poem's characters are the key. Like his poetic mirror image, Paul fell in love with his idealized mate, not Alice; for to fall in love at first sight—as did Paul with a photograph of Alice—is to love a concept of perfection. Similarly, the poem's maiden fair falls for a figment of Alice's perfect mate—the courtly gentleman. When the maid decides the hero is not coarse but "highly bred," she capitulates and the two marry.[3]

Paul's first letter to Alice, dated April 17, 1895, launched their complex courtship. It ended in a secret marriage on March 5, 1898. The two formed their romantic attachment before actually meeting, since they courted strictly by correspondence for almost two years. They courted covertly. The reason may be found in one of Alice's short stories. A barely disguised southern belle being romanced by a famous author through the mail confesses: "My mother had old-fashioned ideas about corresponding with strange men and I did not take her entirely into my confidence as to the number and length of our letters. Nor of the ardent verses he sent to me—and afterwards sold to magazines."[4] In actuality, Alice's mother confirmed this fiction. She wrote that she had no idea that Alice and Paul were romancing by mail; she thought that they were merely friends.[5] Paul and Alice finally met at a party on February 5, 1897. They became engaged and kept that a secret, too, from her family and friends. Correspondence remained the principle means of courting during the engagement period, too, since they lived in distant cities and saw each other infrequently. Loving by mail may not have been unusual for the African American elite. The young activist Ida B. Wells (1862–1931), who would become famous for her staunch antilynching campaign, corresponded with numerous male admirers in several cities. An African American teacher at Spelman Seminary in Atlanta—a school for women of color—contacted her professor beau at Atlanta Baptist College through letters carried by student messengers.[6] And John Hope, the first person of color to be president of Morehouse College in Atlanta, romanced his wife, Lugenia Burns of Chicago, almost exclusively by mail.[7] Often his correspondence mentioned friends teaching in the South who were similarly conducting long-distance romances. School facilities and local environs were not always fertile grounds of mate selection for this corps of teachers. Trusted acquaintances acted as matchmakers for friends living in different cities.

In the culture of nineteenth-century romantic love, letters spoke for and to the missing partner, across distances great and small. These missives have been called "the tongue of the absent."[8] Not surprisingly, Loney Butler, a man of color in Hazelhurst, Mississippi, wrote Sophronia Collins in Carpenter, Mississippi in 1889: "Darling, as I cannot talk to you, please hasten a letter to remove all doubt. . . . [E]very word you write would be a comfort to me."[9] During the five-year courtship of Madame E. Azalia Hackley, an African American concert singer from Detroit, and Edwin Hackley living in Denver, the two met only twice; they married on January 29, 1894. The Hackleys romanced strictly by correspondence, and even the marriage proposal arrived by mail.[10]

The concept of letters as the voices of lovers was common. Etiquette books offered guidance and model love letters, lest the "utterances . . . be rude and unpolished."[11] One mainstream nineteenth-century manual, leaving nothing to chance, reproduced love letters by John Keats.[12] Some African Americans relied on these guides. In his youth, when the soon-to-be-successful African American author Charles Chesnutt earned a meager living as a country schoolteacher, he wrote in his journal on July 20, 1875:

> One of my girls . . . got me to read a love letter to her to-day. It was a proposal of marriage from a young Spartanburg [South Carolina] chap, and nearly all of it was copied *verbatim et literatim* from a letter-writer. It ended up with several verses from popular songs, one of which was "Silver Threads among the Gold."[13]

Opening lines in Loney Butler's letter to Sophronia Collins, a woman of color, closely resemble a guidebook's sample letter of how a "gentleman" might start a love letter to a "lady." Butler's 1889 missive began: "[T]he impression you have made upon me is so deep and powerful that I cannot forbear writing you."[14] The manual further suggested: "I was so impressed by your appearance at the skating carnival last evening that I write to [you]."[15]

Alice and Paul, both educated, talented authors, had no need for correspondence guides, even though their letters follow the form and tendency toward romantic exaggeration sanctioned in the manuals. For example, shortly before they eloped, Paul wrote his future bride: "I can never be satisfied again until you are mine—all mine."[16] The Dunbars' letters also depict a courtship emulating the four conventional stages of romance: attraction, avowal, commitment, and decision to marry. At each stage, the two poets were embroiled in the sentiment of nineteenth-century romantic love and its inherent power dynamics. They experienced intense joy and intense pain. The courtship also evinced patterns of authority and submission that had little to do with romantic love. Race, class, gender-role expectations, and personality determined that aspect of the relationship. Moreover, while a historian of mainstream courting rituals maintains that nineteenth-century middle-class white lovers transcended the constricting attitudes regarding male-female patterns of interaction, this was not true of Alice and Paul. Their letters reveal an intimacy rooted in the traditional rites and rights of turn-of-the-twentieth-century African American elite men and women, a social group that based its values on those of their Euro-American counterparts. However, it was also a social group that attempted to be more conservative in decorum and more zealous in morality, education, and business than their models.

To date, prescriptive literature and the idealized lovers in popular African American Victorian romance novels were the only evidence on courting middle-class couples.[17] Scholars admit that these sources indicated bourgeois goals rather than mimetic representations. The Dunbars' courtship evidences that theory. Their relationship shatters the portrait of perfect people and reveals two very human beings trying to craft a union. Courting letters show Alice, a staunch proponent of propriety, wrestling with ideals and with Paul's often blatant disregard of those niceties. The letters also show Alice and Paul in love, in lust, and at war. Both are sometimes irrational and mean spirited.

The letters further expose Alice and Paul's personalities and foibles, the facades they presented to each other at the beginning of their relationship, and the truer personalities that eventually emerged. Personalities form the essentials of courtship. A love relationship such as Alice and Paul's that defied convention and family asserted the autonomy of both individuals. This assertion of self often resulted in conflicting visions and versions of love and modes of mediation. Ultimately, the Dunbars' correspondence shows two people in love with romantic love—and with illusions. Alice loved a "most loving poet-soul" before she even knew Paul the man; and he loved "the sudden realization of an ideal" before he knew Alice the woman.[18]

Such distorted perceptions were consistent with the emotional intensity characterizing late-nineteenth-century romantic love. Those in love viewed their feelings as an uncontrollable baffling force, an overwhelming experience. This love saturated the worldview of the middle-class and guided its emotional experience and behavior. Romantic love was an intellectual and social force of premiere significance.

The mythology of romantic love was the core of the cult of happiness. It governed courtship, marriage, and the family. Courting couples fell in love and married, with love being the main prerequisite for wedded bliss. Many partners viewed love as the most important element in mate selection, much more important than philosophical, ideological, and religious compatibility—or even those factors combined. Love produced a happy marriage, and marriage yielded a proper middle-class family—the nation's most important social institution. Therefore, marriage, intoned one contemporary mainstream advice giver, "is the most important factor in civilized life. . . . The marriage of one man to one woman, with the intention of a life partnership, is for the best interests of society."[19] Love is one of the greatest events in human life and marriage is a duty, echoed an African American culture critic.[20]

Powerful political leaders endorsed this ideology, with some finding its especially applicable to African Americans. The nation's twenty-fifth president, William McKinley (1843–1901), told black graduates of an industrial school that the loving family and home were the "foundations of good government."[21] A speech by Andrew Carnegie on African Americans portrayed the loving family as "our bulwark in America against revolutionary and socialistic ideas."[22] Mrs. N. F. Mossell, doyenne of Philadelphia's elite African American society, reiterated the marriage-home-nation connection: "Home is undoubtedly the cornerstone of our beloved Republic. . . . Marriage constitutes the basis for the home; preceding this comes courtship."[23]

Courtship and marriage had other monumental ramifications. Marriage was a lifelong experience since divorce generally was unthinkable. Divorce required embarrassing public testimonies of marital cruelty, intemperance, and/or adultery. A good marriage was especially important to the African American middle class. Idyllic unions were symbols of proper conduct, and idealistic behaviors were necessary for racial advancement in a racialized nation. A good marriage countered the racist stereotype that people of color were incapable of loving, sustained relationships. This image of proper married life was so important that W. E. B. Du Bois, and others deeming themselves exemplary, believed that even when relationships failed, couples should remain together.[24] Intact marriages not only negated stereotypes, they also set a model for the underclass—"the majority [of whom] have not made the progress of the elites," wrote Anna Jones, a middle-class woman of color.[25] Jones, a strong supporter of racial uplift, reminded standard bearers that raising "the people by whom we are surrounded [requires] the few [to] show the possibilities of the many." Idealistically, she exhorted: "The ideals of a people determine their destiny."[26] At a time when no blacks had rights that a white needed to respect, elite African Americans tried to use the cultural symbol of marriage as a means of obtaining political goals.

Courtship and marriage were important to this middle class for another reason. Many were the daughters and sons of ex-slaves, and generally slaves had been denied the rituals of romance and marriage that Euro-Americans took for granted, including even mate selection and the delicate art of wooing. One former slave recalled:

> Marse Jim called me and Sam ter him and ordered Sam to pull off his shirt—that was all the McClain niggers wore—and he said to me: "Now do you think you can stand this big nigger?" He had that old bull whip flung acrost his shoulder and Lawd, that man could hit so hard! So I jus said, "yessur, I guess so," and tried to hide my face so I couldn't look at Sam's nakedness, but [Marse Jim] made me look at him anyhow. Well he told us what we must git busy and do in his presence, and we had to do it. After that we were considered man and wife.[27]

Slave marriages were illegal and could be dissolved at the slave owner's whim. Moreover, selling one or both partners to different owners often ended a relationship. The late-nineteenth-century middle class, just a generation removed from bondage, was not unaware of slavery's barbaric history. They treasured their right to mate selection, to court, and to marry.

Romantic love had gained momentum as the necessary ingredient for middle-class marriages by the 1830s, when most African Americans were still enslaved and not necessarily accorded that privilege. People of color coming of age in the postbellum era embraced the concept. To ensure that lovers knew what courtship was all about, an African American advice giver made it clear by writing: "Courtship is the process whereby young people of the opposite sex persuade themselves and each other that they are the complement of the other, and that they should unite in marriage. . . . It is designed that men and women may get well acquainted with those whom they seek to be bound . . . for life."[28]

Most late-nineteenth-century couples did not have this pedantic view of courtship. To them, it was the recognized period for intensifying romantic love. Alice and Paul focused on this grand emotional experience, relishing its ideals. Yet, in a clear division of reality versus prescriptive literature, advice experts seldom mentioned romantic love. Never was it listed as the prime ingredient for mate selection. As one author wrote: "The wooing that goes on year after year is not certain to conduce to the happiest marriages."[29] Couples were told instead to study the sweetheart's religion, health, social class, morality, and character. Compatibility in these areas produced wedded bliss. While it was assumed that love would precede marriage, since a loveless marriage was doomed to failure, advice manuals for blacks and whites gave no attention to the blind all-consuming desire that enveloped Alice and Paul and other starry-eyed romantic lovers. In fact, *The Negro in Etiquette* (1899), one of the few books to mention love, said only of that emotion: "Where there is no jealousy there is no love."[30] Another African American advice book instructed couples to cultivate manliness, womanliness, esteem, intelligence, and good health. The tender affection of love was mentioned only in the context of married life.[31] This minimal discussion of premarital love was not an uncommon practice. When the topic was broached, it was presented as a calm, rational emotion based on esteem. More importantly, love was just one of several factors to be considered in mate selection.

To help seekers in their search for the perfect partner, guidebooks offered requisite characteristics for females and males. These manuals preached an ideology that attributed gender specific qualities to an ideal mate. The best traits in a woman, for example, emanated from her function in life. "The original purpose for which this sex was created [was] . . . providing man with a help-mate," one author intoned.[32] A popular African American journalist reminded readers that "since God made Eve in the fair gardens of paradise as a helpmate unto Adam, it had been woman's task to aid man."[33] She could do this best by being pleasant and having good homemaking skills. African American and mainstream men were advised to look for these qualities in a woman during the courting season. "Seek first a lady who is practical, tidy, industrious, modest, affectionate, steady, has good sense, and a sweetness of temper," men of color were told.[34]

As Paul Laurence Dunbar's love interest, Alice Ruth Moore filled the prescribed bill, although her sweetness of temper may be questioned. She also met another requirement for a future wife. Alice possessed a "sincere disposition to make the happiness of her husband her principal study, the management of her family her constant business, and the education of her children her constant delight."[35] With betrothal, Alice would focus her life on Paul and on her role as his wife. She additionally had those attributes specified in an African American manual as imperative for the wife of a race man: a good physique, moral integrity, education, intelligence, eloquence of language, and musical talent—the latter two to be passed on to her African American babies.[36]

These perfect wives were to mother a generation of perfect children of color. Bishop Daniel Payne of the A.M.E. Church proclaimed that "race considerations require[d] such training."[37] Mrs. M. E. Lee agreed, writing in the church's official journal: "If we Afro-Americans are successful enough to some day measure up equally with the Anglo-Americans, let us not ignore the fact that we owe it chiefly to the unselfish efforts of our mothers."[38] Women of color were to accomplish the "hardest task" and do "the noblest work" by raising exemplary children. By their very nature, these offspring would dissolve racism. Guidebooks like *Floyd's Flowers, or Duty and Beauty for Colored Children,* taught parents how to "turn out . . . good men and women."[39]

Alice was close to the textbook model of the perfect prospective wife. True, she had some traits the advice givers condemned. She was a known flirt and loved dressing exceedingly well. Also, Paul's stature and lifestyle as an internationally famous author comprised a large part of his appeal. In this respect, she was not unlike "some young ladies," admonished a mainstream advice giver. "They think more of the vocation which a man follows than they do of the character he has," the writer complained. "It is what a man *does,* not what he *is* that particularly attracts their notice" (emphasis in original). The author warned that such ideas were "directly at war with human happiness."[40]

Love experts warned women not to marry for money. While they were expected to consider whether a suitor possessed sufficient means, marrying for money, wrote one author of color, was an "insult to nature."[41] No good could come from it. Alice finessed this bit of advice. And one straight-talking guidebook author may have applauded her stance. This African American wife and mother commented that in the real world, "real love—or ambition in its various guises—may be the basis of marriage."[42]

The qualities a woman of color should seek in a mate were outlined in the *Historical Romance of the American Negro* (1902). Women were to accept nothing less than the "Christian Gentleman." Such men were not only religious, they were industrious, highly respectable, brilliantly educated, well trained, and extremely polished. These men were so polished, wrote the author, that they were "as smooth as a mirror, and you can see your face in that mirror as well as the best looking glass."[43] The Christian Gentleman was an asset in the best society, kept company only with refined young Christian people, and encouraged his wife in her good deeds and thoughts. He was a paragon: noble, self-sacrificing, manly in all things. Did such a man actually exist? He did for Hattie Rutherford, an African American music teacher at Spelman Seminary. God had blessed and honored her, she wrote in 1907, by allowing her beau, John Brown Watson—"a noble Christian man"—to love her so devotedly and sincerely.[44]

Paul Laurence Dunbar was far from the prescriptive ideal. Although he professed to be a Christian, was industrious, well educated, and knew his way around a drawing room, Alice would discover that he was neither noble, nor just, nor self-sacrificing. She would also learn that Paul preferred the society of what she termed "low-lifes" rather than the company of refined men preferred by the Christian Gentleman. Moreover, even during the courting years, Paul would exhibit habits and characteristics that no Christian Gentleman would have considered. These indulgences, labeled deleterious by guidebooks, were "intemperate use of intoxicating drinks, smoking . . . licentiousness in every form . . . swearing and keeping late hours at night."[45] Poor health, a teasing or domineering manner, flirting—even mildly—and extremes in dress were also deemed undesirable attributes, which Paul would demonstrate during his courtship of Alice.[46]

Experts advised women never to make a match with men having such egregious traits. Alice admitted to reading prescriptive literature during her courting years. Perhaps, had she not been in love with love, or with Paul's position, she may have more seriously considered the advice givers' wisdom. Manuals reminded women that courting was serious business. It was not just a pleasant pastime, or even worse, wrote one African American author, simply a period of flirtation.[47] A woman was selecting a lifelong partner and the father of her children. A mainstream writer reiterated: "There is nothing more important to the happiness of a lifetime than the right [mate] selection." Unbridled love should not be the basis of that choice. He added: "It is so easy, so delicious to love—the heart learns *that* lesson so readily—but the expression of that love [must be] in accordance with set forms and rules."[48]

One major rule for choosing a husband, according to an African American manual, was: "Be sure he had no habits which may tend to weaken the powers of your children, or in any way debase or lower their being."[49] What were these damaging habits? The same aforementioned traits exhibited by Paul.

Paul was not a suitable beau for Alice, nor for any elite woman, according to the prescriptive literature. But the belief that love conquered all, and that a loving woman could reform a wayfaring soul, was part of the mythology of romantic love and nineteenth-century womanhood. Thus, Paul and Alice courted, with expectations of a happy marriage. During the courting years, other middle-class ideals would be tested, especially sexual purity, emotional fulfillment, and decorum. Alice's and Paul's letters reveal a couple wrestling with duty and desire. They adhered to some ideals, negotiated some, and abandoned others.

The Dunbars' romance was both unique and commonplace. Alice and Paul—like other late-nineteenth-century couples caught up in the concepts of romantic love—idealized each other, integrated love and sex, viewed sex as a sacrament of love, vacillated between joy and gloom, and made each other the paramount symbol of significance in their lives, even above God. Like many in the throes of romantic love, they too idealistically believed that life without the other was pointless. "I feel that if you should throw me out just now I should kill myself," Paul wrote during their engagement.[50] And Alice responded: "If you die—I swear I'll commit suicide. Life would be worse than Hades without you."[51] The editor of the African American magazine *Alexander's Monthly* found this bit of romanticism "absolutely silly. . . . What is the use of . . . giving [a] body to ground worms for so slight a cause as disappointment in love matters?" he asked. "There are plenty of uncaught fish in the sea."[52]

There were other alliances between the Dunbars' distinctive courtship and middle-class relationships in general. Until she committed herself to marriage, Alice, like her female counterparts, was objectified by her suitor and became a sought-after prize. And like other romantics, Alice and Paul believed their true love was predestined, even ordained by God.

There may be an element of even greater importance in the multilevel nature of the Dunbars' courtship. That is its racialized nature. Race literature was the basis of Paul's success, thereby giving him a social stature that appealed to Alice. That same racism caused Paul, a man with a dark complexion, to prefer women like Alice with near-ivory skin. Just as race impacted their romance, so did ideas about gender. Paul's conception of his and Alice's role would strain the relationship.

Winning Alice's love became almost an obsession with Paul from the moment he saw her photograph in the April 1895 issue of the Boston *Monthly Review* magazine. He expressed no such desire in his first letter, however, wisely deeming it best to bide his time. Instead, he penned a chatty and uncharacteristically modest missive. Taking literature—both hers and his—as his theme Paul laid the foundation of the relationship. It proved not to be the solid base that he might have wished. The first exchange of letters revealed a fundamental fissure—opposing views on African American literature. Prophetically, this beginning forecast the rocky rather than rock-solid nature of the Dunbars' courtship and marriage. Paul set this dynamic relationship in motion from his Dayton, Ohio, home, when he took pen in hand to write:

April 17th 1895

Miss Alice Ruth Moore:

You will pardon my boldness in addressing you, I hope, and let my interest in your work be my excuse. I sometimes wonder if in the rare world of art, earthly conventions need always be heeded. I am drawn to write you because we are both working along the same lines and a sketch of yours in the Monthly Review so interested me that I was anxious to know more of you and your work.[53]

Paul proceeded by presenting his "credentials with as little egotism as possible." He, too, was an author and had published in several major newspapers, such as the *Chicago Record and News* and the *Detroit Free Press.* The New York *Independent* had just accepted a short story; and not long ago, *Century,* a most prestigious mainstream magazine, had taken three of his poems.[54]

Paul then moved to that part of the letter Alice would find objectionable—his writing of dialect verse and good times on the old plantation.

He wondered what Miss Moore thought of that form of literature. It had, after all made white writers like Joel Chandler Harris, Thomas Nelson Page, and Ruth McEnery Stuart famous. Did Miss Moore believe, as did many race members, that Afro-Americans should not write "those quaint old tales . . . of our fathers"? Should we ignore this past, this source of "capital literary material"? Paul ended by hoping he had not bored Alice very much, and he expressed a desire for an early response. Then signing his formal name, Paul Laurence Dunbar, the suitor slipped in the envelope two of his recent nondialect poems, "Frederick Douglass" and "Phyllis."[55]

Paul's wish for an early answer was not granted. Unaware of Alice's exact whereabouts, he wrote her in care of her publisher. Eventually the letter reached her home in New Orleans. She knew Paul's name from his many publications in African American journals and newspapers and must have been delighted to receive his missive. Perhaps she, like one of her fictional heroines—a young southern writer whose poem just happened to catch the eye of a famous author—was "thrilled to the very center of my being when the letter came. . . . That he would condescend to notice the amateurish outpourings of a little small-town southern school-girl seemed incredible."[56] Alice must also have been enchanted by Paul's gallant gesture. One of the enclosed poems, "Phyllis," was casually scribbled on the back of an envelope. It was a love poem that Paul had dashed off especially for her, dedicating it to the magazine photograph that had so intrigued him.[57]

Alice was charmed and flattered by Paul's first letter, but pragmatism may have also shaped her reaction and response. As a writer and young woman ever conscious of social stature, she undoubtedly relished an acquaintance with the rising poet. Paul was on the brink of stardom. Although not yet the sensation he would be after William Dean Howells reviewed his poetry volume *Major and Minors* in the *Atlantic Monthly* (1896), the African American intelligentsia had already embraced him. Paul's letter told her that he and the late Frederick Douglass had been friends. The active rumor mill of African American society may also have brought to Alice's ears news of Paul's association with other luminaries.

In spite of her delight, Alice gave no immediate attention to Paul's letter. Just when he "had entirely given up all idea of hearing from [Alice]," her "kind letter" arrived.[58] Offering an unusual apology for the delinquency, she wrote:

Mr. Paul Laurence Dunbar

Dear Sir—

Your letter was handed to me at a singularly inopportune moment—the house was on fire. So I laid it down, not knowing what it was and I must confess not caring very much. After the house was declared safe and the excitement had somewhat subsided I found it laid in my desk and read it somewheres about ten days later. . . . I enjoyed it nevertheless when I did read it, and those dainty little verses have been ringing in my head ever since I read them.[59]

Alice continued by thanking Paul for "those dainty little verses," the poems "Frederick Douglass" and "Phyllis." She sincerely hoped he would send some more. Then she gave attention to some of the questions in his letter. Paul's query concerning people of color writing in Negro dialect was difficult since Alice was not fond of the genre. Later, she would accuse him of wasting his talent and beg him not to "prostitute your art for 'filthy lucre.'"[60]

But none of this condemnation appeared in her first letter. Like Paul, she too had a hidden agenda. Cagily, Alice answered: "Well, I frankly believe in everyone following his bent. If it be so that one has a special aptitude for dialect work, why it is only right that dialect work should be made a specialty."[61] Alice made it clear, however, that no one should expect such dialect from her pen, for she was "absolutely devoid of the ability to handle" it. Nor did she "see the necessity of cramming and forcing oneself into that plane because one is a Negro or a Southerner."[62] On another of Paul's questions concerning the general nature of black literature, Alice was more direct, even bold. The answer required a justification of her fictional texts, which never focused on the plight of blacks and rarely included African American characters. She wrote: "I haven't much liking for those writers that wedge the Negro problem and social equality and long dissertations on the Negro into their stories, Its [*sic*] too much like a quinine pill in jelly." That certainly was not her idea of fiction, she continued. Her characters were human beings, not race types or an idea. Perhaps anticipating that she may have spoken too bluntly, Alice added, "I hope I'm not treading on your corns."[63]

Left: Paul Laurence Dunbar, c. 1900. Courtesy of the Ohio Historical Society. *Right:* Alice Moore Dunbar, c. 1900. Alice Dunbar-Nelson Papers, University of Delaware Library, Newark, Delaware. Courtesy of the University of Delaware Library.

Paul Laurence Dunbar, age 20, before he became famous. Courtesy of the Ohio Historical Society.

Top: Paul Laurence Dunbar with Mrs. Hickerson, a friend, possibly in Dayton, Ohio. Courtesy of the Ohio Historical Society. *Bottom:* Paul Laurence Dunbar with friends, possibly in Dayton, Ohio. Courtesy of the Ohio Historical Society.

Paul Laurence Dunbar in his study in Dayton, Ohio, after the breakup of his marriage. Courtesy of the Ohio Historical Society.

Studio photograph of Paul Laurence Dunbar at the height of his fame. Courtesy of the Ohio Historical Society.

Matilda Dunbar, Paul's mother. Courtesy of the Ohio Historical Society.

Left: A drawing of Alice Ruth Moore that appeared in the *Journal of the Lodge* August 18, 1894. The *Journal* was an African-American newspaper published in New Orleans. Alice, then 19 years old, wrote the woman's column. Alice Dunbar-Nelson Papers, University of Delaware, Newark, Delaware. Courtesy of the University of Delaware Library. *Right:* Alice with an exotic hairstyle. Alice Dunbar-Nelson Papers, University of Delaware, Newark, Delaware. Courtesy of the University of Delaware Library.

Formal studio portrait of Alice Moore Dunbar. Courtesy of the Schomburg Center for Research in Black Culture, New York Public Library.

If Paul had studied Alice's work, he could have anticipated her ary position. Unlike popular African American women writers of the she never wrote about black life. When people of color appeared Alice's short stories, they were Creoles of color with pseudo French Spanish accents. Alice numbered among that near-white aristocracy of Charleston and New Orleans, wrote W. E. B. Du Bois, that denigrated its African heritage and considered it fashionable to pose as Spanish or Portuguese.[64] Her fiction reflected her preferred heritage, focusing on nonracial Creoles and Euro-Americans.

Alice's lack of interest in African Americans as literary material contrasted sharply with the philosophy of other women writers of the race during the 1890s. Popular novels such as *Clarence and Corrine* (1890) and *The Hazely Family* (1894) by Amelia E. Johnson, *Medga* (1891) and *Four Girls at Cottage City* (1898) by Emma Dunham Kelley-Hawkins, *Iola Leroy* (1892) by Frances Ellen Watkins Harper, and *Beryl Weston's Ambitions* (1893) and *Clancy Street* by Katherine D. Tillman interwove the condition and treatment of mainly middle-class African Americans in their tales of romance.[65] These women saw their style of writing as a form and message of race pride and racial uplift.

Alice defied this tradition. She absented herself from that heralded group of "Afro-American women who faithfully portray the lights and shadows of Negro Life."[66] One of her biographers, in an underrated study, vehemently defends Alice's position. The scholar contends that Alice "did not feel the need to wave racial banners in her poems [and] short stories. . . . She wrote from . . . [a] universal sense of life."[67] The author fails to mention that Alice may have adopted the universal perspective because she hated her African heritage and disliked dark-skinned people of color. The biographer also suggests that Alice may have shunned the African American literary tradition because it is based on a "White defined Black experience; dialect, protest and other 'Black' labels.'" Alice decided not to let this racism restrict her writing, the scholar concludes.[68] But Alice did allow racism to restrict her writing. Her hatred of African Americans and refusal to write about black life prevented her from tapping a rich literary vein.

Alice let Paul know that she did not write "race literature" in her very first letter. She closed by telling him that her book *Violets and Other Tales* was in press—and certainly he must want a copy. Citing the cold night

air and the next day's teaching duties as reasons for ending her missive, Alice cordially invited Paul to write again soon.

Paul did. "Your letter . . . was a source of great pleasure to me," he responded happily.[69] He thought he would never hear from her, Paul continued, but because he wanted to know her better, he had searched stacks of newspapers for some of her work or at least a mention of her name. What Paul found was Alice's women's column in a New Orleans newspaper, and "never did [he] devour a woman's column with such avidity."[70] Then, taking issue with Alice's concept of African American literature, he wrote:

> No dear Miss Moore, you did not tread on my corns in expressing your opinion on Negro literature. . . . But I believe that characters in fiction should be what men and women are in real life—the embodiment of a principle or idea. There is no individuality apart from an idea. Every character who moves across the pages of a story in my mind—and a very humble mind it is—is only an idea incarnate.[71]

Contrary to his statement, Alice had not only stepped on Paul's corns, she had jumped on them. Her theory that African American literature should not be based on the plight of the race attacked a major element of what Paul considered his serious work—his consciousness-raising fiction and poems. As Alice would discover much later, Paul was not gracious under attack: he would lash out at any and all who criticized him, including such a notable as Frederick Douglass's widow—coincidentally a white woman. When she criticized his writing of dialect poetry, Paul responded with a scathing letter.[72] His chum, James Weldon Johnson (1871–1938), who would become famous as the executive secretary of the National Association for the Advancement of Colored People (NAACP), knew this side of his friend very well. He recalled: "Under [Paul's] polite tongue, there was a sac of bitter sarcasm that he spat out on people he did not like, and often used in his defense."[73] But this is not the personality Paul wished to present to Alice in this embryonic stage of their relationship. "[L]et us be friendly," he wrote in an ingratiating manner at the end of his discourse on black literature. Perhaps to ward off further discussion of the sticky issue, Paul added, "[L]et us not be literary in our letters."[74]

Literature, however, remained their link. In subsequent letters, Paul

focused on Alice's talent. He encouraged her to write, commented on materials she sent and promised to use his influence to boost her literary career. He made good his promise. During that spring of 1895, while working temporarily as managing editor of the Indianapolis *World,* a newspaper publishing social, literary, and political race matter, Paul used his paper as a forum for Alice's work.[75]

Paul played the role of friend and mentor for almost two months after his initial letter. By June 6, he thought he could reveal his romantic emotions. Suspecting that Alice's feelings were not reciprocal and that he might even be "verging on impertinence or presumption," Paul nevertheless pressed his suit. His was not a forthright declaration of love. Using poetry—the medium in which he excelled—Paul sent "Dear Miss Moore . . . a couple of little lyrics" written for and about her.[76] Both poems evidenced his love. One, a rhapsody on her "beautiful name," began:

> Know you, winds that blow your course,
> Down the verdant valleys
> That somewhere you must, perforce
> Kiss the brow of Alice?
> Where her smiling face you find
> Kiss it gently, naughty wind.[77]

Paul's second poem assessed his unrequited love:

> My lady-love lives far away,
> And, oh my heart is sad by day,
> And, oh my tears fall fast by night;
> What may I do in such a plight?
> . . . .
> But tho' my heart so strongly yearns,
> My lady loves me not in turn.[78]

Despite this heartache, the poem ended with optimism. Inevitably, Paul's lady-love would love him, because he cared so deeply for her. Was it not true that "love breedeth love?"[79]

Paul lapsed into poetry to proclaim his ardor, not only because he was a wordsmith—and one of the best in the land—but also because poetry comprised the culture of nineteenth-century courting letters. Men and women with little or no talent exchanged original rhymes and poems. One such amateur poet was Edwin Hackley, an African American lawyer. While courting his wife, Azalia—a renowned concert singer and one of Alice's friends—Hackley often wrote mediocre poetry for and about his future bride, such as:

> O sweet Azalia,
> But deem me dumb in joyous trance,
> For all my speechless senses
> Turn rapture at thy glance.[80]

Courting couples devoid of Hackley's bravado sent copies of their favorite published works to each other. Poetry had a vital role in public as well as private life. Children recited verses in church programs and at exercises closing the school year. Party goers entertained one another with poems, and elocutionists read them before paid audiences. Paul often presented his poetry in this manner.

Alice's response to Paul's romantic outburst in his letter of June 6, 1895, can only be conjectured. Gaps in the literature preclude certainty. But it is assumed that Alice rebuffed Paul's advances, since neither the poems nor her reaction to them is mentioned in what seems to be the next extant letter (June 13, 1895). That letter finds Paul once again in his role of distant friend and mentor. He addressed her still as "Dear Miss Moore" and ended with his formal name, Paul Laurence Dunbar. In all probability, Alice had replied that she wished only a friendship with Paul.

That stage of the relationship continued until the fall. Generally, Paul curbed all romantic expression, with occasional exceptions—such as a brief poem bidding the "dearest heart goodnight" in a July 25, 1895, letter. The two chatted as acquaintances, still addressing each other as "Miss Moore" and "Mr. Dunbar" in accordance with social custom. They adhered to the ritual for almost two years, probably because etiquette decreed that given names were used only by family or intimate friends. This convention was acknowledged even in secret diaries. Long before gaining prominence as a celebrated journalist, civil rights activist, and antilynching crusader, the young teacher Ida B. Wells (1862–1931) entered in her diary: "[December 29, 1885]—Messrs. Savage & Hodge called this afternoon in the rain & stayed a short while. . . . [January 21, 1886]—Mr. Morris writes a very interesting letter & sends me his picture." Wells makes it clear that in polite society, a gentleman allowed a lady to move the relationship to that level of intimacy where given names were used. "I hate the barren formality of our address to each other," she told her diary on February 14, 1886, about yet another beau. "I want to say 'my dear Charlie' but I hesitate about breaking the ice, tho' I know the advance ought and must come from me."[81] Similarly, Charles Chesnutt (1858–1932), the African American author whom Paul considered his chief rival, used formal names in his secret journals. The exceptions were family members and serious girlfriends.[82]

Alice's letters following Paul's romantic outburst proved the type of relationship she desired. In subsequent correspondence, she discussed general subjects such as literature, teaching duties, and her very important social life. There was a dinner and lake party on the Fourth of July, a "delightful" yet "boresome" event. And "everyone of any consequence" attended the Promenade Concert, but a large crowd made it "next to impossible to get to those whom one wanted to get to."[83]

Paul and Alice exchanged photographs, following the custom of friends and sweethearts. When her professor beau asked Hattie Rutherford, the music teacher at Spelman Seminary, for her picture, she replied that she had one, but not a very good one; perhaps he could wait for a better image.[84] Ida B. Wells traded photographs constantly with her many suitors, as did Paul with his numerous lady friends. Exchanging portraits marked a certain stage in a relationship, since it indicted some measure of endearment. Paul once said smugly of a new conquest: "Minnie McDivett writes she'll send me her picture if I send mine, but I'll let her send first."[85]

Yet Paul was reluctant to send the fair-skinned Alice his portrait. He had internalized the prevailing standard of beauty and hated his looks. Also, he knew of the intraracial hatred between some light-skinned and dark-skinned blacks. Paul pleaded with Alice: "Please do not ask me for my photo or express any desire to know how I look; for I fear that if you knew, our budding friendship . . . would be checked; because women so love beauty—and I do not blame them either—though I have none to offer them."[86]

Paul had good reason to suspect Alice might reject him. Love was not color-blind, and skin tone was a factor in African American romances, regardless of social class. But even this intraracial prejudice was gendered.

Generally the dark-skinned woman was considered an undesirable mate. A successful man with a very brown complexion—someone like Paul—could improve his social status and be more acceptable to high society by "marrying up," that is, marrying a fair-skinned woman. The whiter the skin, the better. But the reverse was not necessarily true for females. A popular rhyme captured popular sentiment:

> My love has sent me a letter,
> Not far from yonder town,
> That he could not fancy me,
> Because I was so brown.[87]

Katherine Tillman, an African American author, reiterated the seriousness of the problem. Her melodramatic poem "Bashy" tells of a dark-skinned woman with no option other than prostitution when her beau rejected her:

> But Bashy, I'll swear, never had a chance;
> A black face never does enhance
> A woman's value in our land.
> Black faces are, well—not in demand.
> . . . .
> Bashy loved, and gave her all.
> The man who caused her awful fall
> Thought her too black to make a wife,
> So she drifted on to a dreadful life.[88]

The intraracial discrimination against dark-skinned women was real, not just fictional. A very brown woman was ugly, and ugliness for woman was sinful. And, oh, what pain it was for a light-skinned man to love such a woman! Much to his chagrin, the author Charles Chesnutt, who was often mistaken for a white man, loved Josie, "a girl who is not strictly speaking, any way good looking. God knows I love you," Chesnutt moaned in his journal more than once. "You are an ugly girl. But love hides a lot, yes, all fault . . . 'charity covers a multitude of sins.'"[89]

Josie was unattractive simply because of her dark complexion, for black was ugly. A Freedmen's Bureau record in 1865, for example, described a Precilla as "black and ugly" and an Emma Hurlbert as "a *very* pretty colored woman nearly white" (emphasis in the original).[90] The public conflation of black and ugly would be demonstrated by the 1920s. Marcus Garvey (1887–1940), a dark-skinned Jamaican, made New York the headquarters for his massive international racial uplift group, the Universal Negro Improvement Association—or UNIA, as it was commonly known. Like Garvey, an overwhelming majority of the organization's members had dark complexions, causing mean-spirited mulattoes to say that UNIA really meant Ugliest Negroes in America.

Like the fictional Bashy and Chesnutt's Josie, Alice's complexion was an important factor in her love life. After all, Paul had fallen in love with her picture in a magazine. This emphasis on a woman's looks was universal. A mainstream magazine article on how to win a man listed beauty as the first of "three primal causes which develop the love of a man."[91] The greater the beauty, the greater a woman's chances of attracting and "catching" a mate. Women of intellect and character were poor runners-up, commented the author.

On receiving Alice's photograph, Paul treated it as he wished to treat her real self, showering affection on the image. He slept with it, kissed it, and gazed at it when he wrote to her. His passion was not unlike that of Charles Chesnutt. In lieu of Josie's photograph—for which he "would give anything"—the then seventeen-year-old fixated on a lock of her hair. On July 10, 1875, he wrote fervently in his journal: "Here is a lock of her hair! I kiss the lock of hair and press it to [my] bosom[.] Would it were she!"[92]

Although Paul was initially reluctant to exchange photographs with Alice, he was never hesitant in sharing good news about his budding career. Having quit his job as elevator boy, Paul scratched out a small living for himself and his mother, Matilda, as a freelance writer and elocutionist. Writing constantly, as well as reading his poetry locally and regionally, he was busy developing and promoting his career. Late in June 1895, he completed one of his favorite and most famous poems, a tribute to his mother called "When Malindy Sings." It is "a lyrical bit in seventy-two lines [that] rather strikes my fancy," he wrote Alice. "I shall add it to my repertoire for recitation."[93] He attended the Western Association of Writers Conference in Indiana, boasting: "I am the only colored member, I am not allowed to feel it. It is boating, fishing, music, poetry and general literature in pleasantly varied layers."[94] With members such as James Whitcomb Riley—a most successful and famous writer of

Hoosier-dialect poetry—and Dr. John Clark Ridpath, author of a widely used history textbook series, Paul relished his association in the prestigious organization. That summer of 1895, he also promoted Alice's book, *Violets and Other Tales,* by telling associates about it. He even sold copies. "Together with payment for my own," Paul wrote in August, I enclose fifty cents for one to be sent to Mrs. Lottie Jackson, Bay View Michigan."[95]

Paul presented himself to Alice as a successful young author, and a harried schedule confirmed that. Yet he was not successful financially—a fact he hid from Alice. At best, he commanded one-tenth of the one hundred dollar fee he would charge for speaking engagements when his career peaked. He even read his poems in recitals when not compensated, just to keep his work before the public. Paul's income as a freelance writer also was not as expected. While he published regularly in newspapers and magazines, he was not remunerated for every item. Prices paid for some stories and poems were often disappointing.

Trying to support himself and his mother in this manner kept Paul in debt and despair. That summer of 1895, during which he was crafting a friendship with Alice, found him close to destitution. Several times influential friends came to his rescue. Creditors dunned him. A local business reminded Paul early in June that he had promised payment when the *Independent* published his story. "I noticed it in the [news]paper several weeks ago," Lorin Wright of Dayton, Ohio, informed Paul. "[A]nd if you can favor me this week, [I] will be greatly obliged . . . I believe the balance is $2.50."[96] Paul may have sighed in relief later that month after paying the Gem City Building and Loan five dollars. If so, his respite was brief. A curt thank-you three days thereafter noted that he still owed $23.14, and it would be appreciated if he would raise it before July 1.[97] The poet's financial situation was so perilous that even his mother, his staunchest ally, urged him to abandon his freelance career and "get something steady."[98]

Paul's meager income was further drained by reckless spending and steady drinking. During this acquaintance stage of the relationship, Alice may not have been aware of these habits, although the small circle of African American intelligentsia kept few secrets. Paul's close friends knew his vices and were both solicitous and angry with him. "Wont you give up that cussed drink, Paul?" asked a longtime Dayton friend. "You are weakening your constitution." Having extended charity, she took him to task, first pointing out the obvious: "Your income is small at present, and you are spending that with nothing coming in." He was extravagant in his spending, she chided, and selfish. He bought fancy clothes and acted the bon vivant. His mother had sacrificed so much for him, and now he was neglecting her needs, as well as other responsibilities. "You have debts," Paul's correspondent reminded him. "You cannot pay your way and drink as you do." Then, in a final attempt at persuasion, she tied him to his destiny, writing: "Unless you alter your mode of living, your race will never have cause to be proud of their poet."[99]

While Paul kept his drinking and spending habits from Alice during the summer of their budding friendship, he made her aware of his serious illness. The poet had a recurring mood disorder and often blamed it for his sometimes maniacal behavior. At first Paul told Alice that the act of writing triggered despondency and mood swings. Creativity placed him "either high on the mountain top or away down in the valley." Surely trying to write affected Alice similarly, he commented.[100] Less than five weeks later, this time for no given reason, Paul was so "away down in the depths of despondency" that it was difficult to answer Alice's letter.[101] He warned her that he could be unkind when depressed, writing: "You will care to hear little from me . . . one of those moods possess me tonight."[102] Evidence of how Paul could act when possessed followed: "I want to quarrel with someone," he railed in a letter, "and as you are at the safest distance for the encounter, I take this opportunity of throwing my venom at you." He was unhappy with Alice's letters. They were infrequent and far too short. "*I want to hear from you,*" Paul stressed (emphasis in the original). "I don't want a note. I want a letter, and if you can't write me a letter, you just try again." Paul spewed venom not only at Alice, but at all mankind and womankind. "Do you know, my little Miss Professor of Human Life that all humanity are cowards at heart[?]" he asked. "What hypocrites we mortals are . . . as well as fools." So too, was dear Miss Moore "by implication [for] you are not immortal—at least not yet."[103]

Paul's erratic conduct and depression may have been alcohol induced. However, it is possible that he suffered with some form of bipolar disorder, a cyclical illness marked by alternating extremes of excitement and depression. He had a strong proclivity for the malady. The evidence suggests that his bouts with depression and rage echoed his father's behavior. Rooted in a chemical imbalance, bipolar disorder was identified by European scientists by the 1890s. Few family doctors, however, would have labeled it as anything other than despondency, nor would they have known how to treat it. There were no special medicines, and certainly no psychotherapy. At best, sufferers were locked away until the more rational phase of the disease recurred.[104]

Paul told Alice about more than his mental illness during the early stages of their relationship. He could be disagreeable "with a vengeance," he cautioned, and he liked associating with what Alice termed "low-lifes."[105] Such letters written during this period seem puzzling. If he were trying to win favor with Alice, why expose these moods and behaviors? Moreover, why would Alice continue a relationship with a suitor who was admittedly unpleasant, verbally abusive, and seriously ill? Since she was not in love at this point, she was not blinded by the irrationality that sometimes accompanies romantic love.

Candor and frankness were major concerns of couples in the 1880s and 1890s. Lovers believed they had a right and duty to tell and be told everything "that went on inside the other's head." Complete openness was a measure of intimacy between engaged couples. More importantly, lovers believed that good marriages were not built on pretenses.

Paul and Alice were not lovers, nor were they engaged in 1895 when he began revealing what went on inside his head. His histrionics were outside the lover's privilege of exposing the "unlovely me's." Paul's boorishness may be attributed in some small measure to role playing. He may, at times, have acted as the mad genius artist. Two of his favorite poets, Byron and Shelley, as well as Edgar Allen Poe were known and romanticized for their sometimes demented behavior.

But Paul's abusive manner was more than role playing. He drank heavily, and alcohol often fueled his demons. Alice would state near the end of their marriage that, when drunk, he behaved "disgracefully."[106]

Paul's boorishness toward Alice in the early stages of their friendship may have also been a manifestation of his poor mental health. Environmental depression—which can be an aspect of mood disorder—frequently engulfed him. During these periods he was sometimes cruel. Depression, which many define as inner rage, may be caused by external realities such as racism. Paul's literary rival, Charles Chesnutt, said he had no white friends because he "could not degrade the sacred name of 'friendship' by associating it with any man who feels himself too good to sit at a [dinner] table with me." Chesnutt seriously considered moving his family to Europe, perhaps to London, so his children would not be warped by racism.[107] William Monroe Trotter, the first African American to graduate Phi Beta Kappa from Harvard College (1895), ended his protracted, painful battle with bigotry by committing suicide.

All turn-of-the-twentieth-century people of color lived in an openly racist society. As already noted, Paul's first major encounter with bigotry came when he sought employment after a stellar high school career. Although a published author, he could get only menial employment in his hometown of Dayton, Ohio. Leading businessmen who knew the poet well spoke bluntly: they could not hire a colored boy for a white-collar job. Later, even at the height of his literary career, Paul would face a form of job discrimination. Critics would love his dialect work and happy tales of life on the old plantation, but novels deviating from the formula would be denigrated. At public poetry readings, Euro-American audiences would demand his dialect verses.

The racism Paul faced was only one cause of his depression. Internal factors—mainly repressed resentment, conflict, and prolonged anger—also contributed to the disease. These emotions are often formed in early childhood, and unless resolved, they may fester into a hostility of which the individual may not be aware. When finally expressed, the anger and resentment may take the form of overt aggression, anger, transference, self-hatred, and suicide. Paul's well-known, biting sarcasm and his abrasive letters to Alice demonstrate hostility. In later stages of their relationship, he would become verbally and physically abusive as well. Even prior to initiating his contact with Alice, Paul spoke of suicide with friends. He would remain suicidal throughout his brief life.

Paul was a man in rage and in pain. Researchers generally trace the source of this form of depression to the family circle. While exploration of the roots of Paul's inner life go beyond the scope of this book, it is known that early relationships with his parents were uneven. Paul was a recognized prodigy, and his mother, Matilda, revered him. She nurtured and indulged him, openly acknowledging him as the favorite of her three sons until he died. By contrast, Paul's relationship with his father was unstable. Joshua was more absent than present during his son's childhood, perhaps causing Paul to feel his father had deserted him. Abandonment can be a major source of childhood inner rage. Children may consider divorce and death as forms of desertion, and this may have been the case with Paul, as his parents divorced before he entered school. Joshua Dunbar later rejoined the family, but after some time, walked out and never returned. He saw his son only when Paul visited him at the local retired soldiers' home. Finally, as Paul approached adolescence, Joshua died.

Anger and resentment emanating from a sense of powerlessness during childhood can also contribute to depression. Paul, a sickly boy who was small for his age, must have felt helpless in his home of intense marital strife. He could neither prevent nor terminate the frequent, violent arguments between his parents. Similarly, he could not prevent neighbors from speaking despairingly about his father, an alcoholic; nor could Paul curb Joshua's turbulent actions when he was intoxicated.

Mental illness may not have been the sole cause of Paul's boorish treatment of Alice during the early stages of their relationship. Some of his antics must be attributed to learned behavior. What nineteenth-century boys were taught about manhood is crucial to understanding adult male attitudes and expectations. Regardless of race or station, young boys were indoctrinated with male privilege.

Urban middle-class America was a gendered world based on male sovereignty. Known variously as the cult of true womanhood, the cult of domesticity, or the world of separate spheres, the doctrine had descriptive and prescriptive components. Women were depicted as inferior to men; they were naturally different with peculiar talents and weaknesses. Thought to have an aptitude for nurturing and serving others, women were intended by God—so it was said—to serve in the private realm, the home. Men were intended to master the public world of commerce and politics. Piety, purity, submissiveness, and domesticity were the virtues prescribed for women. In the United States, as in all societies where men control ownership and distribution of property and certain culturally valued subsistence goods, men dominated and controlled women.

This was also true in intimate relationships. A system of paternalism prevailed based on the care and/or control of the subordinate group—women. Males dictated the behaviors and significant decisions of their loved ones, with the moral framework that credited men with an understanding of their loved ones' best interests. Social custom decreed that women accept this authority. "Good" women learned to comply with and defer to the wishes of male loved ones. Thus, young girls learned at an early age to accommodate the mandates of fathers and husbands and to tolerate "manly" behavior. Wives were to obey husbands, and in matters of the heart, men were the pursuers.

For the African American upper crust, the most conservative group in late-nineteenth-century America, gender ideals were still those of the antebellum cult of domesticity. Women remained the weaker, "gentler" sex, more loving, moral, and caring than men. They were refined and polite. The gender attributes and expectations described in a *Colored American* article in 1839 continued to be gospel in the late nineteenth century:

Man is strong—Woman is beautiful
Man is daring and confident—Woman deferent and unassuming
Man is great in action—Woman in suffering
Man shines abroad—Woman at home
Man talks to convince—Woman to persuade and please
Man has a rugged heart—Woman a soft and tender one
Man prevents misery—Woman relieves it
Man has science—Woman has taste
Man has judgment—Woman has sensibility
Man is a being of justice—Woman an angel of mercy.[108]

Gendering of the species connoted a double standard of conduct in public and private life. Even in romances, dual standards existed. Before and after marriage, men were permitted liberties of which no woman could ever avail herself and keep her reputation. And a woman's premiere attribute, in public and private life, was a stainless reputation.

Male privilege cannot be discounted in Paul's churlish behavior toward Alice. These rites allowed him to act with impunity, just as they allowed men to legally beat their wives. Had Alice exhibited Paul's abusive behavior, she would have harmed her reputation. He would have labeled her uncouth, coarse, and an undesirable shrew, and authors of etiquette books would have upheld his condemnation.

For a combination of reasons, then, Paul hid neither his rude behavior nor his bouts with depression. His state of despondency had worried

Frederick Douglass in 1894, the same year that Paul spoke of suicide to another friend.[109] But symptoms of his illness predated that time. Friends found a strong melancholic strain in Paul's early nondialect poetry, as well as in his later material. His poem, "One Life," according to one corespondent, was exceptionally sad and plaintive:

> Oh, I am hurt to death, my love;
> The shafts of Fate have pierced my striving heart,
> And I am sick and weary of
> The endless pain and smart.
> My soul is weary of the strife,
> And chafes at life, and chafes at life.
>
> . . . .
>
> I know the world holds joy and glee,
> But not for me, 'tis not for me[110]

Paul expected Alice to accommodate his dark moods and behaviors, which he made known in an early letter, writing: "If what you see displeases you, shut your eyes to it, as if you had been my friend always, and like all my friends, were used to making allowances for me."[111] As he battled depression during his get-to-know-Alice summer, friends—usually women—excused his uncharitable behavior. One reminded Paul that he "took delight in saying unkind things"; still, would he please write again soon?[112] Another believed "the dumps" were Paul's "natural curses"; but then, poets could not always feed on ambrosia.[113] When Paul cursed the day he was born, an Indiana corespondent offered balm by speaking of his great talent, which would soon place the world at his feet.[114] Like this friend, others saw the state of Paul's career as the source of his depression. They assured him that when the world acclaimed his great talent, he would lose all self-doubt; he would be rich and despair no more. Streams of letters exhorted: Be not pessimistic! It will happen. You are a gift to "the race"!

Alice turned a blind eye to Paul's melancholia and unpleasantness. Perhaps at this stage, she excused them as artistic temperament, but later, during their first year of marriage, she would find his mood swings galling rather than romantic. In the initial stages of their friendship, however, Alice focused on Paul's talent, charm, and growing professional reputation. Besides, women of her class were trained to accommodate the "harmless whims" of gentlemen and to use their feminine wiles to exact change where needed. Alice and Paul's platonic relationship continued, but after four months he wanted to end that phase. Proclaiming "I can conceal my real self no longer," Paul poured out his heart, boldly and passionately:

Dayton, Ohio, October 13, 1895

Dear Miss Moore:

While I do not wish to apologize for what I am about to write, I do think it needs an explanation. . . . I am sitting here with your picture before me and my heart is throbbing faster than my pen goes. . . . I love you and have loved you since the first time I saw your picture and read your story. I know it seems foolish and you will laugh perhaps, or perhaps grow angry; but I can explain in one sentence. You were the sudden realization of an ideal! Isn't there some hope for me? I wish you could read my heart. I love you. I love you. You bring out the best that is in me. You are an inspiration to me. I am better and purer for having touched hands with you over all these miles. . . . Alice—let me call you that just this time. . . . I am going to pray that God will give you to me.[115]

God did not answer Paul's prayer, for Alice's feelings had not changed. She viewed his letter as a marriage proposal, and while she felt sorry for him and wished she could help him in some way, he "should never, never mention the subject again!"[116]

Paul may have been somewhat puzzled by this second blunt rejection. Women generally found him attractive, and he had always had "a good supply of the fairer sex," according to his best chum, Bud Burns.[117] Paul was a known womanizer and had a reputation for falling in and out of love frequently. Gossip about his amorous adventures could not have escaped Alice because the two shared mutual friends, so this reputation may have been a factor in her rejection of Paul's advances.

And yet Paul's roguish behavior was not totally unacceptable in polite company. His antics were those of a "disengaged man," a man free from restraint because he was not in a serious relationship. Conventional sex roles allowed him to be a rake. He was expected to "take up his time learning what drinking and gambling and betting and swearing and flirting are like."[118] The mainstream author of an 1890s etiquette book lauded the disengaged man, calling his position enviable:

> [He] is wholly irresponsible. He goes where he will, and does what he likes. As someone has said, "Everything is given him on account of his position. If he talks nonsense, it is his high spirits; if he dances incessantly the whole evening. it is that he may please 'those dear girls' . . . if he has a few fast lounging habits, it is held all very well in a fellow like that." Society has a perpetual welcome for him; the men like him for his social qualities, and the women receive him with rapture, if for no other reason than simply because—he is disengaged.[119]

Paul shared elements of his disengaged lifestyle with Alice, especially his fondness for women. "I feel like being kissed," he wrote her, perhaps to raise a little jealousy. She had, after all, rejected his overtures. "So I am going to hurry through the closing lines of this letter and go to see the prettiest, sweetest, daintiest girl who lives on Bruce Street. She will kiss me, but oh how I wish it were you."[120]

Paul's Bruce Street paramour was not the only woman with whom he was entangled while trying to win Alice's love. At least three other women hovered at the center or periphery of his affections, and these amorous relationships overlapped. Their timing makes dubious Paul's ardent declarations of love to Alice. How sincere could he have been when he was concurrently romancing other women, and even offering marriage? Of special interest is Paul's relationship with Maud Clark. It, as well as the others, provides a blueprint for his liaison with Alice.

In March or April 1895, shortly before falling in love with Alice's photograph, Paul broke his engagement to Maud, his hometown sweetheart. To her chagrin and grief, he simply changed his mind about marrying her. This was after compromising her sexually.[121] The reason Paul gave Maud was that she was "an iceberg" and that he could not afford a wife—although within months and without change in fortune he would propose to Alice. His duplicity may not have been as important as his final argument. Telling Maud—as he would demonstrate to Alice—that his work and mother mattered most to him, Paul revealed what would become fundamental sources of tension in his married life. He also ended his break with Maud in a manner that became very familiar to Alice: he got drunk.

Whether or not Maud Clark had the physical attributes Paul admired in women, that is, fair skin and European features, is not certain, for little is known about her. However, she seems not to have had the social stature he required. Maud was not a teacher and seemingly did not have a middle-class occupation: she was not Paul's ideal mate. Although from similar socioeconomic environments, he had outgrown her. Paul had elite aspirations and stood at the rim of his destiny. His vision of wedded bliss included a "cultured mother and father" living with their children in an "elevated ideal of the home."[122] Maud's letters indicate she lacked that form of gentility—she was neither well educated nor cultured according to middle-class African American standards. However, another woman in Paul's life had all the proper graces.

She was Rebekah Baldwin of Washington, D.C., and Alice was her mirror image. Like many African American society belles, Rebekah was a mulatto school marm. She, like Alice, harbored dreams of being a writer. She, like Alice, loved Paul's poetry before she even met the man.[123]

Dunbar scholars contend that Paul and Rebekah were never more than friends,[124] but her letters paint a different picture. The two met initially in 1893, at the Columbian World's Exposition in Chicago and were—in her words—immediately attracted to each other. They began a correspondence spanning Paul's romance with Maud and overlapping his pursuit of Alice. Rebekah and Paul's liaison went through cycles of love and friendship, reputedly evolving into a filial devotion sometime during Alice and Paul's engagement. In fact, the evidence strongly suggests that had Rebekah consented to a sustained amorous relationship, Paul may not have initiated an acquaintance with Alice.[125] During the spring and summer of 1895, in his role as rake, Paul courted both women. Was he in love with both, as he led each to believe? Or was he a deceitful but enterprising suitor, willing to love the one who ultimately loved him? Contrary to what Paul had told Maud Clark, he was in the marketplace—as in his poem, "The Wooing"—and he was shopping for a wife.

Paul courted Rebekah and Alice in the same manner. He wooed Rebekah too, primarily by mail. They discussed literature and exchanged photographs. Paul mentored her creative writing and assured her she was his inspiration. Like the smitten professor at Atlanta Baptist College and his lady-love at Spelman Seminary, Paul read Rebekah's letters "over day after day and sometimes three times a day."[126] He wrote a poem about her and a love poem for her. Paul "talk[ed] soft nonsense," and sang Rebekah's praises: she had "brilliancy" and "aristocratic manners." She was divine![127]

Rebekah in turn idolized Paul. He had genius; he was a gift to the race. She "read his letters again and again—each new reading [was] a source of new delight."[128] To her, Paul's "very memory [was] an ecstasy!" And she loved his moods, too.[129] Rebekah was so enamored of Paul that she declared herself unworthy of him. "I am full of faults," she confessed. "Indeed, I have often wondered how I have kept you interested in me so long. You are so versatile, so poetic, so interesting. I am so monotonous, so prosy and so dull."[130]

Rebekah, however, could not decide what she wanted from Paul. From 1893 to 1895, she vacillated between being Paul's friend—even underlining the word in the letters—and being besotted by him. The year 1895 finally brought resolution to the nature of their liaison, and resolution brought Paul into Alice's life.

Early that year, it appeared that Rebekah might become Mrs. Paul Laurence Dunbar. She was once again in love with Paul. Her January letter invited him to read between the lines to discern "all the appreciation and devotion that my trite and commonplace expressions fail to convey."[131] The following month—while Paul was engaged to Maud Clark—Rebekah visited him and "spent a delightful evening. He brewed divine tea" and enchanted her with his company and "charming conversation."[132] Paul too, may have been thrilled by Rebekah's displays of affection. She queried him about his concept of love, especially his ideal woman. What qualities did his perfect mate need to bring a suitor to his knees? she asked. "Will you not tell me, Paul, that I may learn?"[133]

But Rebekah's passion was short lived. The next month's letter (March 1895) shows no ardor; she had resumed her friendship mode. That Paul sent his first letter to Alice in April suggests he had tired of Rebekah's ambivalence and that he was shopping for a new love. Subsequent behavior lends credence to the theory, as Paul curtailed correspondence with Rebekah and bombarded Alice with letters.

Rebekah, however, was not yet ready to exit Paul's life. Why haven't you answered my letters, she asked in a July 1 missive.[134] Unknowingly, her query initiated a love triangle, for Paul resumed courting Rebekah while pursuing Alice. Did he now love both women? He made both believe so. Yet Paul's actions seem more deceitful and opportunistic than amorous.

He began dispensing tokens of love at random. In the June 6, 1895, letter, for example, he professed love for Alice through his poems "Alice" and "My Lady Love Lives Far Away."[135] By July 10, with "a delicately turned compliment," he convinced Rebekah that her favor had not waned;[136] but in a July 25 letter, Paul bade Alice "the dearest heart, goodnight."[137]

Rebekah finally ended the saga by ending her romance with Paul. In so doing, she influenced the nature of Paul and Alice's relationship. On July 30, 1895, Rebekah proposed that she and Paul engage in a platonic love. "We shall be such friends, as Hannah Moore and Dr. Johnson and Chateaubriand and Mme. Recamier," she wrote, as only a romantic could. "Byron laughs at platonic love, but it has existed and we shall prove that its power is not yet lost."[138]

Paul agreed with Lord Byron, known to some as the archetypical nineteenth-century libertine. He too, wanted passion, not friendship. Moreover, Rebekah's proposal must have angered him because he began mocking her. In his remaining letters, which seem to end in August 1895, Paul spoke constantly of Alice—so much so that the jealous Rebekah snapped: "Now Paul! Please stop talking to me about [Alice] Ruth Moore. I am sure that you needn't be throwing up to me all the time that you like her."[139]

Following Rebekah's suggestion of platonic love, Paul intensified his pursuit of Alice. Perhaps she was now his choice because he was certain he could never have Rebekah. That fall, on October 13, 1895, although they still had not met, Paul wrote Alice that he had loved her since seeing her photograph in the spring issue of a magazine. He wanted the "dearest of girls to know" that she held his future in her hands.[140] Was he now sincere? A year later, while still romancing the recalcitrant Alice in his lyrical but duplicitous manner, Paul proposed to yet another woman. She was Maud Wilkinson, a Euro-American who had aspirations of being an actress. This is not a well-documented relationship. Still, as late as 1956, one of her relatives declared that even though Maud later married a white man, she never forgot Paul and always spoke fondly of him. His proposal to her on October 24,

1896, was strangely reminiscent of his proposal to Alice almost a year earlier. Paul wrote Maud Wilkinson: "Darling, all my dreams of the future hold you. . . . If you will take me, I will marry you now."[141]

Alice's testimony is that she did not know of Paul's wanton nature until after she married him, but evidence points to the contrary.[142] Rebekah, however, acknowledged early in her romance with Paul, the gulf between the man and the author of exquisite letters and poems. She recognized, too, that she loved only the poet and told Paul so, writing: "When I read your letters, Paul I <u>love</u> you. Somehow they touch a something in my heart that warms into love for you . . . [but] *I love you only when I read your letters*" (emphasis in original). Rebekah was well aware that Paul also loved an illusion—the Rebekah of his letters. She continued: "You love *me* when you *write* [to me]."[143]

Rebekah's dilemma was not unusual. Eventually, correspondents had to separate the letter writer from the romantic letters he wrote. The result could be uncertainty. Hattie Rutherford at Spelman Seminary believed the letters of her suitor, John Brown Watson, would charm any woman. Did he love her? Did she love him? she asked.[144] Love letters gave birth to fantasies. Young Ida B. Wells found Mr. Morris wrote "interesting" letters that led her to believe he was "a man." But when she received his photograph, "it was the face of a mere boy." Should she reveal her age to him? she asked her diary. Suppose he were her junior? How improper to give her heart to a younger man! Yet, she confessed: "I feel my scepter departing from me, before him as before no other & it is somewhat humiliating."[145]

Once Rebekah separated the man Paul from the bewitching poet, she knew she could never marry the real Paul. Courtship and marriage were not the same, she told him, and marriage was an iconoclast. It "tears away the veil of romantic illusion, disclosing to our views the rough and jagged edges of character, which first *shock,* then *pain* and then *disgust*" (emphasis in original).[146] While late-nineteenth-century courting couples believed knowledge of the "unlovely me" was necessary for a good marriage, Rebekah realized that she could not build a long-term relationship with a man of Paul's character and mood swings.

There may have been another reason why Rebekah finally rejected Paul. Unlike Alice, she seemingly did not need his stature as a famous man to enter the most elite of African American society, the Washington,

D.C., social set. Although information on her background is limited, she was one of the city's social lights before her association with Paul. Also, since she was a mulatto, her family may have objected to Paul's humble origins and dark complexion. While Rebekah finally concluded that she did not love the real Paul, and perhaps did not need him, she—or her illusion—remained ever attractive to him. Two short months before marrying Alice, Paul was still singing Rebekah's praises—and he sang them to Alice.[147]

Alice recalled that she finally fell in love with Paul sometime in 1897. She called it an incredible year. In the interim—that is, from Paul's October 1895 letter declaring his love to the time she "was won by him" in 1897—monumental changes occurred in both their lives. Alice's sister, Mary Leila, married James Young, a caterer, in 1895. The entire family—bride, groom, Alice, and mother Patsy—moved from New Orleans and set up housekeeping at 55 Jerome Street, West Medford, Massachusetts. Alice had a comfortable life. Her brother-in-law's business was successful, allowing the family to enjoy a middle-class lifestyle, complete with hired "girls." Alice abandoned her school teaching career to pursue myriad interests. She continued her writing and published regularly in African American periodicals. In a quirk of fate, one of her poems preceded a bit of poetry by Paul on the pages of the October 1896 *A.M.E. Church Review*.[148] The pair still had not met. Alice busied herself with social engagements and club work, more now than ever. She was selected secretary of the newly formed National Association of Colored Women in 1896, a major racial uplift organization that was as heavily laden with social life as it was with good works and intentions.[149] More importantly, according to Alice, her immediate and future plans excluded Paul as an imminent factor; she was planning to enter Wellesley College.[150]

Paul's life was also transformed, with 1896 being a banner year. After years of struggle, he became an overnight success when William Dean Howells favorably reviewed his second poetry volume, *Majors and Minors*, in the June *Atlantic Monthly*. Shortly thereafter, Dodd, Mead and Company, a major mainstream publishing house, became Paul's publisher and remained so throughout his life. When the publisher issued his third book of poetry, *Lyrics of a Lowly Life* (1896), Paul had two books before the public in the same year. Both sold well.

Both contained the poems "Alice" and "If," written for Rebekah Baldwin. The latter's response to either book is unknown, but Alice interpreted the inscription in her complimentary copy of *Majors and Minors* as an affectionate statement of her place in his life. She declared the lines were so revealing that she was ashamed to show them to her sister club woman, Mrs. Booker T. Washington.[151] Opposite the title page Paul wrote:

> Jan. 3, 1896
> With the compliments of the author to Miss Alice Ruth Moore.
>> Oft in the darkness of hearts and lives
>>> Comes song that brings joy and light,
>> As out of the depths of Cypress groves
>>> The mocking bird sings at night.
>>>> Paul Laurence Dunbar[152]

Showing Mrs. Washington her personalized copy was Alice's way of alerting high society to her very special relationship with the now famous poet. No doubt she also made all aware that the poem "Alice" was for and about her.

And why not? Among the elite, status was all important. Women gained legitimacy and stature through association with prominent men, especially husbands. With the 1878 marriage of Cleveland socialite Josephine Willson to Blanche K. Bruce, the African American senator from Mississippi, polite society lauded her as Mrs. Senator Bruce, the "Martha Washington of the colored race." Similarly, Mrs. Sarah Dudley Pettey, "the brilliant and accomplished wife of the late Bishop Charles Calvin Pettey," was recognized as Mrs. Bishop Pettey.[153] Alice would be known as Mrs. Paul Laurence Dunbar. But even the knowledge that Paul was courting her elevated her social status. As Alice later recorded in "No Sacrifice," surely an autobiographical short story: "To be receiving letters from him, daily letters, and adorable poems, and passionate outpourings made me the queen."[154]

With success, Paul relocated from Dayton to New York and became even more successful. He was in great demand on the lecture circuit. Prominent magazines commissioned articles and poems. To book his many engagements, Paul hired Major James B. Pond, head of a popular lecture bureau. Pond represented a distinguished clientele that included

Mark Twain, Booker T. Washington, the charismatic cleric Henry Ward Beecher, and Sisieretta Jones (1868–1933). Known professionally as the "Black Patti," this great African American opera singer performed at the White House during Benjamin Harrison's administration. Star status also brought Paul a round of parties and social engagements. It may have been at such an affair that he met Maud Wilkinson, the aspiring Euro-American actress whom he proposed to in October 1896.

It may also have been at such an occasion that Paul met Victoria Earle Matthews, a married mulatto social activist, club woman and author with whom he had more than a passing acquaintance. Mrs. Matthews (1861–1907) was the type of woman who would catch Paul's eye: she had the complexion and features he idolized, as well as status and good reputation. Victoria Matthews is best known for establishing the White Rose Mission (1897), initially a settlement house and community center for "colored working girls" in New York. Later, training classes for children were offered at night and on Saturdays. Alice would work as a volunteer, teaching juveniles manual arts skills. She would also live with Mrs. Matthews during this period.

It was rumored that Victoria Earle Matthews and Paul once had an intimate relationship. Known as Dolores to close friends, to Paul she was "my dusk-eyed Dolores."[155] It was in fact the dark-eyed Mrs. Matthews who finally brought Alice and Paul face to face.

On February 5, 1897, Victoria Earle Matthews hosted a lavish farewell party for Paul in her Brooklyn home at 9 Murray Street. Paul was scheduled to sail the next day for a year-long stay in England, where there was great demand for his literature and recitals. The luminaries W. E. B. Du Bois, Booker T. Washington, and a host of other elites came to bid Paul good-bye. So did Alice. To do so, she traveled overnight by train from West Medford to Boston, and on to Brooklyn.

Alice recalled circumstances surrounding her first meeting with Paul as traumatic. Her family objected to her attending the party; but Paul, as Alice later wrote in a thinly veiled short story, "was pathetic about having to delay seeing his 'Dream Girl' another year. I was torn [with] uncertainty. What if I should never see him? What if he should forget me in Europe?"[156]

Alice's sister club woman, Mrs. Matthews, helped solve the dilemma by inviting Alice to be her house guest for the party weekend. True to social convention, she assured her she would be perfectly chaperoned. Defying family, Alice—in Paul's recollection—"the sweetest, smartest little girl I ever saw . . . ran off from Boston to New York to see me off. . . . She is very much ashamed of having run off, but she said that she could not have gone for a year without seeing me."[157]

That night of their first meeting, Paul and Alice escaped from the illustrious crowd into the Matthews' study. Paul proposed; she accepted and promised to try to learn to love him.[158] As a symbol of betrothal, Paul used "a little gold band" that he "slipped off his finger, which belonged to his mother."[159] Perhaps since it was once customary for the woman to also give a love token, Alice gave Paul a bouquet of violets, her favorite flowers.[160] The two talked of having babies, and vowed to keep the engagement a secret. Paul sailed to England early the following morning. Alice, remaining true to the pledge, did not tell her family that she was engaged. As late as August 1897, Paul warned her not to expect much correspondence from him while she was visiting her family, "as it does not look well for so many letters to be coming from one person, especially when certain things are to be kept secret."[161] He, however, wrote his mother about the engagement while en route to London, telling her: "You will be surprised to hear that Alice Ruth Moore ran away from Boston, and came to bid me good-bye. . . . I hope you will not think it is silly, but [she] and I are engaged. You know that is what I have wanted for two years."[162] Alice would learn that Paul was not discreet. Just as he did not keep their engagement a secret, so he would tell friends about their secret marriage. And he would talk about the most intimate aspects of their lives.

Paul had finally won his "heart's desire," almost two years after falling in love with her photograph. During that time, she had experienced his magnetism and witnessed his talent. Alice had also been introduced to some of his demons. The advice books she was so fond of reading clearly stated that choosing a mate was one of life's important decisions, and that men like Paul who were mentally ill, temperamental, rude, and too fond of drink and women were not husband material. But advice sought —whether from book, family, or friend—is not necessarily heeded. Alice chose to love Paul and consented to be his wife. For the ambitious Alice, a famous husband was the best husband. Also, like other starry-eyed romantics, she believed love was an uncontrollable force that knew no bounds. Even before her association with Paul, Alice, enamored of love, rhapsodized:

> Love, most potent, most tyrannical and most gentle of the passions which sway the human mind, thou art the the invisible agency which rules men's souls. . . . All things are subservient to thee. All delicate intricate workings of that marvelous machine, the human brain; all the passions and desires of the human heart . . . O love thou art all-potent, all wise, infinite, eternal! Behold![163]

With their engagement on February 5, 1897, the couple entered a period of waiting and hoping and planning. It was a period that would irrevocably change both lives. But especially Alice's. During this period, Paul would rape her.

FOUR

One Damned Night
of Folly

I am suffering the tortures of the damned.
Blessed insanity would be a relief—death anything.
We are both paying dearly for one damned night of folly.
　　　　　—Paul Laurence Dunbar to Alice Ruth Moore
　　　　　　　　　　　　　　　　　(December 1, 1897)[1]

A betrothal exacted different prices from the betrothed, depending on gender. During this rehearsal period for marriage, the woman of that time altered her life and began assuming the subservience prescribed for wives. She was expected to relinquish ambitions for worldly achievement, and to prepare for her preordained occupational roles of homemaker and mother. This was especially true for elite women of color, wrote an African American culture critic, for progress of "the race" depended on it.[2]

The engaged woman maintained some autonomy, but she began transferring her independence to her betrothed, entrusting him with her future well-being. This transition period from courtship to marriage was often one of inner doubt and conflict for the engaged woman. Poised between the familiarity and freedom of single life and the greater restrictions, responsibilities, and risks of wedded life, she wondered what marriage would bring. Would hers be a life of deepening love, security, and fulfillment? Would it be a life of confinement and hardship? Even the wedding ceremony—touted as the most beautiful and important ritual for women—would strip her of dignity. The bride's father or some other male authority would "give her away," like something he owned, to her new husband. Moreover, she would have to promise obedience. With the acceptance of an engagement ring, a nineteenth-century middle-class woman made one of the truly fateful choices in her life.

Her companion's life changed very little. He too had insecurities, since the future is unpredictable. But no gender-induced roles required him to abandon career goals for marriage. A betrothed African American male remained free to pursue his very limited employment opportunities. In fact, the engaged male was encouraged to be ambitious, so that he could more readily afford the caretaking of his prospective bride. Unlike his sweetheart, tradition did not require him to forfeit freedom or even curtail his activities. The double standard of conduct allowed him to act with impunity. Moreover, the betrothed male had few duties regarding the business of getting married. His major job was to secure housing and have a new wedding suit made. If he wanted to demonstrate a middle-class or opulent lifestyle, he equipped his home with the appropriate furniture, drapes, "cook stoves, pianos, servant girls, indoor plumbing" and other accouterments proclaiming his station in life.[3] Paul Laurence Dunbar would do just that. In a fine African American section of the nation's capital, he would rent a home for his prospective bride.

In many aspects, the stages of Alice and Paul's engagement mirrored those of other middle-class couples. The evidence suggests that she experienced doubt about her decision to marry Paul once the aura faded— that romantic haze in which the two got engaged when they first saw each other. Her life changed radically that eventful night of February 6, 1897, while Paul's did not. Immediately, Alice began surrendering much of her autonomy, although Paul sailed for England the next day and remained there for eight months. From across the ocean and through the mail, he became her governing force, the authority to whom she responded. For Paul and romantic love, Alice renounced professional goals and defied family and friends. As she followed society's script for betrothed women, her life began imitating her art. Alice acted like the love-struck female in "The Woman" (1895), her essay on the status of females, written before Paul initiated their relationship. Like "the woman," Alice traded independence for dependence—her concept of love. And prophetically, like "the woman," Alice too accepted "a serfdom, sweet sometimes, it is true, but which often becomes galling and unendurable."[4]

The life-altering changes began right after her engagement, when, according to Alice, she abandoned a cherished dream. She told one of Paul's biographers:

> I did not return to Boston [after I got engaged]. I was preparing to enter Wellesley College, but after being engaged, decided to give up my college career. I stayed in New York and within a month had taken a position as teacher in the Brooklyn schools.[5]

Whether Alice seriously planned to attend Wellesley is uncertain. No records indicate that she applied or even inquired about matriculation. In fact, early in their courtship, Alice told Paul of plans to attend Radcliffe, not Wellesley.[6] The Wellesley reference may have been another element in the self fashioning and self-promotion that had changed Alice from the poor illegitimate daughter of a freed slave into a "representative colored woman." By the time she spoke of her engagement to Paul's biographer (ca. 1930), her enviable role as wife of a living legend had vanished, as had her stature as a luminary in the highest circle of African American society. Although she still moved in "society" and was recognized by some as "a shining intellectual light among colored men and women," a writer of "no little repute," Alice was a struggling middle-class matron who had difficulty making ends meet. While she wrote articles, essays, and some poems for African American newspapers, she could not get her material published in mainstream journals. And the white press was Alice's standard of excellence.[7] To tell Paul's biographer that she had given up Wellesley for love conferred some of that awe that had enveloped her at the turn of the twentieth century, when she was the wife of a famous man. Such deference was still important to her. Moreover, surrendering a fine college education for Paul inferred that she had possessed an all-consuming love for her late husband.

If indeed Alice abandoned college plans to prepare for married life, she was still training for a career. Being a suitable wife was deemed a profession, and goals or activities competing with prescribed womanly duties were not encouraged. After her marriage, Alice would abruptly quit her teaching job in the middle of the school year at Paul's insistence. Similarly, when Margaret Murray Washington became the third wife of Booker T. Washington, the noted power broker, she asked his permission to continue her career as an educator at Tuskegee Institute where he was the principal.[8]

That Alice chose matrimony as a career did not mean she was not still ambitious. Her great ambition, rather than great love, caused her to accept Paul's marriage proposal, for on the night of betrothal, she promised to try to learn to love him. That is not to say Alice was not infatuated with the idea of him, or fond of the idea of him. Why would she not be? At twenty-one years of age, she had been romanced by mail for almost two years, by a brilliant, famous man, whose letters, wrote Alice, "make one's very heart leap for joy."[9] He had written love poems for and about her.

Yet Alice's letters to Paul in London were not those of a dewy-eyed fiancée. Although few of her own missives for this period survive, the questions and comments in Paul's letters reflect a passionless lover. He complained that she wrote infrequently. His letters brimmed with affection: he loved and longed for her; he would "love [her] as no man has ever loved before."[10]

By contrast, Alice's letters lacked such effusions. Paul acknowledged what he called the "difference in the intensity of our passions"; but he too found Alice's missives a bit unusual.[11] "If you do really care for me, let me know it," he wrote during the first month of their engagement.[12] He begged her to display some ardor: "Tell me over and over again that you love me. . . . Love me, dear, and tell me so."[13] While Paul wrote that he yearned for the magic of her presence and the thrill of her kiss, Alice thought she should not have even kissed him good-bye.[14] Her only display of passion was jealousy, when Paul continued to write about his "friend and companion," a young English woman married to an African American from his hometown of Dayton.

If two extant letters are typical, Alice did not love Paul. She sent no kisses and displayed no ardor. She did not even write that she missed her betrothed. Her letters four months into the engagement were those she could have written to a friend. In fact, Alice even referred to Paul as her "correspondent" rather than her beloved. In a chatty June 8, 1897, letter she wrote: "Dearest Paul—I have been a long time writing you, haven't I? But really I have been busy, up to my eyes in work of all sorts, and treating all my correspondents shabbily." Alice then spoke of the *glorious* time she had during a five-day Boston visit, and how "recklessly busy" she had been for the past two months.[15] Similarly, the self-centered Alice wrote "Paul dearest" on June 19, 1897, about her approaching birthday. He must save his pennies and farthings because she wanted a pretty gift—her sister said she deserved one. Alice continued with news of the approaching Harvard-Yale boat race, where she planned to root for Harvard "with all possible zeal." Then she talked about her pretty living quarters and a testimonial dinner for Victoria Earle Matthews, with whom she was living. In what seemed to be an afterthought, the future Mrs. Dunbar closed "[w]ith tenderest love."[16]

Perhaps Alice was in that stage of uncertainty that was common for newly betrothed women. Her lack of affection may have indicated doubt about being engaged, as was the case with the brown-haired, brown-eyed mulatto Lugenia Burns of Chicago in 1896. Misgivings plagued her during her secret engagement to John Hope, a southern professor. Like Alice in her period of quandary, Lugenia—called Genie—sent letters that were short, indifferent, infrequent, and cold. Theirs too, was a long-distance romance, one mainly crafted through years of letter writing dating from 1893 until their marriage in 1897.

The miles between Genie and John, and the fact that they were secretly pledged to each other, gave her second thoughts. Such a concealed relationship put her in a precarious position. At a time when a lady's character could be ruined simply by being seen frequently in the company of one man, John's visits to Chicago—in which he monopolized her time—"embarrassed" and "humiliated" her, Genie complained. Although he had not publicly declared his intentions, gentlemen friends, suspecting she was engaged, kept their distance. If he were not serious, Genie wrote John, he was compromising her reputation and ruining her chances of making a good match. Just what is the depth of your emotion? she asked in a June 1896 letter.[17]

John Hope's response from Augusta, Georgia, went to the core of Genie's anxiety. She was the one with uncertainties, not he. "Here is the time for you to examine yourself closely," he replied, "to see whether, after all, you are capable of yielding to all the demands our present relations silently but inexorably make upon you." Hope urged Genie to search both heart and mind to see if she had been too hasty in making her commitment to him. He had examined himself *thoroughly*, he assured her, and knew how he felt and just what he was willing to do. He urged her to do the same. "I want you to know *yourself* in the same way," he added, "and not to doubt yourself at all" (emphasis in original).[18]

John knew that he loved Genie, he concluded, and believed that she loved him as well. He failed to mention, however, that their secret engagement did not harm his reputation nor impair his marriageability.

Like Genie Burns, Alice pondered her relationship with Paul soon after their engagement. Her love was faint, but she had great expectations for her life as Mrs. Dunbar "We'll be rich . . . won't we?" she later asked him as she spun fantasies of visiting Paris.[19] Goals and resources once channeled toward her public career were directed toward being Paul Laurence Dunbar's wife. She intended to be a model wife and studied advice literature and home-decorating books in preparation. Alice believed she had sacrificed her career goals with her engagement, and she expected to be handsomely rewarded for her forfeiture. When in a characteristic period of self-doubt, Paul told Alice that he was a mediocre wretch of a writer, was sick of fame, and just wanted to make a living, she fired back:

> I do not agree with you in saying that your ability is mediocre and that you are content to merely make a living. You are not mediocre, and I will not let you be content. I shall spur you on like a whirl-wind whip until you work or quiver from exhaustion. . . . To be content with a little would be mediocre and vain—to aspire ever higher . . . until you can survey the world from the top of the latter [*sic*], this is what I want my Paul to do. What ever ambition I may have had for myself I have lost in you.[20]

Ever mindful of her designated duties as an engaged woman, Alice told Paul that her only ambition now was to be his comforter, inspiration, and helpmate.

Alice lied. She wanted a great deal more. Despite what she told Paul, she still wanted to succeed as a professional writer and knew that he could help her. Poetry and fiction still flowed from her pen, but her work was not readily accepted for publication. On receiving yet another rejected manuscript, she told her fiancé: "It would be a good idea if it had . . . your dialect—and your name."[21]

Alice wanted the accouterments and social deference due Mrs. Paul Laurence Dunbar. She made that clear to Paul during their betrothal. When Paul talked of renting a six-room house, Alice insisted on one with eight rooms. She was, however, more than satisfied with their compromise home located at 1934 Fourth Street (North West) in Washington,

D.C. Washington was the capital of elite African American society. "It is a three storey brick with seven rooms," Paul reassured her, "with pretty alcoves on the upper floors and with all modern improvements. It is just next to Bob Terrell's."[22]

Alice must have been thrilled. Bob Terrell was Judge Robert H. Terrell, an African American Harvard graduate. His wife, Mary Church Terrell, had the very best credentials. She was of course, extremely fair skinned. She was wealthy and very well educated. Mollie, as her friends called her, had a bachelor's degree from Oberlin College, at a time when few women of either race even graduated from high school. Also, Mollie had taken the rigorous four-year "gentleman's course" rather than the two-year "ladies' program," and had capped her education with study in Europe. Mollie and Bob Terrell were one of the premier couples of African American society, along with the sons of Frederick Douglass and their wives, the Princeton-educated cleric Francis Grimke and his prominent wife, Charlotte Forten Grimke, and a few other "best families."[23]

Alice could not have asked for more prestigious neighbors than the Terrells. During the latter stage of the engagement, when Paul, who hated high-society rituals, would not return Mollie and Bob's social calls, Alice would beg him to do so. Offending the Terrells made it impossible for her to enter that rarefied strata of society as his wife, she would tell him. Perhaps thinking that she sounded selfish and manipulative, Alice would add: "We owe it to ourselves to create and maintain an unquestioned, looked-up to social position."[24]

Alice readily admitted that Paul's status was important to her, and that she valued his name and reputation more than he. While Paul was certain that Alice did not care for him only because of his success, he felt compelled to ask: "Could you still love me and would you marry me if I [were] . . . a failure? If instead of a laurel to wear I should come . . . with a grief to share, darling would you share it?"[25]

Perhaps Alice was opportunistic. If so, Charlotte Perkins Gilman, Thorstein Veblen, and other late-nineteenth-century mainstream critics of traditional marriage would have applauded her stance.[26] They argued that American courtship was not a process of love seeking; it was a marriage market, where women presented themselves as merchandise for men to marry. Women's wares were certain feminine virtues or wiles, like graciousness and beauty. In Alice's case, it was light skin and a look of refinement. Paul's autobiographical poem, "The Wooing," relating his courtship of Alice, confirms the theory. While shopping in the marriage mart, he was bowled over by a lady with a near ivory complexion, auburn hair, and hazel eyes.[27] The critics of nineteenth-century traditional marriage further argued that even the popular term "marriage market" implied mercenary, materialistic motives. It connoted an exchange of love for financial support, since middle-class women were bred to become economically dependent wives. This too is evident in "The Wooing." Paul's maiden fair is not only a commodity to be purchased like any other item, but she can be had at a bargain price:

> He bought a rose and sighed a sigh,
> "Ah, dearest maiden, would that I
> Might dare the seller too to buy!
>
> "I'm not, sir, in the market yet . . ."
> "Tho' much I sell for gold and pelf,
> I'm yet too young to sell myself."
> . . . .
> Then loud he cried, "Fair maiden, if
> Too young too sell, now as I live,
> You're not too young yourself to give."[28]

Veblen and Gilman's scathing commentaries on courtship and marriage mocked the culture of romance that is manifested in Paul's poem. The love critics noted that since courtship allowed men to select the best buy for the money, women should trade at their best price. They should evaluate and select prospective husbands in terms of earning power. Once married, the critics concluded, middle-class wives entered an institution of male domination that kept them dependent on husbands for survival.[29]

Veblen and his culture experts may have been serious or writing tongue-in-cheek. But some women subscribed to their ideas. Including Genie Burns. She angrily reminded John Hope, then a modest, salaried college professor, that he had made the better bargain in the marriage market. She had "turn[ed] from those with money" to him who offered only love, for he had "*nothing else*" to give (emphasis in the original).[30]

By the same token, it is doubtful that the status-conscious Alice would have become engaged to Paul if he had offered only love rather than an enviable lifestyle for African Americans.

Marriage for social gain was neither unexpected nor unacceptable in late-nineteenth-century America. Despite the aura of romantic love enveloping courtship and marriage, some took a practical approach. Mrs. N. F. Mossell, a Philadelphia woman of color who was married to a medical doctor, believed wedded bliss could be also based on "ambition in its various guises. . . . [R]ight principles, morality, Christian living and due regard for heredity and environment" produced a happy, lasting union.[31]

Alice's letters to Paul during their engagement spelled out her expectations as Mrs. Paul Laurence Dunbar. Similarly, he revealed what he wanted from married life. Theirs was to be the standard middle-class patriarchal household in which the husband-father as family provider was the authority figure; and the wife-mother, as the nurturer, was responsible for child rearing, housework, and emotional support. This division of labor created a power imbalance that reified male supremacy and validated a husband's power over his wife. His was a position of economic strength, while hers was that of economic and status dependency. Alice and Paul, true believers in patriarchy, began practicing their faith immediately after betrothal.

But not all women of color accepted the submissive harness as easily and readily as Alice. Some argued that race men and women were equal, because both had come from slavery and both had endured its barbarity for more than two centuries. Thus, neither sex had an advantage over the other. Club woman and activist Fannie Barrier Williams further explained:

> In our development as a race, the colored woman and the colored man started even. The man cannot say he is better educated and has a wider sphere, for they both began school at the same time. They have suffered the same misfortunes. The limitations put upon their ambitions have been identical. The colored man can scarcely say to his wife, "I am better and stronger than you are," and from the present outlook, I do no think there is any danger of the man getting very far ahead.[32]

In Williams's thesis, the racial experience eradicated male superiority. According to her theoretical framework, Alice and Paul were social equals: both were the children of freed slaves; both entered school as members of freedom's first generation; both had triumphed over poverty; both were authors; and both were gifted people whose opportunities were limited by the color line.

Paul and Alice did not subscribe to such radical ideology. Paul had been introduced to sexism by society in general and his father specifically, and he relished his patriarchal role. In letters from London, he promised to protect Alice and provide for her. He would give her an easy and pleasant home, a life devoid of outside employment so that she would have the leisure to write. Paul promised to work his fingers to the bone for his queen, which he did at a feverish pitch. The month following their betrothal, he wrote Alice from his small room in London: "I am myself writing very hard and very steadily, the last few evenings past having seen me do sixteen thousand words in prose and about a half dozen poems. This is hustling. But a fellow who is thinking of taking a wife and making a home will hustle."[33]

The sixteen thousand words of prose included a draft of his first novel, *The Uncalled* (1898), an autobiographical tale. Paul began it on arrival in London in February and had finished it by July. Among the half-dozen poems composed early in his London stay was "Little Brown Baby with Sparkling Eyes," one of his most popular works. He liked it, too, telling Alice, it is "the best and tenderest bit of verse that I have done since I came here."[34] Another bit of creativity found him writing lyrics for "Dream Lovers," a romantic operetta by the black British composer, Samuel Coleridge Taylor.

Paul offered his high level of productivity as proof that he could meet his patriarchal obligation of providing for Alice. Such evidence was required of a man engaged to be married. But as head of household, he would not only be the bread winner, he would be the authority figure as well. This too, was expected and usually accepted. Accordingly, Paul relegated Alice to her subordinate role. He began by addressing her constantly in the diminutive. His letters now began "Dear Little Girl" and "Girlie." While these may be viewed as terms of affection, other popular nongendered endearments such as "darling" and "beloved" expressed similar ardor but without denigration. John Hope, the blue-eyed African American graduate of Brown University, frequently addressed his sweetheart as "Little Genie" and "Little Girl." It did not matter that she was twenty-five years old when they got engaged and had sometimes supported her entire family. Perhaps it was in retaliation that Genie gave John the pet name of "Snooks," the same name she had given her dog.[35] John Hope was an unabashed sexist who publicly called on African American men to be more manly, and women of color to be more womanly. He further opposed female leadership in organizations with male members, and thought women should not ride bicycles—a popular sport that Alice and even Frederick Douglass's daughter-in-law enjoyed.[36]

Hope's brand of sexism was widespread. A writer in the prestigious black journal, the *A.M.E. Church Review* (1892)—an organ dedicated to the principle of male supremacy—castigated women who did not "stay in their place." This included cyclists. "She is not the object of admiration, speeding as a jockey on the tract," the patriarchal journalist intoned. "She never looks so well upon a bicycle as she does upon a throne." Such inappropriate activity demeaned "woman's exalted station!"[37] Lest women even contemplate the abandonment of their narrow sphere, he added: "She may endeavor to put herself in man's place, and may do so many things as he does them . . . but it is to be remembered that grace and beauty belong unto woman, and that she must occupy such positions in which she can most conspicuously display those virtues."[38]

Paul, like John Hope and countless other men, did not count his betrothed as his equal. Alice was well educated and, like him, an author. He even praised her achievements in those acceptable ladylike endeavors such as creative writing. But Paul demanded that Alice stay in her place. In a letter written just days after their engagement, he began laying down the rules for her role as his wife. At social gatherings, for example, she would make the requisite idle chatter while he "looked wise."[39]

Alice became Paul's possession. "I consider you mine already," he wrote early in the engagement period.[40] She agreed: "[Y]ou are the undisputed possessor of me. . . . *Je tu* [*sic*] *fait mon obeisance.* [I am yours obediently.]"[41] And so Paul commanded her at will. "Now I am going to be your husband," he reminded Alice, "so you might as well learn to obey me now as later."[42] This authority allowed him to determine her associates, since there were people, even in the highest of high society, he would not permit her to know, as he informed Alice from London. Eventually she chafed under his domination. She came to see that he wished to dictate virtually every aspect of her life, including her thoughts. When this control irritated her, Alice asked:

> Wont you let me love New Orleans as you love Dayton? Wont you let me love home-folks as you love your friends of high school days? Wont you respect my traditions as I respect yours. . . . Wont you let me cherish girlhood memories as I hear you cherishing yours? Wont you think kindly of those girls I care for as I think kindly of the boys you like? Wont you let me speak of old things dear to me—or must I be silent?[43]

There was only one area in which middle-class women like Alice were given authority and deemed superior to men. Social custom engendered women with high moral principles. Men were considered far less virtuous, if not libertines. This made women the moral guardians of public and private life, and nineteenth- century America became a land of reform movements.

African American socialites attacked the problems of being black and female. The National Association of Colored Women, formed in 1896, became the major vehicle through which women attempted reform. With protecting and developing women of color as a major aim, the organization stressed self-help and racial solidarity. Mother Clubs to disseminate information on child rearing and homemaking, and day nurseries and kindergartens were established. The organization also focused on lynching. Since racial segregation was an organizing principle of the mainstream Women's Christian Temperance Union, African American women fought against the curse of alcohol through their churches, clubs, and settlement houses. Elite women were also suffragettes, although their struggle for the right to vote involved racism and sexism simultaneously. And zealous women attempted to reform the black Baptist church by challenging examples of gender inequity during the last two decades of the nineteenth century.

In private life, the ideology of the very moral middle-class female and the morally weak male allowed for a dual standard of sexual behavior, which was the foil of feminists throughout the century. Whether married or single, men could indulge their manly urges without disdain or loss of stature. Single women, however, were to remain chaste until marriage. Neither they, nor married women, could engage in an activity that might blemish their reputation. Also, these women were expected to tolerate the peccadilloes of male family members, and to forgive them. Paul once reminded an angry Alice of her role in this regard, writing: "You are far stronger than I am, don't be hard upon the weak."[44]

Paul enjoyed his socially sanctioned pleasures. Seemingly, he kept few roguish activities from Alice. "I hope you are not acting as badly as I am dear little girl," he wrote four months into the engagement.[45] Of course, she was not. He would not allow it, cautioning: "[I]f you are ever unfaithful to me, it would kill me. I can conceive of you [as] careless, blind, unthinking, but unfaithful—it would be awful."[46]

Even the slightest possibility of an impropriety caused Paul to assert his authority and reiterate Alice's position. "I shall not complain about your being in New York," he responded to her plans to visit that city, "although I do not like it. It is a dangerous place. But I know, darling, that you will do me no injustices, and yourself no dishonor, so I am content."[47] In a similar gender-related comment, Paul wrote that propriety for a woman of Alice's station was more important that humanity.[48]

It was also important for Alice, in her role as moral guardian, to reform Paul. She was "great hearted, pure souled," he said, while he had a fondness for alcohol and women. He depended on her to keep him on the straight and narrow. Time and again, Paul wrote from London: "Darling, I wish you were here. I have gone through another severe temptation and see that it is going to be so to the end of my stay. . . . You could keep me out of a great deal of mischief. . . . Pray that I will be real good. . . . For your sake I will be true and pure."[49] Later, he asked in a plaintive tone: "Dear, won't you help me be good? I believe I am worth saving."[50] His reformation was more important than that of most men. "[Y]ou owe it to my future, to your future, and to the good of the race which we both dislike . . . [to] make me the best man it is possible for me to be."[51]

Ultimately, Paul took no responsibility for his conduct. Just as he would blame God when he abused Alice (God should have stopped him), so he blamed Alice for his womanizing. Women throwing themselves at him were also at fault. There was "one girl [who] took possession of me and made me dance with her and her alone, while a little married woman who is <u>crooked</u> tried to be attractively suggestive" (emphasis in original).[52] Under such circumstances, what was a fellow to do?

Alice tackled her reform mission with zeal. Constantly, she prayed,

that people in the olden days were happier, cautioned a mainstream culture critic. They meant instead that Americans, especially women, were now "less tolerant of misery." He continued:

> It has not been so long since men only were supposed to have just causes for divorce, since their rights and sentiments alone could be infringed or wounded by conjugal derelictions. . . . [But] the idea of justice and equality of opportunity in pursuit of happiness has . . . so permeated modern society that women as well as men feel impelled to escape from . . . incompatibility, infidelity or a general perversion of marriage which degrades and poisons existence and renders the higher purposes of life unfruitful.[10]

One contribution to the sky-rocketing divorce rate was the concept of companionate marriage. Many men went kicking and screaming into this type of union. Most, like Paul, refused to accept the ideology, could not or would not meet its standards of wife as best friend and a softening of patriarchy. Perhaps that was the reason why mainly women sought divorces. They rebelled against the conditions of marriage to which the majority of husbands still held fast. Irate wives refused to be considered as property, to be commanded or treated badly at will.

Taking note of wifely rebellion, a late-nineteenth-century social commentator attributed it to the current wave of womanly self-respect. It made wives less tolerant of those trials that past spouses considered "pre-ordained, inevitable and, if not acceptable, at least offering no basis for public support," he surmised.[11] One such condition was spousal cruelty—verbal, psychological, and physical. Spousal assault has been viewed as a traditional male privilege in patriarchal cultures. Some societies even incorporate abusive rituals in marriage ceremonies, thereby underscoring masculine authority and the devaluation of women. In pre-industrial Russia, for example, it was customary for a father to gently strike his daughter with a new whip on her wedding day and then present the instrument of control to the groom.[12]

Census Bureau records show that many turn-of-the-century American women were fed up with abusive forms of male marital frustration. In 1902, the year Alice and Paul permanently separated after four years of marriage, 61,480 divorces were granted. By and large, it was women (41,424 of them) who initiated these legal actions, with a solid and growing core citing cruelty as the main reason.[13] From 1867 to 1906, wives charging spousal aggression received 218,520 divorces; men, 39,300.[14] Companionate marriage and social reform generated the more lenient court rulings that recognized mental or physical torture as sufficient grounds for divorce. The explosion in cruelty cases proved that women expected more than the intolerable bonds of traditional matrimony. They were willing to seek legal redress when physical violence or threats, "ingenious malice . . . humiliating assaults and annoyances" endangered their health and life.[15]

Once again, census records on divorce indicated neither race nor class. But African American taste arbiters could find no reasons for upper-crust women to dissolve their marriages. Nothing was considered serious enough to break holy vows or hinder the racial goal of stable, cultured relationships. Katherine Davis Tillman, an influential black journalist and author, ranked wedlock as the third most important factor in the course of human events. It took a back seat only to birth and death.[16] Stable unions situated in homes of morality, education, and refinement were imperative for the proper upbringing of race children; for, by example and mental acuity, these children would solve the race problem. So wrote Alice's neighbor, the prominent black socialite, Mary Church Terrell.[17] Since many people of color born in disadvantaged circumstances had found paths of distinction, community leaders believed that offspring born and nurtured in the virtuous middle-class tradition would accomplish miracles.

These important race goals meant that aristocratic marriages had to remain intact, regardless of spousal role frustration. African American newspaper editors were appalled that women of color would dare to leave their husbands. Journalists especially chided lower-income wives, even those who were abused. The *Savannah Colored Tribune* (1876), tried to make women seeking release from brutish husbands feel guilty by reporting: "White families quarrel and disagree as much as colored do [,] but you never hear of a white woman however low they may be running to the magistrate." The *Richmond Planet* (1890) advised wives to "[s]tay out of the police court with your petty quarrels."[18] An editorial in the popular middle-class journal, *A.M.E. Church Review* (1892), addressed the religious issue of broken marriages. Conceding that some action was needed when a spouse with "a beastly, disreputable character" endangered the other partner's life, the journalist

advocated separation rather than divorce, since "the Bible does not forbid it."[19]

Some race leaders would not even countenance separation. W. E. B. Du Bois claimed he suffered fifty-three years in a miserable marriage,[20] yet he believed wedded aristocrats should remain together, regardless of marital dissatisfaction. It was their duty as proponents of racial uplift to set an example for the less enlightened. Besides, conflict and disappointment were integral to marriage, according to authors of race manuals, especially "after the first transports of affection have subsided into quietness."[21]

African American etiquette books seldom addressed companionate marriage. They ignored the rising trend of wives divorcing their husbands. These authors, espousing traditional wedlock, blamed failed relationships on wives. Since marriage was woman's career and vocation, married women were held accountable for their "business," just as those toiling in the outside world. Moreover, these advice givers judged wives by similar standards. If a husband were unsuccessful in his vocation, it was because he was ill-prepared, did not work hard enough, or did not know his trade. So it was with the true woman and her career. A faltering or failed marriage reflected her ineptitude.

This popular conception of marriage as woman's business was an illogical offshoot of sexism. The prescribed ingredients for success in woman's decreed vocation spelled failure for entrepreneurs in the outside world. While achieving capitalists fixed their eyes on great profits from little investment, "the true wife . . . enters marriage not thinking how much she can get out of it, but how much she can put into it," wrote one African American advice giver.[22]

Woman's role in the marriage business differed markedly from that of a successful entrepreneur. Despite platitudes proclaiming her love to be a potent agent that made men leap to her bidding, a wife had little or no power, even in the home. Also, the exalted business model—the robber barons—became rich through assertiveness and ruthless tactics. A woman practicing her true vocation was to be submissive and demure. When relations were not harmonious, it was her job to set the good example, to take "the initiative in refraining from the trying speech, the quick remark, the sharp retort."[23] Perhaps this was not fair, argued a marriage expert of color. But injustice was inherent to woman's career.

He continued: "Men are impetuous; they have the care and support of the family on their hands. Masculine nerves are not always stronger than feminine ones." Wives were expected to diffuse their personal anger and accept the verbal assaults of husbands with "gentleness and patience, the two chief virtues of the . . . homemaker."[24]

Paul Laurence Dunbar's vitriolic poem, "Parted," a lyrical assault on his wife's character, reflects the patriarchal notion that marriages fail because of flawed wives. The melodious rendition of his marital breakup restates accusations found in his personal correspondence. Alice is responsible for she failed to live up to his expectations for Mrs. Paul Laurence Dunbar.

Writing "She wrapped her soul in a lace of lies / With prime deceit to pin it," Paul tells the audience his wife was not the model of morality a gentleman (like him) expects to marry. Rather, she was a deceitful liar. However, he did not realize this duplicity during their courtship, for he writes: "I thought I was winning a fearsome prize / So I staked my soul to win it."

In the lines, "We wed and parted at her complaint / And both were a bit of barter," Paul again comments on Alice's lack of ladylike virtues. She forced him into marriage, as he would write of their elopement. And instead of being a proper wife who keeps the marriage together, her actions caused the separation. While Paul concedes some culpability in the marital disunion—smugly evoking in one letter the male privilege of being a "human man"—Alice is not blameless and deserves no sympathy. For he writes: "Tho I'll confess that I'm no saint / I'll swear that she's no martyr."[25]

"Parted" is Paul's vengeful testimony of his disappointment with love. It is also a statement of his character and of cultural norms. Generally, middle-class men of color had unrealistic expectations of wives. Many journalists described the perfect wife as queenly; others envisioned obsequious handmaidens. Community leader L. A. Scruggs believed a wife lived mainly for her spouse. Serving, loving, and obeying him were part of the joys of her life and the aspirations of her soul.[26] Paul agreed, telling Alice on their first wedding anniversary, "A woman's care of her husband is the romance of married life."[27]

Unlike Paul, Alice published no poetic descriptions of his failure to meet her ideals. She did, however, leave thinly veiled short stories relat-

ing constant verbal, psychological, and physical abuse. In one, "The Decision," a couple meet and fall in love through the mail. The husband, an extremely successful author, lashes his wife with "the most scathing scorn that his ready tongue was capable of. . . . She felt the fineness go out of her soul like the gold dust out of the heart of a flower. When he struck her, she scarcely even wondered."[28]

Alice's correspondence further testifies to Paul's brutal behavior. This aggressiveness is curiously absent in his poem "Parted."[29] Paul may have omitted his dastardly doings because it was irrelevant in his view of marriage. To him, spousal chastisement was a husband's right, and submission a wife's duty. His father had been a wife beater, and none of Paul's writings suggests he disapproved of the practice.

African American manuals gave the impression that nothing as odious as physical assault occurred in upper-crust marriages. Perhaps that is the reason why wives were urged to stand by their men. Wife beating is never mentioned, not even in chapters with ominous titles like "Home as Hell on Earth."[30] According to the sources on gracious living, home as hell was the married couple having little spats, and children of the race living in coarse, uncultured homes.[31]

Despite public denial, spousal abuse was a reality for elite women of color. And they knew it. Four months before eloping, Alice told Paul of a society woman who had run away because her husband beat her. "You'd better not do me such a trick," Alice wrote prophetically.[32] Genie Burns, who was engaged to the southern professor, John Hope, had a wife beater in her family. She feared that John would treat her similarly. "Oh! Genie," Hope responded in an 1897 letter, "I am so afraid you fear me. . . . [D]on't compare me with Sam." He hastened to assure her that he would never harm her. "A man's self respect will keep him from being cruel," Hope wrote. "I shall break no heads . . . only ruffians assault women. . . . *Gentlemen* do not *beat* them" (emphasis in original).[33]

But Genie Burns had an even greater reason to fear her prospective husband. While John Hope found wife beating loathsome and would never dishonor himself in that manner, he believed that murdering an unfaithful wife was justifiable. He wrote Genie:

Gentlemen sometimes kill wives who are unfaithful. . . . Othello in the ecstasy of jealousy did not strike Desdemona. When he became certain in his mind that she was untrue, he killed her. . . . Only *great* causes render gentlemen otherwise than gentle to their wives; and when they have to be *un*gentle, *honor* is at stake. Then they commit a great deed. (Emphasis in original)[34]

John Hope's conception of the "great deed" emanated in ancient Roman law, which allowed husbands to kill wives for any number of supposed offenses, especially adultery. It was part of the divinely ordained order of things. Hope obviously still subscribed to the divine right of husbands. Had he and Genie been married at the time he laid down the law, and had she filed a complaint, many courts would have called his statements threatening. Threats and intimidation were forms of mental cruelty. If constant, they were grounds for divorce in the latter half of the nineteenth century.

Male privilege and elite African American society's portrait of the dutiful wife sanctioned Paul's anticipation of a perfect Alice. Anything less would have resulted in conflict and role frustration. If indeed Paul's violent behavior stemmed from conflicting role expectations, then his discontent began on March 9, 1898, just three days after the elopement. Ironically, the secret wedding was the source of this initial disgruntlement. As his poem "Parted" indicated, he was not in favor of it.

An essay on eloping in a mid-nineteenth-century mainstream newspaper severely criticized the practice. "Pre-mature marriages are among the greatest evils of these times," the journalist strongly opined, "and it would not be a bad idea in these days of reform if an anti-marry-in-a-hurry society were formed."[35]

Although romantics relished the secret marriage of the British poets Elizabeth Barrett and Robert Browning, middle-class Americans despised the very idea of eloping. As true romantics, Alice and Paul, in the ecstatic aftermath, cast their wedding in that light. They called it their private "Mr. and Mrs. Browning affair."[36] Still, to those members of society who set the code of conduct for those of lesser civility, hasty marriages—as they were also called—were so unacceptable that they were not even discussed in books on gracious living. A survey of African American and mainstream etiquette books reveals only one reference to premature marriages. Another Euro-American author too, castigated them, arguing there was nothing memorable about the ceremony—no attending friends, "no marriage formalities," nothing to make it shine like a star.[37] In other words, eloping eliminated the very important ritualistic display of conspicuous consumption and grand manners.

Ministers to prominent families often refused to marry runaway lovers lest they incur the wrath of parents and social acquaintances. Secret marriages implied something furtive, unclean, dishonorable—something like pregnancy or worse. Small wonder, then, that on hearing her daughter had eloped, the wife of a prominent mainstream medical doctor "fainted three times in succession, and her screams could be heard almost anywhere."[38]

Alice's mother, Patsy Moore, probably reacted similarly. Then her grief and disappointment turned to rage. Twenty days after the wedding, "Mama" was still furious and unrelenting. "[S]he hasn't opened her mouth or made a single comment," Alice moaned. "I have no mother now."[39] The wedding shattered Alice's family. Her older sister, Leila, was grief stricken. When calm returned, she wrote Paul a nasty letter.

By the third day of his honeymoon, the groom was having second thoughts about the elopement. He and Alice had vowed to keep the marriage secret until the end of the school year, thereby enabling the new Mrs. Dunbar to fulfill her teaching contract. But Paul did not honor the agreement. On returning home to Washington, he told two friends that he had married over the weekend, and they were appalled. His confidantes, Dr. Daniel Hale Williams and Ella Smith, a well-to-do Newport, Rhode Island, mulatto with a master's degree from Wellesley, stripped the elopement of romanticism and revealed its tawdriness.

Paul's friends informed him that he and Alice had breached propriety, that they had jeopardized their position in society. Quality people simply did not elope. That type of ceremony was the domain of "criminals or two plebeians with the fear of disgrace hanging over them."[40] Ella and Dr. Dan—as Paul called him—urged the groom to publicly announce the marriage straight away, and to bring Alice to Washington immediately. "Society" had to see that she was not pregnant. If Alice remained in Brooklyn until the end of the school year as planned, "society" would assume that she had aborted the fetus.[41]

Convinced by friends that his secret wedding was a social sin and that the wages of sin were social death, Paul blamed the marital impropriety on Alice. From his Washington home, angry accusations flew: "You made me do something I did not want to do. . . . In your intoxicating presence, I had to give way or seem selfish or uncaring. . . . Had you cared very deeply for me, it seems you would not have placed me in such a position!"[42] Now that prime movers in Washington's African American aristocracy knew they were married, Paul demanded that Alice terminate her position and join him in Washington immediately.

Many elite men of color probably sanctioned Paul's anger and subsequent demands. Etiquette books and middle-class society declared woman to be man's civilizing force. Manners and refinement were her domain. Thus, Alice had led Paul astray. Surely she knew the etiquette of weddings; Paul, as a man, was naturally ignorant of such things. It was Alice's duty to guide him in the art of gracious living. This secret wedding was all Alice's fault!

Public knowledge of the Dunbars' elopement not only questioned Alice's degree of refinement, it also invoked the moral issues of premarital sex and pregnancy. Moreover, knowledge of the secret marriage challenged Paul's manhood. Married middle-class women were not supposed to work outside the home, for husbands provided for the family's genteel lifestyle. For Alice to remain at her Brooklyn teaching post was to suggest an unsavory reality of many elite African American homes— including the Dunbars': the world-famous poet and his wife needed her salary of sixty dollars per month.[43] However, since they too embraced the prevailing social ethos, Paul insisted on Alice quitting her post at once and taking her rightful place at his side.

The appearance of cultivated living, as well as the divine right of husbands, supported Paul's demands. The third Mrs. Booker T. Washington had to ask her husband's permission to continue working as an educator at the institution he built. Bishop L. J. Coppin, a noted African American minister, "desired that my wife should give up teaching at once" when they married in 1881.[44] But Fanny Jackson Coppin, a brilliant teacher and innovator, was forty-four years old and entering her first marriage. Since 1869, she had been principal of the Institute for Colored Youth, a prestigious Philadelphia high school. Also, Fanny had no interest in "high society." She refused to abandon her career and join her husband in Baltimore, where he pastored a church.

The bishop commuted weekends for three years, before relocating to

Philadelphia. Again he asked Fanny to come home and be a full-time wife. Again she refused. Fanny Jackson Coppin gave up her job when she retired in 1902, twenty-one years after marrying the bishop. She cited declining health as the reason for terminating her career.

The stalwart Mrs. Coppin was not the sort of wife preferred by men like Paul. Nor was she the preference of the conventionally minded. Despite her tenacity, the boards of education in most cities did not allow married women to work full-time as educators. They were forced to resign after their weddings. It would be 1918 before married women could work as teachers in the vast segregated school system of Washington, D.C., where the Dunbars would spend most of their short married life.

Advocating the husbands' often selfish cause, African American journalists—themselves mainly men—told married women to stay home and be true wives. Too many men plodded day in and day out, only to come home to cold suppers, an editor of the *Colored American Magazine* wrote in 1908. He suggested a men's convention to discuss means of keeping women homebound. At stake was the "destruction of our American homes, because of its abandonment by its queen," the editor pontificated. "Nowhere else . . . has home life meant more, and to have it abandoned by the very member of society who can do the most to make it a place of happiness and refinement, is a thing to be regretted."[45]

Alice acknowledged that her place was in Washington at Paul's side. But she also knew the reality of their financial situation and wanted to contribute as long as possible. "No one realizes more than I do the swiftness with which an income like yours can be eaten by bare necessities," she told Paul. Alice explained the limitations of her earning power as Mrs. Dunbar:

> The only things I can do are write . . . and be a stenographer, and keep books and give lessons in some things. I can do fancy work too, but it is slow and doesn't pay, and folks don't take lessons in things much, and you wouldn't want me to be at some other man's elbow taking dictation, would you?[46]

Their best course of action, Alice believed, was for Paul to tell no one else about the marriage so that she could keep her job. Besides, honor, duty, and racial uplift required her to stay at her post. As the only professional woman of color in her Brooklyn school, she could not depart abruptly. To do so would "close an avenue. . . . [M]y going leaves a vacancy which <u>must</u> be filled by a white teacher as there is no colored lady ready" (emphasis in original).[47]

Alice urged Paul not to worry about society's interpretation of their secret wedding, nor about suspicions of pregnancy. Their place in the aristocracy was inviolate because they had the very best credentials. Was he not a world-famous poet? Was she not his wife? "As for the world," Alice wrote haughtily, "why we can make it bow when we choose."[48]

Paul erupted! Clearly Alice was not acting as a proper wife. What about your duty to honor and obey me? he demanded. And what about my conjugal rights? Paul's last question changed into sexual threats, as he tried to make Alice bow to his commands.

He began in honeyed tones. "[D]o you think that just marrying me and living away from me means my safety[?]" he asked. "Why darling I am the same man, surrounded by just the same dangers that I was before. . . . I want to be true to you," he later confessed, "[but] you know my nature." During that same week, Paul reminded his bride that he was "human and man human. . . . [B]ut if you don't come soon, I will not be responsible for what I do." Then, when his so-called gentle touch lacked results, Paul unleashed his anger, telling Alice: "The situation is simply this, I am placed under the responsibility of a married man without either his comforts or privileges. I refuse to accept the anomalous situation." Paul threatened: "I shall hold myself responsible for nothing that happens during an enforced separation . . . from my wife. Do not think me hard or cold," he added self-righteously, "but believe me just."[49]

A sexual threat can be a powerful weapon. Paul's attack was two pronged. He berated Alice for not performing her wifely duties, and convinced her that in her absence he would take his pleasures elsewhere. Alice capitulated. On April 17, 1898, roughly six weeks after eloping, she quit her job and joined Paul in Washington.

Manipulative sexual threats were not uncommon among the self-righteous. John Hope, who promised never to beat his wife but found honor in killing an unfaithful spouse, used verbal sexual coercion to achieve his goal. His approach differed from Paul's heavy-handedness. Hope's coercion was an iron fist in a velvet glove.

Weeks before her marriage to Hope, Genie Burns wavered. She reminded her fiancé that she supported her mother financially. To marry him and move south was to leave her mother destitute. Hope responded ever so graciously. He understood Genie's dilemma. He would never ask her to choose between him and her mother. But Hope knew his beloved's vulnerability. In a twenty-one-page letter, he titillated her with memories of past sexual experiences. Hope promised to "fill [her] again with those ecstasies" as her husband. In fact, sex would be so much better then, for he had given her only "a slight idea of what it means to love and be loved." Hope assured Genie that even that infinitesimal knowledge made it impossible for her to live without him as a sex partner. Genie and John married on December 29, 1897, as originally planned.[50]

Sex is the hydra of intimate relationships. While it is a channel of love and pleasurable sensations, sex can be a mode of empowerment and manipulation. Feminist historians contend that the passionlessness ascribed to nineteenth-century middle-class white wives was actually an authoritative control mechanism. By refusing to provide sex on demand, they limited their chances of pregnancy and the dangers of childbirth. Wives then controlled their bodies and sexuality.

Sex could also be a political commodity among the African American elite. Their socialized erotic expressions could foster problematic conjugal relations. While middle-class ideology viewed sexual intercourse as an important aspect of marriage; marriage was more than physical intimacy. It was love, affection, respect, economic support, and child rearing. Still, for some elite people of color, sex was the site of unfulfilled expectations and subsequent marital frustration.

This was the case for W. E. B. Du Bois, on a theoretical and personal level. The great scholar contended that middle-class sexual indoctrination made conjugal love a common battleground for the African American aristocracy. Du Bois married in 1896. After fifty-three years of wedded life, he bitterly condemned his wife, Nina Gomer Du Bois, for their sexual incompatibility. He complained that while he was a "normal" and "lusty" man, Nina had no interest in sex. Declaring that he had exercised great care and restraint, it had all been for naught, he said. "My wife's life-long training as a virgin made it impossible for her ever to regard sexual intercourse as not fundamentally indecent."[51] Du Bois hinted that his spouse had been socialized in accordance with the early-nineteenth-century teachings that delicate, refined ladies abhorred sex. If they thought of it at all, it was with horror rather than desire. Sexual passion was ascribed to men, prostitutes, and the lower classes. At the very best, sex for ladies was a conjugal duty.

Du Bois never forgave his wife for not fulfilling his desires. He refers to her by name only once in his 448-page *Autobiography of W. E. B. Du Bois*. In the few remaining references, Nina is "my woman . . . wife . . . hausfrau."

This coldness surfaced early in the marriage. None of the couple's courting letters, nor any others speaking of wedded bliss, are available to researchers. This infers deliberate destruction or document manipulation. But Nina Du Bois's turn-of-the-century missives of her famed husband—for which there are no replies—evidence little or no affection. The correspondence is polite, businesslike, almost pathetic:

> November 13, 1910. Dear Will; I suppose you are very busy. I was going to write for a couple of copies of the *Crisis* [the NAACP journal Du Bois created and edited], but learned they had all been sold. . . . There's a fine editorial in this week's *Independent* on you. I suppose you've seen it. Carrie wants to know just when and how long you will be here. I believe you said you would be here at Christmas. How are you these days[?] I am only fairly well. Yolanda has a bad cold. . . . Nina[52]

Du Bois blamed his failed marriage and unfulfilled sex life on Nina, perhaps in accordance with the nineteenth-century creed of accusing wives for marital woes. One wonders how much he contributed to their incompatibility. The African American sociologist Allison Davis described Du Bois as a man who was uncomfortable with women, one who confessed to feeling "free" when his mother died suddenly. Davis wrote that Du Bois "seems to have been as emotionally detached from her as he was from his wife later."[53] And while the great scholar sang the praises of African American women in his acclaimed book *The Souls of Black Folk* (1903), he was generally rude to them and had a "rigid sexual defense system." Moreover, Davis believed Du Bois was "poor at courtship and at giving himself over to a love relationship. . . . [H]e was inexpressive—perhaps even cold—towards women," and actually feared them.[54]

The evidence suggests that the sensual life may have haunted the marriage of another representative African American couple. John Hope barraged Genie Burns with erotic love letters during their courtship, and since she sometimes asked him to write her some "trash," she obviously enjoyed his titillating missives. Both also relished their premarital sexual experiences. But as a married man, John did an about-face, proposing that he and his bride place little emphasis on sexual intercourse. Hope argued that an overindulgence led to depression and sorrow. Rather than sex, he suggested they concentrate on literature, conversation, and "pretty things." They were to be a "bible and prayer loving couple."[55]

How disappointed Genie must have been after such a sensuous courtship. Hope's actions are puzzling, unless he had always been a closet worshipper of early-nineteenth-century values regarding conjugal relations. Then, many moralists—and later some feminists—advocated sexual restraint within marriage as a means of focusing the relationship on spirituality rather than the husband's baser instincts. For it should be remembered that, theoretically, ladies abhorred sex while men had an inherent need for it. A marriage emphasizing spirituality helped protect the wife from her predator husband.

Hope's argument that "excessive" intercourse spawned depression is reminiscent of an early-nineteenth-century belief that sex drained vital organs and caused rapid physical deterioration in men. Dr. William Acton, a famous mainstream advice giver of the time, noted that intellectuals (such as Hope) had delicate constitutions and should make love no more than once every seven or ten days. Exceeding that rate was deadly, since both brain activity and orgasm strained the nervous system. For those men who insisted on overindulging (regardless of occupation), the physician prescribed the restorative treatments of Spanish fly—now considered a dangerous drug—and cauterization. The latter involved flushing the penis internally with nitrate of silver.[56] To have sex as often as twice a week was to court an early death, Acton preached, and no medicine could prevent that. Perhaps it was John Hope's belief in this message of doom that caused him to ration conjugal love. But for whatever reasons, he is rumored to have had many affairs during his marriage. This although Hope hinted at killing Genie should she be untrue.

It is likely that sex was also problematic in the marriages of still another prominent leader. Booker T. Washington had three wives, yet the famed educator and power broker frequented houses of prostitution and died of syphilis. Washington's dalliances suggest a certain sexual dysfunction in his households. Then again, he and/or his spouse may have believed in limited conjugal intercourse, either for the sake of marital spirituality, or to accommodate the much-trumpeted wifely abhorrence of sex.

At first glance, the sensual life seems not to have been a problem for Alice and Paul Laurence Dunbar. Letters reveal a mutually gratifying intimacy, one so powerful that the couple named their sex organs "Miss Venus" and "Sir Peter." And even these were reduced to the pet names of "Miss V" and "Sir P." If Nina Gomer Du Bois disliked conjugal love, Alice's letters give the impression that she relished it. Her correspondence challenges the myth that middle-class women lacked passion and sensuality.

The Dunbars wrote about their sex life during Paul's extended lecture tours. In March 1901, for example, "Wifelums," as Alice styled herself, wrote: "Sweetheart Hubbins . . . Miss V. rose up early this morning before I was awake and demanded Sir P." Five days later, "Lonesome Wife-Bird" asked: "Sweetheart Hubbins . . . How is Sir P.? Tomorrow will be two weeks since he and Miss V. had a visit together and she has been making some solicitous inquiries as to his health." The following month, "Wife-bird" assured "Husband, hubbins, darlingest one," that Miss Venus would "extend cordial hospitality to Sir Peter when he comes. Yum-yum!"[57]

Similarly, Paul passed on messages about Miss V.'s missing companion: "Sir P. is so obstreperous this morning. . . . Sir Peter is in awful condition this morning, tearful and unruly." Sir Peter, Paul wrote, was beginning to influence his dreams.[58]

Such comments paint a picture of blissful sex, and perhaps ecstasy enveloped the Dunbars' conjugal life. But is the sex life in their letters an accurate picture? Were the meetings of Miss Venus and Sir Peter fully consensual, or was there some coercion? Paul had raped Alice during their courtship. Was marital rape a factor in the Dunbars' marriage?[59]

Conjugal violence was common in turn-of-the-twentieth-century America. While reform laws during the latter part of the nineteenth century made cruelty, physical assault and verbal abuse grounds for divorce, sexual violence was excluded. Marital rape did not warrant legal separation or divorce; but through liberal interpretations of cruelty laws, small numbers of divorces were granted to wives who proved that violent spousal sex threatened their health. A California plaintiff in 1890 swore that her husband "would force me to submit to him . . . many times so that often I could not get out of bed. I would beg him not to do it as I was very sick. The only answer he gave me was 'you damned bitch, you have no business to be a woman.'"[60] While this petition was granted, most were refused. Even worse, some marital rape divorces were later challenged and overturned.

Generally, jurists and the populace found no crime in husbands having sex with resistant spouses. Wives were considered sexual property, and it was their duty to accommodate husbands' needs and desires. Moreover, the laws inferred that nonconsensual sex did not harm the wife, thus no crime was involved.

Despite legal rulings, abused wives and feminists recognized marital rape as a criminal act, a vicious, hateful display of power. One husband's boastful testimony in 1890 made that clear:

> I jumped into bed, forcing her on her back, drove my prick up her. It must have been stiff, and I violent for she cried out that I hurt her. . . . I felt that I could murder her with my prick, and drove and drove. . . . I hated her— she was but my spunk-emptier.[61]

Moral reform societies targeted marital rape, defining it beyond today's standard of sex obtained by force, fear, or threat of physical assault. Nineteenth-century conjugal violence included oral sex, excessive sex, disregard for women's pleasure, and forced relations when the husband was intoxicated or diseased. Reformers made patriarchy the culprit, citing rape as the obvious consequence of excessive male power. Furthermore, the traditional marriage ceremony propitiated male dominance by requiring wives to obey husbands in or out of bed. Accordingly, a common feminist slogan proclaimed that wife status equaled victim status.

The reformists' argument was flawed, as are all arguments blaming women's social problems solely on patriarchy. Not all husbands rape their wives. However, the context of male supremacy is valid; male domination characterizes marital rape.

Paul firmly believed in male supremacy and the rights to a wife's body. He shared some broad characteristics with husbands most likely to commit spousal rape. Paul was violent, liked a woman in a woman's place, believed they should obey husbands, and subscribed to the double standard of sexual conduct.[62]

As a husband, Paul brandished power and sexual intimidation. While still a groom, he demanded his conjugal rights. He promised to seek pleasure elsewhere if Alice did not quit her Brooklyn job and join him in his bed in Washington immediately. Moreover, just weeks after they eloped, a demonic display of behavior caused Alice to write that she was "thoroughly frightened" at the prospect of living with him.[63] Fear made it unlikely that she denied her husband sex. Using the broadest definition of marital rape—sex coerced by physical assault, threat or fear of bodily harm—and factoring Paul's premarital sexual assault of Alice when he could not evoke spousal privilege, marital rape seems a certainty in the Dunbars' wedded life.

Alice recognized Paul's savage rape during their courtship as a dastardly crime. Would she have considered herself a victim of marital rape? Perhaps not, for even today many twenty-first century wives with comparable experiences chose other paths of interpretation. When a man uses restraint to obtain sex from a nonconsenting woman, it is rape. But if a husband restrains his wife's arms or body with his arms or body during nonconsensual sex, wives will not call it rape. While women categorize beatings and threats during arguments as inappropriate behavior, when the same accompanies unwanted sex, wives refuse to see it as wrong, and certainly not as rape. Many still cling to the early nineteenth-century theories of a husband's sexual rights and a wife's duty. Others are persuaded by the myth that only unwanted sex with a stranger constitutes rape, and still more are as influenced by their husband's view of sex as they are by his worldview. His word is law.

As a wife rape victim, Alice may have experienced any or all of these sexual situations. Undoubtedly, she held the same beliefs. It is certain that Paul's view of rape shaped hers. Rape was what he said it was—love and not a crime. Soon after sexually violating her during their courtship, Paul convinced Alice that he had committed an act of love, writing: "Only let my love in some measure condone my weakness. . . . I was a drunken brute who let his passion obscure his love."[64] Eventually, both glorified the crime. Alice declared that the ordeal had "strengthened, purified, and beautified" her love. The rape made them one in the eyes of God. "[F]or we are married, dear," wrote Paul, "heart to heart and soul to soul, and 'whom God hath joined together let no man put asunder.'"[65]

As Mrs. Dunbar, Alice cast herself in the role of the dutiful, self-sacrificing wife. This was expected of women in her class. She masked her efforts to accommodate Paul's behavior with a tolerant facade. Following one of his frequent tongue lashings, a bruised, unhappy Alice shouldered the blame, writing placidly: "I am ridiculously tender-hearted and sensitive. Slight words and looks hurt me for days, although I may laugh it away apparently. Won't you try to remember this dear?"[66] Would such an abusive husband stop short of marital rape? Would such a cowered wife call it by its true name? How much of the Miss Venus dialogue scripted by Alice was genuine? How much was what an intimidated wife thought her husband wished to believe?

Was Alice a typical victim of wife rape? There is no profile of such women. They inhabit each time period, socioeconomic class, ethnic group, and continent. But frequently these women share one denominator. Most often, wife rape victims are battered wives, for the latter are the easiest adult group to intimidate. Alice Dunbar was a battered wife.

There is no doubt that physical assaults were a constant in the Dunbars' marriage. Alice's life with Paul, she said, was "a dog and cat existence."[67] Just when her husband became a wife beater is uncertain. As the dutiful wife, Alice protected his reputation—and simultaneously hers. She told no one, especially not her mother and sister, about the turbulence in her household.

By the second year of the marriage, however, the episodes—as Alice called them—were an open secret among their friends. Paul vented his hostility in public and with impunity. That elite circle of African American society that was so important to the status-conscious Alice witnessed and broadcasted her degradation.

The Reverend Francis Grimke and Charlotte Forten Grimke reported one beating that occurred in the Catskills. The Princeton-educated theologian and his wife, a descendant of a wealthy abolitionist family, were vacationing there during the summer of 1899, along with others of the Washington aristocracy. The Dunbars were, too, combining their holiday season with a rest cure for Paul, who had recently suffered a near fatal bout of pneumonia. Whether the Grimkes witnessed Paul's assault on Alice is uncertain, but "they did their share of commenting on the Catskill Mountain business," remembered Alice, "more than I would have thought either of them would." So did the local minister, "the little Mr. Mitchell [who] never was known to keep his mouth shut."[68]

Paul's brutality began to stoke the rumor mill. While in Denver that fall and winter, continuing his rest cure, he reportedly slapped Alice. "[She] didn't seem to mind," Paul supposedly told a friend.[69] From that point on, the battering intensified. Alice admitted when the marriage ended: "We had some scenes right in [our Denver] house where no pains were taken to keep it quiet. . . . Our affairs [were] conducted in the broad light of day."[70] Denver society mavens wrote Washington and New Orleans counterparts about what they saw and heard. Washington and New Orleans gossips wrote Alice seeking confirmation. The news traveled to the East Coast, eventually reaching Alice's family.

When Alice and Paul returned to Washington in the spring of 1900, he was an acknowledged wife beater, and she, a stoical victim. Friends claimed they were not surprised by any aggression that they witnessed in the Dunbars' home. Paul's male cronies especially commented on his behavior. One said he hated to see the Dunbars at social gatherings, since it was only a matter of time before Paul would hit Alice. Another claimed to have actually witnessed this at a dance.[71] Dr. A. M. Curtis, a physician in the Dunbars' social circle, conceded euphemistically that Paul "flew into ungovernable rages and ill-treated his wife."[72] And Christian Fleetwood, Civil War Medal of Honor winner and a Dunbar neighbor, noted angrily that Paul gave Alice "an aggravated repetition of the same treatment . . . anytime his condition gave him the excuse."[73]

The "condition" to which Fleetwood referred was Paul's drinking. He drank heavily, sometimes remaining drunk for days. Since beatings occurred often while he was inebriated, Alice, her family, and friends blamed Paul's brutality on "demon drink."

Theirs was a common assumption, and it propelled the late nineteenth-century temperance movement. Americans believed that alcohol loosened inhibitions and caused the loss of self-control that made drunk men beat women and children. Today anthropologists refute the theory. Comparative studies of societies show that liquor alone does not lead to aggression. Alcoholic behavior may vary from culture to culture, indicating that liquor-induced violence is a learned response.

Paul's constant abuse of Alice had Fleetwood seething with rage. Angrily, he wrote Alice, "his dear persecuted" friend: "[A] few years ago, I remarked, 'I wish I was either his brother or hers[.] If I was his brother I'd thrash him within an inch of his life[.] If I was hers I would not stop at that inch[!]'"[74]

No one intervened. In fact, it is doubtful that anyone even spoke to Paul about mistreating Alice. Fleetwood gave a partial explanation: "[B]eing related to neither [of you], for me to take public action would only further complicate matters."[75] Besides, many believed it was a husband's right to chastise his wife.

One may wonder why Alice endured such savagery when wife beating was grounds for divorce. The code of middle-class wifery suggests one reason: to eject a husband and live independently was heresy. Woman's proper role was that of a wife.

For Alice, as for any woman contemplating divorce, there were personal considerations. Although battered, she was still Mrs. Paul Laurence Dunbar, wife of a living legend. At his side, little was denied her in the constricted world of African American life. Then, too, when Paul was sober—for "there were times when he was not . . . [and] was a different man altogether, brutal in fact. . . . [But] when he was himself, he was a charming companion," Alice recalled, "and those sporadic moments and days . . . were delightful beyond compare. It was the memory of those happy days that gave me strength to stand the others."[76]

At least one other factor kept Alice in her abusive relationship: pride. "I always hated the idea of the publicity of an open rupture," she added. "Then too, as my family had bitterly opposed the marriage—for my mother knew that he drank—I did not like to give them the satisfaction of knowing I had made a miserable failure."[77]

Alice would have received little sympathy or moral support if she had filed for divorce. Although wife beating had been outlawed in most states by 1870, it was still considered appropriate behavior for husbands. This may account for Christian Fleetwood's reluctance to intervene in Alice's situation. Few considered spousal abuse a serious crime. In a time when reformers tackled heinous social problems, not even those spearheaded by feminists—black or white—attacked spousal abuse. The few rights and laws addressing female victimization were by-products of other social crusades that affected women's lives, such as temperance, child welfare, and social purity.

Since spousal abuse was a serious issue only in some divorce courts, law enforcement agents—mainly men—treated it as a minor offense. Convicted husbands might spend the night in jail or pay light fines. In Chicago in 1904, for example, the "slapping list" fine in one local court included "$1 for a left handed slap, $2 for a right handed slap [and] $5 when standing up." The document's misogynistic author noted that the penalties classed wife beating as a "luxury within the reach of the humblest income."[78] A husband obeying the "rule of thumb" law used by many communities escaped all wife-beating punishments. He committed no crime as long as the stick used in the assault was no thicker than his thumb.

Wife beating was literally a joke to some, including members of the United States Congress. An opponent of a national bill for the flogging of abusive husbands quipped in 1906: "More women are in pain because they are unmarried, than are in pain because they are married and beaten." Another suggested that if the bill became law, the president, cabinet members, senators, and congressmen should be exempted.[79] Wife victimization was the theme of songs and jokes.

Finding this cavalier attitude abhorrent, staunch moralists, vigilantes, and feminists enacted more stringent punishment. Maryland (1882), Delaware (1901), and Oregon (1905), passed whipping-post laws for the public flogging of wife beaters.[80] When not murdering and maiming innocent African Americans, branches of the Ku Klux Klan terrorized "Wife-beaters, Family-deserters, [and] Home-wreckers." Frontier Baptist churches were known to excommunicate frequent spousal abusers, and women like Susan B. Anthony aided and sheltered runaway wives.[81]

Alice probably never received any aid. Like Christian Fleetwood, who consoled her, family and friends believed they had neither the right nor desire to intervene in domestic conflagrations. Alice endured them for a minimum of three years, from 1899—using the Catskill episode as a gauge—until January 25, 1902. That night, in a drunken rage, Paul nearly beat her to death. Later he boarded a train to New York, and the Dunbars never saw each other again.

The final story is best told by Alice: "He came home [that] night in a beastly condition. I went to him to help him to bed—and he behaved . . . disgracefully. He left that night, and I was ill for weeks with peritonitis brought on by his kicks."[82] In the pre-penicillin era, peritonitis was a deadly disorder.

Like other beatings, this one too had an audience, for Paul enjoyed humiliating his wife. Her mother, Patsy Moore, and her sister, Mary Leila Moore Young, were house guests and no doubt witnessed the horrible event. Paul took the word abroad, telling listeners in the corner saloon that Alice had wronged him and had therefore been chastised. He told the same story when he reached New York. One of his drinking buddies, T. Thomas Fortune, editor of the African American newspaper *New York Age,* was in Washington on business when he heard the news. He passed it on to his Alabama correspondent, Booker T. Washington.

Despite the vicious beating and her public degradation, Alice was willing to forgive Paul. So conditioned was she to his brutality, so enveloped was she in false pride, ambition, and the requisites of true womanhood, that she confessed: "I could have overlooked the brutal treatment." It was her reputation, that most vital element of proper womanhood, that made her sever their relationship. "[H]e went . . . and spread a vile story about me," said Alice, "and that was the reason I broke up my home . . . the slander I could not stand."[83]

Paul and Alice neither saw nor spoke to each other again following that night. Paul stayed angry for months. Like the typical wife beater, he blamed Alice for the altercation. "She is in the wrong," he wrote his mother.[84] But three months later, he wanted to reconcile and asked Alice by telegram: "April 12, 1902 . . . Will you over look everything and come to New York[?] Answer at once."[85]

Why Paul contacted Alice at that time is curious. According to the Dunbar love legend, his note marked the beginning of an intensive two-year campaign to regain her affection. But when he wrote his wife, the duplicitous Paul was already in more than a platonic relationship with someone known only as Rose. "Paul dearie," she wrote on April 29, 1902, "have you missed me a wee bit to-day you dear, dear bad boy? [Y]ou seen like a naughty school boy, and I laugh at your merry pranks, though I confess at times your ears *should* be *boxed!*"[86] The smitten Rose thought Paul was her "Soul-mate." Near summer's end, she assured him: "[T]hough we are struggling against what seems hopeless odds, we will win out and you shall find rest [,] peace [,] contentment and best of all, happiness with Your Rose."[87] The romance faded, for later the gallant Paul on two occasions sent two dozen pink roses to an unknown Dayton love.[88]

Alice did not respond to her husband's initial request for a reconciliation. She also ignored the other forty-two letters, poems and messages that he sent during the next two years. Throughout his campaign that begged forgiveness, Alice replied only once and in one word: "No!"[89]

The years following the breakup "were like a bad dream to Paul," wrote one Dunbar biographer.[90] He lived briefly in New York and Chicago before returning to Dayton in 1903, to die of tuberculosis. Paul wrote poignantly:

Say, it's nice a-gettin' back
When your pulse is growin' slack,
And yore breath begins to wheeze
Like a fair-set valley breeze;
Kind o' nice to set aroun'
On the old familiar groun'
Knowing that when Death does come
That he'll find you right at home.[91]

Despite his declining health, Paul wrote constantly. He published eight poetry volumes, two collections of short stories, and numerous articles.[92] When health allowed, he traveled extensively, giving readings of his poetry. But as his reputation for being drunk at lectures increased, the audiences dwindled. "I am not doing so much reading here as I anticipated," he wrote his mother, Matilda, from Kansas in 1903.[93] His fortunes similarly declined: "You know that I haven't got $50.00 to my name," he confided later that year.[94] The stellar poet was again struggling to survive in his hometown, just as he had prior to gaining international fame. On August 11, 1904, the Dayton Gas Light Company threatened to discontinue service because of an outstanding bill of thirty dollars.[95]

Yet Paul continued to drink heavily. Although biographers claim he imbibed because of the common fallacy that liquor cured tuberculosis, Paul was an alcoholic. His liquor bills indicate a man nursing a serious malady. In March 1905, he purchased eight dozen bottles of beer from the Schwind Brewery in Dayton; in April, thirteen dozen.[96] Thereafter, a monthly statement shows his consumption was heavy:

August 1, 1905
The Fred Kette & Sons Co.
Wholesale Dealers in Wines and Liquors

July	14	1 qt. rye	75
	15	1 qt. rye	75
	17	1 qt. rye	75
	18	1 qt. rye	75
		1 qt. gin	75
		1 bot. burgundy	35
	22	1 qt. rye	75
	27	1 qt. rye	75
	29	1 qt. rye	75
	31	1 qt. rye	75

$7.10[97]

Paul's drinking habits could have only hastened his death. Following a period of declining health, he died at 3:30 P.M. on Friday, February 9, 1906, in his Dayton home. While the death certificate listed tuberculosis, romantics claimed he died of a broken heart. Paul was thirty-three; or as his doting mother calculated, thirty-three years, 7 months and 12 days old.[98] Matilda Dunbar was at her son's bedside. She reported a heroic deathbed scene that has become lore. Paul expired in her arms. "He died so peaceful and was conscious until just 10 minutes before he breathed his last breath," Matilda told a neighbor, who later recorded the scene for posterity:

These were his last words. He said to his mother he was going, she in her sorrow begged him not to go away from her. He said, "I have made a brave fight—and now the Lords [*sic*] will be done." He says, "I am not suffering[.] The Lord is my shepherd I shall not want." These were his last words.[99]

Other words of Paul followed him in death, word corrupted by the racism that had twisted him in life. The dialect verses so loved by white audiences—and eventually so hated by Paul—became his epitaph. Misguided men of power declared lines from his poem "A Death Song," published the year before he died, as Paul's self-proclaimed memorial. They conveniently overlooked other death poems he had written in standard prose. A bronze plate on a granite monument reads:

Parted

Paul Laurence Dunbar
1872   1906

LAY ME DOWN BENEAF DE WILLERS IN DE GRASS,
WHERE DE BRANCH'LL GO A-SINGIN' AS IT PASS.
AN' W'EN I'S A-LAYIN' LOW
I KIN HEAH IT AS I GO,
SAYIN' SLEEP MA HONEY, TEK YO' RES' AT LAS'[100]

No one told Alice of her estranged husband's death. She read about it in a newspaper the next day while riding a streetcar in Wilmington, Delaware. Alice had moved there following her separation from Paul and taught in the city's segregated school system. She was shocked, and angry that neither in-laws nor friends had informed her of Paul's demise. Death rituals were taken seriously in the African American community. As a widow, Alice should have been in seclusion and mourning. Instead, she had been seen in public, blithely conducting her normal affairs. Alice worried what high society would think.

The widow was especially angry on reading Paul's death was neither sudden nor unexpected. Had she known he was terminally ill, she would have gone to his bedside, she confided to friends remorsefully. She had promised herself and Paul's best chum that she would not let the poet die without telling him she still loved him. Why had not the curs in Paul's family warned her of her husband's eminent demise? His friend Bud Burns had promised to wire if Paul were terminally ill. Why had he not kept his word? Alice fired off a scathing letter to Burns reminding him of their agreement. But what Alice did not know was that Burns had died several months before Paul.

In the anguish of her husband's death, Alice blamed herself for the failed marriage and Paul's violent behavior. How it pained her that Paul never knew she had forgiven him. And yet, it seems the distraught widow did not attend her husband's funeral, which was the largest the city of Dayton, Ohio, had ever seen. While today Dunbar scholars still debate Alice's presence, a Cleveland *Gazette* reporter wrote with disdain on February 17, 1906: "Despite the announcement from Wilmington, Dela. that Mrs. Alice Dunbar wife of the deceased, would attend the services [,] her presence was not noted, and she did not make herself known to any of the family or immediate friends."[101]

Alice blossomed following her separation from Paul in 1902. Initially, she taught temporarily in the Washington, D.C., segregated school system and continued her busy social schedule of teas, sports events, and parties. Later that year, Alice moved with her mother, sister, and her sibling's four children to Wilmington, Delaware, to work as a teacher. Her sister, Leila, recently deserted by her husband, reactivated her teaching career, and she and Alice taught at Howard, the only African American high school in the city. Alice worked there for eighteen years. During that time, she was also a scholar, studying at the University of Pennsylvania and Cornell, and publishing an article on Milton in 1909.[102] Alice resumed the hectic schedule she had prior to marriage, becoming active in Republican party politics, owning and editing the *Wilmington Advocate,* an African American newspaper from 1920 to 1922, working for women's suffrage, and serving as executive secretary of the American Friends Inter-Racial Peace Committee from 1928 to 1931

As she had while still with Paul, Alice wrote constantly, basing much of her fiction on life with him. In her short stories "Ellen Fenton" (1902?), "The Decision" (1902–1909), and "No Sacrifice" (c. 1928–1931), beleaguered wives suffer with brutal mates who are too fond of women and drink.[103] In "A Modern Undine," a lengthy tale that Alice called a novelette, she reversed the roles. The heroine receives Paul's characteristics, and the hero, hers. Marion, the female protagonist, has

> the impenetrable mask of bitter reserve [her husband] could not hope to pierce, yet heroically, devoutly he did serve her, patiently did he strive to interest her. In despair he racked his heart for some reason for her grim silence. Perhaps it was her suffering; perhaps he had not tried to understand her in their earlier years together. . . . He blamed himself bitterly, and strove to do penance at her side, while he worshipped her as one would the shrine of the Virgin.[104]

Alice never became the great author she hoped she would be. Mainstream publishers regularly rejected her fiction, and it was their acceptance she craved. As was usual, a New York firm returned a manuscript on February 18, 1903, deeming it not "of sufficient value to publish."[105] Finding the Dunbar name no longer magic, she submitted work under the pseudonyms of "Al Dane, Alicea Nelson," and other aliases.[106] These too were rejected.

Editors of African American journals were kinder. Perhaps because she was Mrs. Dunbar, and perhaps because of her education and refinement, she represented the best of the race. These editors readily accepted her poems and essays, and she wrote a syndicated news column for the Associated Negro Press from 1926 to 1930. Alice edited a race book, *Masterpieces of Negro Eloquence* (1914), and later *The Dunbar Speaker and Entertainer,* a collection of her late husband's work (1920).[107]

Paul's widow took his material on the lecture circuit, reading poems and selections from his novels. She also spoke of his heroic rise to fame. In doing so, she faced the same racism that her husband had encountered. Despite the "burning messages" she brought to the audiences, fumed Alice in her diary, "they want me to recite a dialect poem! . . . gingham aprons and headhankerchief and Suwanee River, Old Black Joe stuff. Sickening. Tiresome. But that white audience seemed to like it; it tickled their vanity."[108]

Eventually, Alice forgave Paul for his cruelty. Although she seldom mentions him in her diary kept from 1921 to 1931, her musings were without rancor. In a March 6, 1927, entry, Alice wrote: "It was a Sunday that March 6, fell in 1898, twenty-nine years ago when Paul and I were married! 29 years!"[109] The entry for Monday, July 2, 1928, read: "Marvin . . . showed me a picture of Paul . . . before he died. He was seated in a chair under the grape arbor of the Dayton home. It was the last picture he ever had taken."[110] And on Sunday, March 30, 1930, Alice noted: "I re-read those poems of Paul . . . *Lyrics of Love and Sorrow.* Exquisite things."[111]

Alice did not allow her ambivalent relationship with Paul to sour her on love and companionship. She married twice more, to men of mark. Alice eloped in Wilmington, Delaware, with one of her teaching colleagues, Henry Arthur Callis, on January 19, 1909. She kept this marriage a secret, too. They divorced later, although the date is uncertain. Callis became a successful Chicago physician. On April 20, 1916, Alice wed Robert J. Nelson, political activist and journalist. He was rumored to be a black descendant of Horatio Nelson. Alice adopted the surname of Dunbar-Nelson, by which she is best known in today's literary circles. In this marriage to Bobbo, as she called him, Alice had a stable, admiring, supportive companion. Finally, she had a union that would last her lifetime. And she was ever so grateful, writing: "I have had a lot to be thankful for. Bobbo, first, last and always, the best."[112]

Alice died on September 18, 1935, of heart failure. In death she was once again Paul's wife. An African American newspaper headlined, "Body of One-Time Wife of Dunbar Cremated"; another carried the banner: "One time Wife of World-Famous Poet Is Buried from Philadelphia."[113] In death, she remained the elegant, romantic lady of status she had been in life. There was a magnificent funeral service. The body, attired in a champagne evening gown that matched the interior of the mahogany casket, stood in the midst of fifty-one floral tributes. There were twenty flower bearers and a mile-long funeral cortege. A romantic to the end, Alice requested that her ashes be strewn to "the four winds, either over land or sea."[114] Family members tossed them from the banks of the Delaware River.

CONCLUSION

The nature of courtship and marriage defies precise explanations. Love, mate selection, and decisions made regarding a relationship are often unfathomable to the outsider. This may be especially true of one examining a romantic liaison from another century. However, one may examine evidence that has been left behind to see what a courtship and marriage reveals of similar past experiences.

The courtship and marriage of Paul Laurence Dunbar and Alice Ruth Moore Dunbar demonstrate the difficulties that could befall elite African American relationships in the late nineteenth century. While the Dunbar liaison was a highly personal one driven by their personalities, it was also a union shaped and influenced by social forces. In their attempt to construct a model relationship based on the romantic ideal and middle-class values, Alice and Paul experienced the pressures of racism, gender role expectations, and unequal power relations. By taking a close look at the Dunbars' relationship, our understanding of the intimate lives of elite African American men and women may be enhanced.

Unlike their Euro-American middle-class counterparts, people of color had love lives pervaded by racism. American attitudes taught the inferiority of an African heritage. This racism engulfed the nation, determining the economic, social, and political rights of African Americans. Bigotry created a dynamic in these courtships and marriages that was unparalleled in mainstream liaisons. This xenophobia privileging white over black caused many African Americans to insist on mulatto partners and to denigrate those of a darker hue. This could be a source of palpable tension—if not disgust—in couples like the Dunbars. Racism poisoned their relationship. Both were consumed with racial self-hatred. Paul viewed himself as an ugly, black boy at a time when black and ugly were synonymous. But he rejoiced when he was treated in England as if "I am entirely white!"[1] Meanwhile, Alice constructed a self that emphasized a nonracial Creole essence. Their racial self-hatred was not limited to themselves since both exhibited great dislike for African American others. Paul simultaneously loved and hated mulattoes, while the mulatto Alice spoke in unflattering terms of people with dark skin tones. Their dislike of the African self encompassed all people of color. Do this for "the good of the race which we both dislike," wrote Paul to Alice.[2]

Racism circumscribed the life blood of upwardly mobile African Americans. It determined how male partners could structure realistic goals and limited the means in which men could support families in the patriarchal society of late-nineteenth-century America. Marriage experts agree that economic and financial strain can ruin relationships. The fact that Paul could best maintain his chosen lifestyle by writing dialect material disparaging blacks fueled the hostility he so often directed toward Alice. And she, who hated the genre and could be most contentious, accused him of prostituting his great art.

Other social forces shaped the Dunbars' romance. Alice and Paul believed their relationship was based on the ideology of romantic love, a concept cultivated during courtship. Believers imbued love and sex with morally and emotionally charged meanings. Love was an overwhelming sensation; it was the only legitimate basis of marriage; it was the key to domestic harmony. Romantic love involved mutuality, commonality, and sympathy between men and women. The class- and gender-driven society of separate spheres that Paul and Alice inhabited was not compatible with the concept of romantic love. Under separate spheres, men were superior to women, with the latter confined to a narrow circle of domestic life focusing on children, husband, and home. This world was subordinate to men's world of commerce and politics. Piety, purity, submissiveness, and domesticity were the virtues widely prescribed for women. In most respects, their situation was one of extreme dependence. Unequal partnerships between men and women are ill-suited to romance and marital happiness. Feminist Susan B. Anthony recognized this incompatibility of love and separate spheres. Love could never exist where man ruled woman, man owned woman, she wrote. Anthony saw a harmonious relationship as the "real marriage of souls when two people take each other on terms of perfect equality, without the desire to control the other. . . . [This] is a beautiful thing. It is the truest and highest state of all."[3]

The gender-segregated lives of men and women generated emotional distances between them. This limited communication and inhibited the practice of romantic love. Early in her marriage, Alice would write that she and Paul were not confidential friends. How could men and women leading emotionally separate lives be intimate as peers and marriage partners? Historian Carroll Smith Rosenberg's well-known theory holds that this extreme cultural separation caused middle-class women to develop emotional relationships with other women—those with whom they shared everyday lives and cares. She argues that women shared a common experience based on gender roles and biological rites of passage, and their relationships functioned as mutual support systems providing security, companionship, and self esteem. As these are attributes of romantic love, one wonders how satisfying were heterosexual African American and mainstream romances under separate spheres.

Alice and Paul's romance reiterates the destructiveness of this mode of life. It challenges the myth of separate spheres as the ideal model for domestic bliss, revealing it instead to be a flawed paradigm for love and connubial felicity. Given the world the Dunbars inhabited, it is difficult not to view Alice as a victim of society and of her relationship with Paul. Because of her choices, she seemed trapped in the suffocating bonds of true womanhood, trapped in a demeaning, savage relationship. Alice did not reign supreme in the home, that supposed female citadel. Hers was an abode of abuse and ego mutilation.

Yet today's feminist ideology indicates that women in Alice's circumstances are not mere victims. They are always empowered to some degree and can be resistant rather than passive participants in brutal situations. Alice's experiences with Paul lend credence to this theory. Her survival indicated an inner strength, a power that made complete passivity impossible. That she was a periodic warrior further supports this thesis. Alice once described her life with Paul as a dog and cat existence, thereby conjuring an image of two snarling opponents rather than a batterer and a hapless, helpless victim. Early in their marriage she warned him that she would no longer let his antics and insufferable behavior make her life miserable. During his periods of "sheer, morbid nonsense, preceding from an unhealthy mental and physical condition," wrote Alice, "I shall regard you as an unfortunate, unhealthy, uncontrolled child, to be humored a little, pitied a great deal, and dealt sternly with at the right time."[4]

The Dunbars' courtship and marriage suggests the need to examine on a larger scale the intimate relationships of elite people of color during the late nineteenth century. Although there are obvious limits to the general conclusions that may be drawn from the experience of one couple, Alice and Paul are analytical constructs that are useful in highlighting certain typical though by no means uniform cultural patterns. Alice's rape and brutal marriage, for example, begs the question of the commonality of abuse in upper-crust liaisons. Wife torture, as it was called, was an accepted aspect of American culture, although reforms were underway. Alice wrote that she knew of a woman of society who left her husband because he beat her. Genie Burns, married to the African American college professor John Hope, had a brother who abused his wife. Moreover, the fact that Paul's brutal treatment of Alice was not a secret, yet no one intervened, suggests that while some may have abhorred his behavior, it was not uncommon, and he was within his rights.

The Dunbar courtship was basically one of correspondence, as were others'. Alice's friends Azalia Smith of Detroit and Edward Hackley of Denver reportedly met only twice during their five-year romance by mail. John Hope, living in the South, and Genie Burns in Chicago, exchanged letters for more than three years before marrying. When Hope could afford to, he visited Genie three times a year—Christmas, Easter, and summer vacations.

This courtship by correspondence needs further investigation, for it may have been common among teachers. Scattered across the nation, this educated band of race missionaries often had to look beyond local environs for partners. Near the end of the nineteenth century, Miss Cora Jackson, an Indianapolis teacher, "had a beau down from Chicago."[5] Helen Brown of Chicago, "a mercenary gold-hunter . . . went east on a beau hunt" in 1897. A year later, John Hope's friend W. T. B. Williams—an African American Harvard graduate teaching in Indianapolis—romanced a New England woman by mail. The next year, Williams was fond of a woman in Augusta, Georgia, whom he rarely saw because of the distance and expense of travel.[6] How successful were these long-distance romances? And what determined a successful relationship?

The Dunbars' courtship and marriage reveal a relationship shaped by the ideologies of romantic love, race, class, and gender. While on one level it is a highly personal story shedding light on the character of the individuals, it also provides an analysis of a broader social pattern. The Dunbar tale is a means of probing the ideas, feelings, and behavior of people of color in the past.

NOTES

Notes to the Introduction

1. Louis Harlan and Raymond W. Smock, eds., *The Booker T. Washington Papers,* VI, 1901–1902 (Urbana: University of Illinois, 1977), 388–389. Dunbar and Fortune's drinking escapades were deemed injurious to racial advancement as well as an embarrassment to prominent African Americans like Washington who functioned as self-appointed moral arbiters of the "race." See pp. 50, 345, 347–348. But in 1911, even Washington's impeccable public character was questioned. An encounter in a New York "neighborhood of high class prostitutes" reached the newspapers, bringing humiliation and shame. See David Levering Lewis, *W. E. B. Du Bois: A Biography of a Race, 1868–1919* (New York: Henry Holt, 1993), 430.

2. Harlan and Smock, *Booker T. Washington,* VI, 391. For a fascinating study of Fortune's turbulent life, see Emma Lou Thornbrough, *T. Thomas Fortune: Militant Journalist* (Chicago: University of Chicago Press, 1972).

3. Dunbar's first book was the poetry collection *Oak and Ivy* (New York: Dodd, Mead, 1893). The book was actually printed and released in December 1892. However, since the printer did not expect to meet his stated 1892 deadline, 1893 was printed on the title page. See Jean Gould, *That Dunbar Boy: The Story of America's Famous Negro Poet* (New York: Dodd, Mead, 1958), 138.

Other works published by Dunbar by 1902 include poetry: *Majors and Minors* (1895); *Lyrics of a Lowly Life* (1896); *Lyrics of the Hearthside* (1899); *Poems of Cabin and Field* (1899); *Candle-Lightin' Time* (1901); novels: *The Uncalled* (1898); *The Love of Landry* (1900); *The Fanatics* (1901); *The Sport of the Gods* (1902); short-story collections: *Folks from Dixie* (1898); *The Strength of Gideon and Other Stories* (1900); unpublished plays: *Winter Roses* (1899); *Robert Herrick* (no date); *Old Elijah* (c. 1900). For information on the plays, see Peter Revel, *Paul Laurence Dunbar* (Boston: Twayne, 1979), 97–98; and New York Public Library, Schomburg Center for Research in Black Culture, *Calendar of the Manuscripts in the Schomburg Collection of Negro Literature* (New York: Andronicus, 1942), 139. Thorough listings of Dunbar's works are found in Virginia Cunningham, *Paul Laurence Dunbar and His Song* (New York: Dodd, Mead, 1963), 267–276; and Eugene W.

Metcalf, *Paul Laurence Dunbar: A Bibliography* (Metuchen, NJ: Scarecrow, 1975). By 1902, Dunbar had also been the lyricist for several of Will Marion Cook's popular musical shows. For information on this aspect of Paul's career, see Henry T. Simpson, *The Ghost Walks: A Chronological History of Blacks in Show Business, 1865–1910* (Metuchen, N.J.: Scarecrow, 1988), 149, 153, 227, 240, 267, 291, 531.

4. Felton O. Best, "Crossing the Color Line: A Biography of Paul Laurence Dunbar, 1872–1906" (Ph.D. diss., Ohio State University, 1992), 171; citing an unpublished Dunbar essay on Denver in the manuscript collection, The Life and Works of Paul Laurence Dunbar, Dayton Public Library, Microfilm Edition, reel 7.

5. Paul describes elocutionists as "Dunbareans" in a letter to Alice Dunbar, April 8, 1901, in Eugene W. Metcalf, "The Letters of Paul and Alice Dunbar: A Private History," (Ph.D. diss., University of California, Irvine, 1973), II, 874. Felton Best comments on "Dunbareans" although he does not use the term. See his "Crossing the Color Line," 178.

Hereafter, Metcalf's dissertation is cited as Metcalf, "The Letters." The principals are cited as PLD (Paul Laurence Dunbar) and ARM (Alice Ruth Moore). After her marriage Alice is cited as AMD (Alice Moore Dunbar).

6. PLD to AMD, April 1, 1901, in Metcalf, "The Letters," II, 883. It would be difficult today to find an African American community without a school, apartment house, bank, or some other institution bearing Paul Laurence Dunbar's name; see, for example, Willard B. Gatewood, *Aristocrats of Color: The Black Elite, 1880–1920* (Bloomington: Indiana University Press, 1990), 329; Charles M. Astin, *Paul Laurence Dunbar's Roots and Much More* (Dayton: Sense of Roots, 1989), 74–88; Geneva C. Turner, "For Whom Your School Is Named," *Negro History Bulletin* 16 (May 1953), 188; W. E. B. Du Bois, "The Dunbar National Bank," *The Crisis,* November 1928, 370–387.

7. On Dunbar as the only African American participant in McKinley's presidential inauguration, see Best, "Crossing the Color Line," 182–183; and Tony Gentry, *Paul Laurence Dunbar* (New York: Chelsea House, 1989), 90. On Dunbar's relationships with Presidents McKinley and Roosevelt, see Benjamin Brawley, *Paul Laurence Dunbar: Poet of His People* (Port Washington, NY: Kennikat, 1967), 90–91. Dunbar also participated in Theodore Roosevelt's inaugural parade on March 5, 1905. See Gentry, *Paul Laurence Dunbar,* 95.

8. The African American Judge Robert Terrell, husband of Mary Church Terrell, described Alice in this manner. See Gatewood, *Aristocrats of Color,* 378, note 89.

9. G. F. Richings, *Evidence of Progress among Colored People,* 12th ed. (Philadelphia: George S. Ferguson, 1905), 419.

10. Richings, *Evidence of Progress,* 419.

11. *Violets and Other Tales* (1895) was the first book by young Alice Ruth Moore. The second, *The Goodness of Saint Rocque* (1899), bore the name Alice Dunbar. For a more thorough presentation of Alice's writings, see Gloria T. Hull, ed., *The Works of Alice Dunbar-Nelson,* 3 vols. (New York: Oxford University Press, 1988); Ruby Ora Williams, ed., *An Alice Dunbar-Nelson Reader* (Washington, DC: University Press of America, 1979); Ora Williams, "Works by and about Alice Ruth (Moore) Dunbar-Nelson: A Bibliography," *CLA Journal* 19:3 (March 1976), 322–325.

12. Quoted in Metcalf, "The Letters," I, 12–13.

13. On the image of African Americans at the turn of the twentieth century, see Fannie Barrier Williams, "The Negro and Public Opinion," *Voice of the Negro,* January 1904, 31–32; Fannie Barrier Williams, "The Colored Girl," *Voice of the Negro,* June 1905, 400–403; George Fredrickson, *The Black Image in the White Mind: The Debate on Afro-American Character and Destiny, 1817–1914* (Middletown, CT: Wesleyan University Press, 1971).

14. "A Southern Authoress," undated, untitled newspaper in Paul Laurence Dunbar Collection, Ohio Historical Society, Microfilm Edition, reel 7. This source is hereafter cited as PLD Collection.

15. PLD to ARM, December 29, 1897, in Metcalf, "The Letters," I, 319. Other references comparing the Dunbars' relationship to that of Robert and Elizabeth Barrett Browning are PLD to AMD March 14, 1898, in Metcalf, "The Letters," II, 509; ARM to PLD, March 26, 1898, in Metcalf, "The Letters," II, 555.

16. PLD to AMD, March 14, 1898, in Metcalf, "The Letters," II, 509.

17. AMD to PLD, March 16, 1898, in Metcalf, "The Letters," II, 515.

18. AMD to PLD, March 27(?), 1898, in Metcalf, "The Letters," II, 555. Robert Browning published his dramatic poem "Pippa Passes" in 1841. Elizabeth Barrett Browning published her poem "Aurora Leigh" in 1857.

19. Harlan and Smock, *Booker T. Washington,* VI, 388–389.

20. Metcalf, "The Letters," I, 12.

21. Gloria T. Hull, in *Color, Sex, and Poetry* (Bloomington: Indiana University Press, 1987), 45, and Best, in "Crossing the Color Line," 162, make reference to the rape but fail to label it as such.

22. PLD to ARM, December 1, 1897; PLD to ARM, December 2, 1897; PLD to ARM, December 7, 1897—all in Metcalf, "The Letters," I, 262, 266, 276–277, respectively.

23. Metcalf, "The Letters," I, 21.

24. Best, "Crossing the Color Line," 203.

25. Gossie Harold Hudson, "A Biography of Paul Laurence Dunbar" (Ph.D.

diss., Ohio State University, 1971), 150; Pearle H. Schultz, *Paul Laurence Dunbar: Black Poet Laureate* (Champaign, IL: Garrard, 1974), 138.

26. Williams, "An In-Depth Portrait," 57; Hudson, "A Biography," 152.

27. There is one scholarly article on elite African-American intimacy: see Vicki Howard, "The Courtship Letters of an African-American Couple: Race, Gender, Class, and the Cult of True Womanhood," *Southwestern Historical Quarterly* 100:1 (1996), 64–80.

28. The seminal work on the importance of gender as a historical analytical concept is Joan W. Scott, "Gender: A Useful Category of Historical Analysis," *American Historical Review* 9:5 (December 1986), 1053–1075.

29. Scott, "Gender: A Useful Category," 1068.

30. Scott, "Gender: A Useful Category," 1068–1069.

31. Metcalf, "The Letters," I, II.

32. Dunbar manuscript collections used for this study are the Paul Laurence Dunbar Collection, Ohio Historical Society, Microfilm Edition; the Paul Laurence Dunbar Collection, Schomburg Center of Research in Black Culture, New York Public Library; the Life and Works of Paul Laurence Dunbar, Dayton Public Library, Microfilm Edition.

33. Elizabeth Crook, "Sam Houston and Eliza Allen: The Marriage Mystery," *Southwestern Historical Quarterly* 94:1 (1990), 1–36; Karen Rosenberg, "An Autumnal Love of Emma Goldman," *Dissent* 30:3 (1983), 380–382.

Other articles on late-nineteenth, early-twentieth-century relationships of Euro-Americans include George M. Anderson, "'Premature Matrimony': The Hasty Marriage of Bertie Anderson and Philemon Crabb Griffith," *Maryland Historical Magazine* 83:4 (Winter 1988), 369–377; Virginia Hamilton, ed., "'So Much in Love . . .': The Courtship of a Bluegrass Belle—Rosalie Stewart's Diary, December 1890–July 1891," *Register of Kentucky Historical Society* 88:1 (1990), 24–44; Walter Harding, "Henry Thoreau and Ellen Sewall," *South Atlantic Quarterly* 64 (1965), 100–109; Victor Hicken, "A Congressional Romance: Or Victorian Love by Mail," *Old Northwest* 4:1 (1978), 35–48; Shan Holt, "The Anatomy of a Marriage: Letters of Emma Spaulding Bryant, 1873" *Signs* 17:3 (Autumn 1991), 187–204; Charles Howe, "Daniel and Mary Livermore: The Biography of a Marriage," *Proceedings of the Unitarian Universalist Historical Society* 19:2 (1982–1983), 14–35; Ginette Merrill, "The Meeting of Elinor Gertrude Mead and Will Howells and Their Courtship," *Old Northwest* 8:1 (1982), 23–47; Marilyn Motz, "'Thou Art My Last Love': The Courtship and Remarriage of a Rural Texas Couple in 1892," *Southwestern Historical Quarterly* 93:4 (April 1991), 457–473; Annegret Ogden, "Love and Marriage: Five California Couples," *The Californian* 5:4 (July–August 1987), 8–19; Leland S. Person, "Hawthorne's Love Letters: Writing and Relationship," *American Literature* 59:2 (May 1987), 211–227.

34. Howard, "The Courtship Letters of an African-American Couple," 64–80.

35. Ellen K. Rothman, *Hearts and Hands: A History of Courtship in America* (New York: Basic Books, 1984); Karen Lystra, *Searching the Heart: Women, Men and Romantic Love in Nineteenth-Century America* (New York: Oxford University Press, 1989).

36. See, for example, PLD to ARM, December 7, 1897, in Metcalf, "The Letters," I, 73.

37. Biographies on Paul Laurence Dunbar are too numerous to list. See, for example, Addison Gayle, Jr., *Oak and Ivy: A Biography of Paul Laurence Dunbar* (Garden City, NY: Doubleday, 1971); Tony Gentry, *Paul Laurence Dunbar* (New York: Chelsea House, 1989). For a biography of Alice, see Ruby Ora Williams, "An In-Depth Portrait of Alice Dunbar-Nelson" (Ph.D. diss., University of California, Irvine, 1974). The only published work on the Dunbars' courtship and marriage is a newspaper essay: see Andrew Alexander, "The Dunbar Letters: The Tragic Love Affair of One of America's Greatest Poets," *Washington Post Magazine,* June 28, 1981, 24–29.

38. PLD to ARM, January 16, 1898, in Metcalf, "The Letters," I, 370; ARM to PLD, February 28, 1898, in Metcalf, "The Letters," II, 484.

39. ARM to PLD, January 23, 1898, in Metcalf, "The Letters," I, 392.

40. Scholarship on the exploitation of slave women is voluminous. See, for example, Deborah Gray White, *Ar'n't I A Woman? Female Slaves in the Plantation South* (New York: Norton, 1985), 27–46; Angela Davis, "Reflections on the Black Woman's Role in the Community of Slaves," *Black Scholar* 3 (December 1981), 3–15; Eugene Genovese, *Roll, Jordan, Roll: The World Slaves Made* (New York: Vintage, 1976), 25–49, 413–462.

Scholarship on the rape/lynch syndrome is also immense. See, for example, Jacqueline Dodd Hall, *Revolt against Chivalry: Jessie Daniel Ames and the Women's Campaign against Lynching* (New York: Columbia University Press, 1979); Joel Williamson, *The Crucible of Race: Black-White Relations in the American South since Emancipation* (New York: Oxford University Press, 1984); Elizabeth Pleck, *Rape and the Politics of Race, 1865–1910, Working Paper no. 213* (Wellesley, MA: Wellesley College Center for Research on Women, 1990).

41. Darlene Clark Hine, "Rape and the Inner Lives of Black Women in the Middle West: Preliminary Thoughts on the Culture of Dissemblance," *Signs* 1:4 (1989), 912–920; Catherine Clinton, "Bloody Terrain: Freedwomen, Sexuality and Violence during Reconstruction," *Georgia Historical Quarterly*

76:2 (Summer 1992), 313–332; Laura F. Edwards, "Sexual Violence, Gender Reconstruction and the Extension of Patriarchy in Granville County, North Carolina," *North Carolina Historical Review* 68:3 (July 1991), 237–260.

Notes to Chapter 1

1. The four lines of the poem that appear here as an epigraph are found in Virginia Cunningham, *Paul Laurence Dunbar and His Song* (New York: Dodd, Mead, 1953), 14–15; and Jean Gould, *That Dunbar Boy: The Story of America's Famous Negro Poet* (New York: Dodd, Mead, 1958) 34–35.

Cunningham states that Paul wrote the poem for the engagement of his half-brother, Robert Murphy. Gould, however, believes it was written initially for Paul's half-brother William Murphy, the first brother to marry, then later revised for Robert's engagement. Gould also gives a different version of the poem's last line, writing: "To me it's thin as tissue."

2. William Wordsworth (1770–1850) was Poet Laureate of England from 1843 to 1850.

3. Paul was designated the "rising laureate of the colored race" in an 1892 newspaper article several years before he actually became famous. See Jay Martin, "Foreword: Paul Laurence Dunbar," in *A Singer in the Dawn: Reinterpretations of Paul Laurence Dunbar,* ed. Jay Martin (New York: Dodd, Mead, 1975), 14. However, a powerful group of nineteenth-century writers and influence peddlers is credited with naming Paul the "Poet Laureate of the Negro Race." They were William Dean Howells, Edmond Clarence Stedman, Eugene Field, James Whitcomb Riley, James Lane Allen, and Robert Ingersoll. See Charles Austin, *Paul Laurence Dunbar's Roots and Much More* (Dayton: Sense of Roots Publications, 1989), 15.

4. Austin, *Paul Laurence Dunbar's Roots,* 15.

5. Walker M. Allen, "Paul Laurence Dunbar: A Study in Genius," *Psychoanalytic Review* 25 (1938), 53.

6. Cunningham, *Paul Laurence Dunbar,* 14.

7. Joshua's birthdate is uncertain. The year 1816 is the date given in Peter Revel's, *Paul Laurence Dunbar* (Boston: Twayne, 1979), 38. Felton O. Best's dissertation, "Crossing the Color Line: A Biography of Paul Laurence Dunbar, 1872–1906" (Ph.D. diss., Ohio State University, 1992), gives Joshua's birthdate as 1823 (p. 29). Austin, in *Paul Laurence Dunbar's Roots,* cites the years 1816–1825 as the period of Joshua's birth (p. 16).

8. Eliot is quoted in Jean Lloyd, Raymond Mack, and John Pease, *Sociology and Social Life,* 6th ed. (New York: Van Nostrand, 1979), 4.

9. James D. Corrothers, *In Spite of the Handicap: An Autobiography* (1916) (reprint, Freeport, NY: Books for Libraries, 1971), 104.

10. On African American life in Ohio, see David A. Gerber, *Black Ohio and the Color Line: 1860–1950* (Chicago: University of Illinois, 1976); Grace Goulder, *Ohio Scenes and Citizens* (Cleveland: World Publishing, 1964); Charlotte Conover, *Dayton and Montgomery County* (New York: Lewis Historical Publishing House, 1932).

11. Frank U. Quillan, *The Color Line in Ohio: A History of Race Prejudice in a Typical Northern State* (1913) (Reprint, New York: Negro Universities Press, 1969), 139.

12. Quillan, *The Color Line,* 139.

13. Quillan, *The Color Line,* 140.

14. Lloyd et al., *Sociology and Social Life,* 147.

15. Gossie H. Hudson, "A Biography of Paul Laurence Dunbar" (Ph.D. diss., Ohio State University, 1970), 124; citing a letter from Martha Evans to Dunbar, n.d., Paul Laurence Dunbar Collection, Ohio Historical Society, Microfilm Edition, reel 1. This source is cited hereafter as PLD Collection. Paul is cited as PLD.

16. Gilberta S. Whittle, "Paul Dunbar," *A.M.E. Church Review* 18 (April 1902), 322; Hudson, "A Biography," 31; Best, "Crossing the Color Line," 32.

17. Ruth Brinson, "The Powerful Influence of Heredity: Its Effect Upon Individuals and Races," *A.M.E. Church Review* 11 (January 1895), 406.

18. Wordsworth's line is from his poem "My Heart Leaps Up" (1807).

19. On Paul's birth, see Patricia C. McKissack, *Paul Laurence Dunbar: A Poet to Remember* (Chicago: Children's Press, 1984), 9. Charles Austin, in *Paul Laurence Dunbar's Roots,* shows that Matilda Dunbar lived in her grandmother's house at 311 Howard Street in 1872, the year of Paul's birth (p. 15). For data on Matilda's grandmother, Rebecca Porter, see Austin, *Paul Laurence Dunbar's Roots,* 20.

20. From an interview with Matilda Dunbar, c. 1930, in Boyd, "An Appreciation of Paul Laurence Dunbar," 13, unpublished manuscript in the collection, The Life and Works of Paul Laurence Dunbar, Dayton Public Library, Microfilm Edition, reel 3. The statement "This child will be great someday and do you honor" was supposedly spoken by Joshua Dunbar. It is found in Lida Keck Wiggins, *The Life and Works of Paul Laurence Dunbar* (Naperville, IL: J. L. Nichols, 1907), 26. Wiggins states that she too interviewed Matilda in preparation for her biography of Paul (p. 19). Paul's aunt, Rebecca Voss, named him after her son, Laurence Spencer Voss.

21. The marriage license of Matilda and Joshua Dunbar is reproduced in

Austin, *Paul Laurence Dunbar's Roots,* 14. It is not true that Bishop Wright, the father of Paul's childhood friends Wilbur and Orville Wright, married Joshua and Matilda, as reported in Best, "Crossing the Color Line," 45, and Gould, *That Dunbar Boy,* 45.

22. Boyd, "An Appreciation," 12, The Life and Works of Paul Laurence Dunbar, reel 3.

23. Information on the Murphy brothers is found in Austin, *Paul Laurence Dunbar's Roots,* 22; Hudson, "A Biography," 21, 29–30. It is possible that Robert Small Murphy was named in honor of the African American Civil War hero Robert Smalls. However, one Dunbar biographer cites Robert's middle name as Snell, rather than Small. But this could be a typographical error. See Boyd, "An Appreciation," The Life and Works of Paul Laurence Dunbar, reel 3.

24. Boyd, "An Appreciation," 14, The Life and Works of Paul Laurence Dunbar, reel 3.

25. Paul Laurence Dunbar, *The Uncalled* (1901) (reprint Miami: Mnemosyne, 1969), 7. Paul's wife, Alice, said *The Uncalled* was his autobiography. See Saunders Redding, "Portrait against Background," in *A Singer in the Dawn,* 42.

26. Gossie H. Hudson, "The Crowded Years," in *A Singer in the Dawn,* 231.

27. Brenda Stevenson, "Distress and Discord in Virginia Slave Families, 1830–1860," in *In Joy and in Sorrow: Women, Family and Marriage in the Victorian South, 1830–1900,* ed. Carol Blesser (New York: Oxford University Press, 1991), 103–124, 293–297. Also, Deborah Gray White, *Ar'n't I a Woman? Female Slaves in the Plantation South* (New York: Norton, 1985), 152–153.

28. Cited in Dorothy Sterling, ed., *We Are Your Sisters: Black Women in the Nineteenth Century* (New York: Norton, 1984), 340.

29. Sterling, *We Are Your Sisters,* 338–340.

30. United States Bureau of Census, *Historical Statistics of the United States: Colonial Times to 1970* (Washington, DC: U.S. Department of Commerce, 1975), 165.

31. See, for example, Best, "Crossing the Color Line," 33; McKissack, *Paul Laurence Dunbar,* 15.

32. Undated newspaper article, "The Story of Paul Laurence Dunbar by a Southerner," Installment VI, Benjamin Brawley Manuscript Collection, Moorland-Spingarn Research Center.

33. On Matilda's marital problems, see Boyd, "An Appreciation," 14–15, The Life and Works of Paul Laurence Dunbar, reel 3. For information on Matilda's mother, Eliza Burton, see Austin, *Paul Laurence Dunbar's Roots,* 19.

34. Boyd, "An Appreciation," 16, The Life and Works of Paul Laurence Dunbar, reel 3.

35. Gilberta S. Whittle, "Paul Dunbar," *A.M.E. Church Review* 18 (April 1902), 322.

36. Boyd, "An Appreciation," 22, The Life and Works of Paul Laurence Dunbar, reel 3.

37. Joanne Braxton, ed., *The Collected Poetry of Paul Laurence Dunbar* (Charlottesville: University of Virginia Press, 1993), 254–255.

38. Paul Laurence Dunbar, *The Complete Poems of Paul Laurence Dunbar* (New York: Dodd, Mead, 1948), 307–309.

39. Stevenson, "Distress," 115–116.

40. Boyd, "An Appreciation," The Life and Works of Paul Laurence Dunbar, reel 3.

41. Best, "Crossing the Color Line," 33–34.

42. These poems are in Braxton, ed., *Collected Poetry*, 294–295, 293–294; 50–52, respectively. "Colored Soldiers" is also found in Dunbar, *Complete Poems*, 77–79.

43. Paul Laurence Dunbar, *The Fanatics* (New York: Dodd, Mead, 1901).

44. "The Story of Paul Laurence Dunbar by a Southerner," Installment VI, Benjamin Brawley Collection.

45. Austin, *Paul Laurence Dunbar's Roots*, 16.

46. Boyd, "An Appreciation," 17, The Life and Works of Paul Laurence Dunbar, reel 3.

47. Boyd, "An Appreciation," 11, The Life and Works of Paul Laurence Dunbar, reel 3.

48. Paul Laurence Dunbar, "The Ingrate," in *The Strength of Gideon* (1900) (reprint, Miami: Mnemosye, 1969), 96.

49. Ibid.

50. See a copy of the marriage license in Austin, *Paul Laurence Dunbar's Roots*, 14.

51. On African American troops in the Civil War, see James M. McPherson, *The Negro's Civil War: How American Negroes Felt and Acted during the War for the Union* (New York: Vintage, 1967), 143–244; Benjamin Quarles, *The Negro in the Civil War* (Boston: Little, Brown, 1953); Dudley Taylor, *The Sable Arm: Negro Troops in the Union Army, 1861–1865* (New York: Longmans, Green, 1956); R.J.M. Blackett, *Thomas Morris Chester: Black Civil War Correspondent* (Baton Rouge: Louisiana State University Press, 1989).

52. Hudson, "A Biography," 22; Boyd, "An Appreciation," 7, The Life and Works of Paul Laurence Dunbar, reel 3.

53. Hudson, "A Biography," 22; Boyd, "An Appreciation," 7, The Life and Works of Paul Laurence Dunbar, reel 3.

54. Dunbar, *Complete Poems*, 79.

55. Most of Paul's biographers portray Matilda as a widow at this stage of her life; but she clearly says in a 1930s interview that she was abandoned. See Boyd, "An Appreciation," 10–11, The Life and Works of Paul Laurence Dunbar, reel 3.

56. Eugene W. Metcalf, "The Letters of Paul and Alice Dunbar: A Private History," 2 vols. (Ph.D. diss., University of California, Irvine), 1973, I, 12. This source is cited hereafter as Metcalf, "The Letters." Paul is cited as PLD (Paul Laurence Dunbar), and Alice before her marriage as ARM (Alice Ruth Moore). After marriage she is cited as AMD (Alice Moore Dunbar).

57. For a fascinating narrative of Matilda's slave life, see Boyd, "An Appreciation," 99–111, The Life and Works of Paul Laurence Dunbar, reel 3.

58. Boyd, "An Appreciation," 100, The Life and Works of Paul Laurence Dunbar, reel 3.

59. Pearle Schultz, *Paul Laurence Dunbar: Black Poet Laureate* (Champaign, IL: Garrard, 1974), 14.

60. Boyd, "An Appreciation," 102, The Life and Works of Paul Laurence Dunbar, reel 3.

61. Different sources give different names for Matilda's first husband. See Boyd, "An Appreciation," 105, The Life and Works of Paul Laurence Dunbar, reel 3; Austin, *Paul Laurence Dunbar's Roots*, 11, 50; Gayle, *Oak and Ivy*, 8; Hudson, "A Biography," 21.

62. Boyd, "An Appreciation," 108, The Life and Works of Paul Laurence Dunbar, reel 3.

63. Boyd, "An Appreciation, 109, The Life and Works of Paul Laurence Dunbar, reel 3; McKissack, *Paul Laurence Dunbar,* says knowledge of a Back-to-Africa movement spurred Matilda's emigration activities (p. 22). Cunningham, *Paul Laurence Dunbar,* says Matilda ran away after sassing her owner, and hid until Emancipation Day (p. 17–19).

64. Boyd, "An Appreciation," 110–111, The Life and Works of Paul Laurence Dunbar, reel 3.

65. Cunningham, *Paul Laurence Dunbar,* 18.

66. On Joshua Dunbar's height, see Best, "Crossing the Color Line," 31.

67. Cunningham, *Paul Laurence Dunbar,* 19.

68. Boyd, "An Appreciation," 23–24, The Life and Works of Paul Laurence Dunbar, reel 3.

69. *Dunbar News,* March 7, 1934, 1.

70. Paul M. Pearson, "Paul Laurence Dunbar," *Talent,* March 1906, 13.

71. Sterling, *We Are Your Sisters,* is a very readable source on laboring freed women (pp. 331–338, 355–362).

72. Sterling, *We Are Your Sisters,* 255.

73. The best source on the economic struggles of African American women after freedom is Jacqueline Jones, *Labor of Love, Labor of Sorrow: Black Women, Work, and the Family, from Slavery to Freedom* (New York: Vintage, 1985).

74. Boyd, "An Appreciation," 125, The Life and Works of Paul Laurence Dunbar, reel 3.

75. Robert Murphy to Paul Laurence Dunbar, March 13, 1899, PLD Collection, reel 1.

76. Boyd, "An Appreciation," 122, The Life and Works of Paul Laurence Dunbar, reel 3.

77. Lida Keck Wiggins, *The Life and Works of Paul Laurence Dunbar* (Naperville, IL: J. L. Nichols, 1907), 39. See also Benjamin Brawley, *Paul Laurence Dunbar: Poet of His People* (Port Washington, NY: Kennikat, 1936), 32; Hudson, "A Biography," 57.

78. Hudson, "A Biography," 58, citing PLD to Matilda Dunbar, May 7, 1893, PLD Collection, reel 1.

79. See, for example, PLD to ARM, July 4, 1897, and PLD to ARM, December 7, 1897, in Metcalf, "The Letters," I, 173, 274, respectively.

80. PLD to Matilda Dunbar, May 7, 1893, PLD Collection, reel 1.

81. PLD to Matilda Dunbar, May 26, 1893, PLD Collection, reel 1.

82. PLD to Matilda Dunbar, June 6, 1893, PLD Collection, reel 1.

83. Dunbar, *Complete Poems,* 127–128.

84. Quoted in Hudson, "A Biography," 26. Hudson incorrectly identifies Amelia Douglass as Frederick Douglass's daughter. She was his daughter-in-law, married to his son, Louis.

85. Alice Dunbar-Nelson to Benjamin Brawley, incomplete, undated letter, Benjamin Brawley Collection.

86. Allen, "Paul Laurence Dunbar," 79.

87. Dedication cited in Cunningham, *Paul Laurence Dunbar,* 137.

88. Dedication cited in Cunningham, *Paul Laurence Dunbar,* 137.

89. Dunbar, *The Uncalled,* dedication page.

90. The dedication in *Lyrics of the Hearthside* is reproduced in Dunbar, *Complete Poems,* dedication page.

91. Boyd, "An Appreciation," The Life and Works of Paul Laurence Dunbar, reel 3; Hudson, "A Biography," 29–23.

92. Quoted in Best, "Crossing the Color Line," 38.

93. Best, "Crossing the Color Line," 36.

94. "An Easter Ode" is found in Braxton, *Collected Poetry,* 306.

95. "Our Martyred Soldiers" is found in Braxton, *Collected Poetry,* 293–294.

96. The class song appears as "Farewell Song" in Braxton, *Collected Poetry,* 299–300.

97. Best, "Crossing the Color Line," 50, says the *Tattler* was published December 13, 20, and 27, 1890. However, Schultz, in *Paul Laurence Dunbar*, says there were six issues (p. 36).

98. Braxton, *Collected Poetry*, 300, cites Paul's graduation date as June 16, 1891. Hudson, "A Biography," 44, gives the date as June 17. Although Paul was an excellent student, he flunked math his senior year (1890), because illness had kept him out of school for three weeks. On returning, he performed brilliantly in all other classes but was still required to repeat the senior year.

99. Charlotte Reeve Conover, *Some Dayton Saints and Prophets* (N.P.: N.p., 1907), 186.

100. Allen, "Paul Laurence Dunbar," 57.

101. The museum of Dunbar memorabilia is located in Dayton at 218 Summit Street, the house where Paul died.

102. Cunningham, *Paul Laurence Dunbar*, 54.

103. Cunningham, *Paul Laurence Dunbar*, 56.

104. Paul Laurence Dunbar, "One Man's Fortunes," in *The Strength of Gideon* (1900) (reprint Miami: Mnemosyne, 1969), 129–163.

105. Dunbar, "One Man's Fortune," 160.

106. McKissack, *Paul Laurence Dunbar*, 39.

107. Conover, *Some Dayton Saints*, 179–180.

108. See Cunningham, *Paul Laurence Dunbar*, 99–100, for Paul's poem in the Hoosier dialect.

109. James Weldon Johnson, *Along This Way: The Autobiography of James Weldon Johnson* (New York: Viking, 1933), 159.

110. "A Banjo Song" is found in Dunbar, *Complete Poems*, 30–32.

111. Conover, *Some Dayton Saints*, 184.

112. Much of Howells's review is found in Best, "Crossing the Color Line," 127–128.

113. Best, "Crossing the Color Line," 128.

114. Best, Crossing the Color Line," 129.

115. Best, "Crossing the Color Line," 129–130.

116. Best, "Crossing the Color Line," 88.

117. Paul's thank-you note to Howells is found in Hudson, "A Biography," 82.

118. Quoted in Best, "Crossing the Color Line," 140.

119. Quoted in Gayle, *Oak and Ivy*, 59.

120. Peter Revell, *Paul Laurence Dunbar* (Boston: Twayne, 1979), 40; Allen, "Paul Laurence Dunbar," 57, 67.

121. Wiggins, *Life and Works*, 29.

122. "My Best Girl" is found in Braxton, *Collected Poetry*, 296–297.

123. Hudson, "A Biography," 7.

124. Brawley, *Paul Laurence Dunbar*, 76, 37; Wiggins, *Life and Works*, 81; Gould, *That Dunbar Boy*, 182–183.

125. Cunningham, *Paul Laurence Dunbar*, 97.

126. Paul's poem, "The Crisis," tells of his life after publication of *Majors and Minors*. See Cunningham, *Paul Laurence Dunbar*, 150. The poem is found in Dunbar, *Complete Poems*, 179.

127. Gayle, *Oak and Ivy*, 11.

128. Gayle, *Oak and Ivy*, 39; Brawley, *Paul Laurence Dunbar*, 39; Cunningham, *Paul Laurence Dunbar*, 132.

129. Austin, *Paul Laurence Dunbar's Roots*, 58; Best, "Crossing the Color Line," 82.

130. Cunningham, *Paul Laurence Dunbar*, 140.

131. E. B. Taylor, "When Dunbar Came to Baltimore," *Afro-American*, October 1933.

132. Johnson, *Along This Way*, 152.

133. Gayle, *Oak and Ivy*, 117.

134. Alice Dunbar-Nelson to Benjamin Brawley, undated, partial letter, Benjamin Brawley Collection.

135. Johnson, *Along This Way*, 159–160.

Notes to Chapter 2

1. Paul Laurence Dunbar to Alice Ruth Moore, October 13, 1895, in Eugene W. Metcalf, "The Letters of Paul and Alice Dunbar: A Private History," 2 vols. (Ph.D. diss., University of California, Irvine, 1973), I, 68–69. Hereafter this source is cited as Metcalf, "The Letters." The principals are cited as PLD (Paul Laurence Dunbar), and ARM (Alice Ruth Moore). After her marriage, Alice is cited as AMD (Alice Moore Dunbar).

2. PLD to ARM, January 28, 1898; PLD to ARM, December 29, 1897, in Metcalf, "The Letters," I, 403, 319, respectively.

3. Alice Dunbar-Nelson, "People of Color in Louisiana," *Journal of Negro History* I, 1:4 (October 1916), 367.

4. PLD to ARM, October 8, 1897, in Metcalf, "The Letters," I, 204.

5. PLD to ARM, August 16, 1896, in Metcalf, "The Letters," I, 105.

6. PLD to ARM, December 29, 1895, in Metcalf, "The Letters," I, 75; also PLD to ARM, September 26, 1897, in Metcalf, "The Letters," I, 195.

7. Gloria T. Hull, ed., *Give Us Each Day: The Diary of Alice Dunbar-Nelson* (New York: Norton, 1984), 91. Juno was the ancient Roman queen of heaven, the sister and wife of Jupiter.

8. Gloria T. Hull, "Dunbar-Nelson, Alice Ruth Moore (1875–1935)," in *Black Women in America: An Historical Encyclopedia,* ed. by Darlene Clark Hine et al. (Bloomington: Indiana University Press, 1993), I, 359.

9. This conversation occurred in the Ardmore, Delaware, home of Ms. Young in 1981.

10. Alice Dunbar-Nelson, "The Goodness of St. Rocque," in Gloria T. Hull, ed., *The Works of Alice Dunbar-Nelson* (New York: Oxford University Press, 1988), I, 5–6.

11. PLD to AMD, March 14, 1898, in Metcalf, "The Letters," II, 510.

12. PLD to ARM, August 29, 1897, in Metcalf, "The Letters," I, 193.

13. "Paul to Virginia," in Hull, *The Works of Alice Dunbar-Nelson,* I, 83–84. Alice wrote the poem before making Paul's acquaintance. It appeared in her first book, *Violets and Other Tales* (Boston: Monthly Review, 1895).

14. Hull, *Give Us Each Day,* 95. Alice kept a diary from 1921 to 1931. Periodically, she reflected on her "halcyon days," as she called them—her youth in New Orleans.

15. Hull, *Give Us Each Day,* 268.

16. See Alice's essay, "The Woman," in Hull, ed., *The Works of Alice Dunbar-Nelson,* I, 28. On the concept of the New Woman for mainstream middle-class Americans, see Carolyn Forrey, "New Woman Revisited," *Women's Studies* 2 (1974), 37–56.

17. Alice Dunbar, "Tony's Wife," in Hull, *The Works of Alice Dunbar-Nelson,* I, 21–22. Like Alice, Wiletta Johnson, a late nineteenth-century African American writer, gives a romanticized picture of New Orleans during this period. See Wiletta Johnson, "A Southern City: Reflections," *A.M.E. Church Review,* July 1893, 163–171.

18. Feminist educator Anna Julia Cooper described the mainly mulatto elite in this manner. See her *Voice from the South* (1892); reprint (New York: Negro Universities Press, 1969), 207. Cooper was a remarkable woman despite her belief in the prevailing theory of social classes. For a fine biography of this figure, see Louise Daniel Hutchinson, *Anna Julia Cooper: A Voice from the South* (Washington, DC: Smithsonian Institution Press, 1981).

19. On racial uplift among the elite, see, for example, Cynthia Neverdon-Morton, *Afro-American Women of the South and the Advancement of the Race, 1895–1925* (Knoxville: University of Tennessee Press, 1989).

20. Cooper, *Voice from the South,* 207.

21. PLD to ARM, June 25, 1895, in Metcalf, "The Letters," I, 51.

22. Azalia Hackley, *The Colored Girl Beautiful* (Kansas City: Burton Publishing, 1916), 49, 157. On the social construction of African American woman-

hood, see also Alexander Crummell, "The Care of Daughters," *Tracts for the Negro Race* (Washington, DC: The Author(?), 1899).

23. Paul enclosed the poem "Phyllis," which he wrote on the back of an envelope. See ARM to PLD, January 29, 1898, in Metcalf, "The Letters," I, 407. The poem later appeared in his *Lyrics of a Lowly Life*, published by Dodd, Mead in 1896; see Addison Gayle, Jr., *Oak and Ivy: A Biography of Paul Laurence Dunbar* (Garden City, NY: Doubleday, 1971), 54.

24. Barbara Welter, writing about white middle-class women, has an enlightening chapter on the subject. See "Coming of Age in America: The American Girl in the Nineteenth Century," in *Dimity Convictions: American Women in the Nineteenth Century* (Athens: Ohio University Press, 1976), 17.

25. ARM to PLD, July 6, 1895, in Metcalf, "The Letters," I, 55–56. Although Alice protested that she did not draw well, both she and Paul were considered competent amateur artists.

26. *Woman's Era*, November 1894, 6, 8, 10. Records show that Alice was sales agent and correspondent for *Woman's Era* by 1894. See *Woman's Era*, November 1894, 5–7; also December 1894, 13–14. Alice's address at the time was 55 Palmyra Street.

Josephine St. Pierre Ruffin of Boston is credited with starting the New Era Club in February 1893. The organization's monthly newspaper, *Woman's Era*, was the first one published by an African American woman. The paper was "devoted to the interests of the Women's Clubs, Leagues and Societies throughout the country." See *Woman's Era*, November 1894, 8. See also Elizabeth Fortson Arroyo, "Ruffin, Josephine St. Pierre (1842–1924)," in *Black Women in America*, II, 994–997.

27. *Woman's Era*, November 1894, 8.

28. Alice began writing this column in 1895. The newspaper was published in New Orleans by the Colored Knights of Pythias. See Metcalf, "The Letters," I, 42, note 15.

29. ARM to PLD, May 7, 1895, in Metcalf, "The Letters," I, 37.

30. ARM to PLD, May 7, 1895, in Metcalf, "The Letters," I, 37. *Violets and Other Tales* was published sometime between May and August 1895. For Paul's comments on the book, see PLD to ARM, August 14, 1895, in Metcalf, "The Letters," I, 63.

31. Jasper Johns, "Body of One-Time Wife of Dunbar Is Cremated," [Philadelphia] *Afro-American*, week of September 28, 1935, 2; Walker Allen, "Paul Laurence Dunbar: A Study in Genius," *Psychoanalytic Review* 25 (1938), 62; Gloria T. Hull, "Alice Dunbar-Nelson: Delaware Writer and Woman of Affairs," *Delaware History* 17 (Fall–Winter 1976), 92.

32. ARM to PLD, February 16, 1897, in Metcalf, "The Letters," I, 448.

33. Alice Ruth Moore, "In Our Neighborhood," in Hull, *Works of Alice Dunbar-Nelson*, I, 124. There are many similarities between the Moore family and this story's fictional family. Since much of Alice's literature was autobiographical, she undoubtedly used herself and her sister as models for the daughters in the story.

34. PLD to ARM, October 13, 1895, in Metcalf, "The Letters," I, 68–69.

35. Hull, *Give Us Each Day*, 266.

36. Larsen married a prominent physicist. There are many parallels between her life and Alice's. See Larsen's stunning biography by Thadious M. Davis, *Nella Larsen, Novelist of the Harlem Renaissance: A Woman's Life Unveiled* (Baton Rouge: Louisiana State University Press, 1994).

37. This sparsely documented letter was enclosed in another letter dated September 13, 1898. See Metcalf, "The Letters," II, 674, 678, 680.

38. Benjamin Brawley, *Paul Laurence Dunbar: Poet of His People* (Chapel Hill: University of North Carolina Press, 1936), 114.

39. John Blassingame, *Black New Orleans: 1860–1880* (Chicago: University of Chicago Press, 1973), 174.

40. Blassingham, *Black New Orleans*, 174.

41. Arthe A. Anthony, "The Negro Creole Community in New Orleans: 1880–1920" (Ph.D. diss., University of California, Irvine, 1978), 41. This is an outstanding source on New Orleans Creoles of color.

42. Birth Certificate of Alice Moore, Recorder of Births, Marriages and Deaths in and for the Parish and City of New Orleans, 1875, no. 974. The place of Alice's birth seems to have been the 300 block of Second Street. Copy of birth certificate in possession of the author. My thanks to Sybil Kein for providing me with a copy of this document.

43. Anthony, "Negro Creole Community," 139.

44. *Soards' New Orleans City Directory for 1874* (New Orleans: L. Soards and Company, 1874), 560.

45. Birth Certificate of Alice Moore, Recorder of Births, Marriages and Deaths in and for the Parish and City of New Orleans, 1875, no. 974.

46. *Soards' New Orleans City Directory for 1876* (New Orleans: L. Soards, n.d.), 708; *Soards' New Orleans City Directory for 1877* (New Orleans: L. Soards, n.d.), 672.

47. *Soards' New Orleans City Directory for 1880* (New Orleans: L. Soards, n.d.), 779.

48. U.S. Department of Commerce, Bureau of Census, 10th Census (1880), vol. 8, Enumeration District 9, 2nd Ward, Orleans Parish, Sheet 32, lines 46–48.

49. Blassingame, *Black New Orleans*, 95.

50. *Soards' New Orleans City Directory for 1883* (New Orleans: L. Soards, n.d.), 779.

51. *Soards' New Orleans City Directory for 1887* (New Orleans: L. Soards, n.d.), 623.

52. *Soards' New Orleans City Directory for 1892* (New Orleans: L. Soards, n.d.), 593.

53. In a short story, "Dexter's Debut," Alice so describes the house at 56 1/2 Palmyra. See Gloria T. Hull, "'Two-Facing Life': The Duality of Alice Dunbar-Nelson," *Collections* 4 (1989), 34.

54. Violet Harrington Bryan lists Alice's address in 1892 as 56 1/2 Palmyra Street. See *The Myth of New Orleans in Literature: Dialogues of Race and Gender* (Knoxville: University of Tennessee Press, 1993), 144, note 49.

55. Leila was born in New Orleans at 2 P.M., December 25, 1869, at 236 Carondolet Street, the residence of her maternal grandmother, Mary Wright. See Birth Certificate of Mary Moore, Recorder of Births, Marriages and Deaths in and for the Parish and City of New Orleans, 1869, no. 389. Author has a copy of the document.

56. Hull, *Give Us Each Day*, 114.

57. "Tony's Wife," in Hull, *Works of Alice Dunbar-Nelson*, I, 19–36.

58. Birth Certificate of Mary Moore, Recorder of Births, Marriages and Deaths in and for the Parish and City of New Orleans, 1869, no. 389. Also, Violet Harrington Bryan, "Race and Gender in the Early Works of Alice Dunbar-Nelson," in *Louisiana Women Writers: New Essays and a Comprehensive Bibliography*, ed. by Dorothy H. Brown et al. (Baton Rouge: Louisiana State University Press, 1992), 102.

59. AMD to PLD, March 7, 1899, in Metcalf, "The Letters"; also Gloria T. Hull, "Shaping Contradictions: Alice Dunbar-Nelson and the Black Creole Experience," *New Orleans Review* 15:1 (1988), 35.

60. Telephone conversation of Sybil Kein and Eleanor Alexander, June 19, 1994.

61. ARM to PLD, October 10, 1897, in Metcalf, "The Letters," I, 207.

62. Hull, *Give Us Each Day*, 95.

63. "Little Miss Sophie," in Hull, *The Works of Alice Dunbar-Nelson*, I, 140–152.

64. Blassingame, *Black New Orleans*, 84, 94.

65. AMD to PLD, March 22, 1898, in Metcalf, "The Letters," II, 538; AMD to PLD, April 10, 1898, in Metcalf, "The Letters," II, 583.

66. Hull, *Give Us Each Day*, 337, 449, 442, 202, respectively.

67. Hull, *The Works of Alice Dunbar-Nelson*, I, 47, 124, 126, respectively.

68. Mary Wright died in New Orleans. She was buried there April 10, 1896.

Alice's diary indicates she was very fond of her grandmother. See Hull, *Give Us Each Day,* 176.

African-American servants received even less pay than their Euro-American counterparts. See: Mabel Collins Donnelly, *The American Victorian Woman: The Myth and the Reality* (New York: Greenwood, 1986), 9; also Sterling, *We Are Your Sisters,* 359–360.

69. Blassingame, *Black New Orleans,* 216.

70. Jacqueline Ann Rouse, *Lugenia Burns Hope: Black Southern Reformer* (Athens: University of Georgia Press, 1989), 26–27.

71. U.S. Department of Commerce, Bureau of Census, 10th Census (1880), vol. 8, Enumeration District 9, District 1, 2nd Ward, New Orleans Parish, Sheet 32, lines 46–48.

72. Alice Dunbar-Nelson, "Brass Ankles Speaks," in Hull, *The Works of Alice Dunbar-Nelson,* II, 314.

73. Dunbar-Nelson, "Brass Ankles," in *The Works of Alice Dunbar-Nelson,* II, 315, 314, respectively.

74. Mrs. E. C. Hobson and Mrs. C. E. Hopkins, A Report Concerning the Colored Women of the South (Baltimore: Trustees of the John H. Slater Fund, 1896), 7; Miss E. B. Emery, *Letters from the South on the Social, Intellectual, and Moral Condition of the Colored People* (Boston: Beacon, 1880), 14.

75. Emery, *Letters from the South,* 14–15. On the education of freed people and their offspring, see Brenda Stevenson, ed., *The Journals of Charlotte Forten Grimke* (New York: Oxford University Press, 1988), 381–511; Jacqueline Jones, *Soldiers of Light and Love: Northern Teachers and Georgia Blacks, 1865–1873* (Chapel Hill: University of North Carolina Press, 1980).

76. Blassingame, *Black New Orleans,* 125, 127. Straight University was charted in 1869 by the state of Louisiana. The following year, the school came under the auspices of the American Missionary Association. Like many of the new schools of higher learning for African Americans, this one also had grammar and high school departments. Straight is now known as Dillard University.

77. *Catalogue of Straight University, New Orleans, LA, 1894–1895* (New Orleans: University Press, 1895); *Catalogue of Straight University, New Orleans, LA, 1897–1898* (New Orleans: University Press, 1898).

78. *Catalogue of Straight University, New Orleans, LA, 1894–1895,* 36.

79. Emery, *Letters from the South,* 14.

80. G. F. Richings, *Evidences of Progress among Colored People,* 12th ed. (Philadelphia: George S. Ferguson, 1905), 420.

81. For other socially acceptable jobs, see Katherine D. Tilman, "Paying Professions for Colored Girls," in *The Works of Katherine Davis Chapman Tilman,* ed. by Claudia Tate (New York: Oxford University Press, 1991), 116–121.

82. Sharon Harley, "Beyond the Classroom: The Organized Lives of Female Educators in the District of Columbia, 1890–1930," *Journal of Negro Education* 51:3 (1982), 255.

83. Hull, *Give Us Each Day*, 178.

84. Dickson D. Brice, Jr., *Black American Writing from the Nadir: The Evolution of a Literary Tradition, 1877–1915* (Baton Rouge: Louisiana State University Press, 1989), 131.

85. "A Southern Authoress," undated, unidentified newspaper clipping, PLD Collection, reel 7. Reviews of *Violets and Other Tales* appeared in the following African American newspapers: Boston *Daily Standard*, July 27, 1895; *Texas Freeman*, August 10, 1895; New Orleans *Daily Crusader*, August 24, 1895; Denver *Statesman*, September 14, 1895; New York *Age*, October 3, 1895; San Francisco *Western Outlook*, October 14, 1895. The book was also reviewed in the *New York Sun*, October 10, 1895. See PLD Collection, reel 7.

86. *Soards' New Orleans City Directory for 1895*, 665. The school was located at "old" 201 Marigny. Alice lived at "old" 55 Palmyra. In 1892, Alice lived at 56-1/2 Palmyra. In 1895, she lived at 55 Palmyra. The houses may have been renumbered.

87. Hackley, *The Colored Girl Beautiful*, 156.

88. George Washington Cable, *Madame Delphine* (New York: Charles Scribner's Sons, 1881), 43.

89. Alice Dunbar-Nelson, "People of Color in Louisiana," *Journal of Negro History* I, 1:4 (October 1916), 361.

90. Charles Austin, *Paul Laurence Dunbar's Roots and Much More* (Dayton: Sense of Roots Publications, 1989), 58.

91. John James Audubon was born in Haiti. His father, Pierre Audubon, was French, and his mother, Jeanne Rabine, was a mulatto servant.

92. Hackley, *The Colored Girl Beautiful*, 33, 32, respectively.

93. Henry Louis Gates, Jr., ed., *Bearing Witness: Selections from African-American Autobiography in the Twentieth Century* (New York: Pantheon, 1991), 15, 17.

94. E. Franklin Frazier, *Black Bourgeoisie: The Rise of a New Middle Class in the United States* (New York: Collier, 1970), 112.

95. Joanne M. Braxton, ed., *The Collected Poetry of Paul Laurence Dunbar* (Charlottesville: University of Virginia Press, 1993), 149.

96. "Brass Ankles Speaks," in Hull, *The Works of Alice Dunbar-Nelson*, II, 321.

97. ARM to PLD, January 28, 1898, in Metcalf, "The Letters," I, 347.

98. ARM to PLD, January 11, 1898, in Metcalf, "The Letters," I, 354.

99. ARM to PLD, January 12, 1898, in Metcalf, "The Letters," I, 359.

100. ARM to PLD, January 29, 1898, in Metcalf, "The Letters," I, 406.

101. Hull, *Give Us Each Day*, 260, 54, respectively.

102. Hull, *Give Us Each Day*, 434.

103. Dorothy Sterling, ed., *We Are Your Sisters: Black Women in the Nineteenth Century* (New York: Norton, 1984), 429; citing *Voice of the Negro*, July 1904.

104. Blassingame, *Black New Orleans*, 178.

105. Quoted in Blassingame, *Black New Orleans*, 180–181.

106. Cable, *Madame Delphine*, 7.

107. Dunbar-Nelson "People of Color in Louisiana," *Journal of Negro History*, I, 367.

108. Dunbar-Nelson, "People of Color in Louisiana," *Journal of Negro History*, I, 367.

109. Bryan, *Louisiana Women Writers*, 121.

110. Literary critic Robert Bone ranked Toomer's *Cane* in the class with Richard Wright's *Native Son* and Ralph Ellison's *Invisible Man*.
Scholars still debate Toomer's solution to his identity. See, for example, Nellie McKay's fine book, *Jean Toomer, Artist: A Study of His Literary Life and Work, 1894–1936* (Chapel Hill: University of North Carolina Press, 1984).

111. Dunbar-Nelson, "People of Color in Louisiana," *Journal of Negro History*, I, 361.

112. Harnett Kane, *Queen New Orleans: City by the River* (New York: William Morrow, 1949), 185; Joel Williamson, *New People: Miscegenation and Mulattoes in the United States* (New York: Free Press, 1980), xii.

113. Blassingame, *Black New Orleans*, 201.

114. ARM to PLD, April 28, 1896, in Metcalf, "The Letters," I, 93; Ann Allen Schockley, *Afro-American Women Writers, 1746–1933: An Anthology and Critical Guide* (New York: Meridian, 1989), 263.

115. Violet Harrington Bryan, "Race and Gender in the Early Works of Alice Dunbar-Nelson," in *Louisiana Women Writers: New Essays and a Comprehensive Bibliography*, ed. by Dorothy H. Brown et al. (Baton Rouge: Louisiana State University Press, 1992), 124. See also Hull, "Shaping Contradictions," 34–37.

116. Anthony, "Negro Creole Community," 141.

117. Violet Harrington Bryan, *The Myth of New Orleans in Literature: Dialogues of Race and Gender* (Knoxville: University of Tennessee Press, 1993), 178–179, note 67.

118. ARM to PLD, May 7, 1895, in Metcalf, "The Letters," I, 38.

119. Alice's characterizations of immigrants have been described as racist. See Roger Whitlow, "Alice Dunbar-Nelson: New Orleans Writer," in *Regionalism*

and the Female Imagination: A Collection of Essays, ed. by Emily Toth (University Park: Pennsylvania State University Press, 1985), 109–125.

120. Hull, *Works of Alice Dunbar-Nelson,* I, 14–176.

121. Paul Laurence Dunbar, "One Man's Fortunes, in his *The Strength of Gideon and Other Stories* (1900) (reprint, Miami: Mnemosyne, 1969), 160.

Notes to Chapter 3

1. Joanne M. Braxton, ed., *The Collected Poetry of Paul Laurence Dunbar* (Charlottesville: University of Virginia Press, 1993), 55–56; Paul Laurence Dunbar, *The Complete Poems of Paul Laurence Dunbar* (New York: Dodd, Mead, 1948). "The Wooing" appeared initially in Paul's third book of poetry, *Lyrics of a Lowly Life* (New York: Dodd, Mead, 1896).

2. Braxton, *Collected Poetry,* 56; Dunbar, *Complete Poems,* 87.

3. In her autobiographical story, "The Decision" (c. 1902–1909), Alice (the heroine, Marion) discovers that Paul (Marion's husband, Burt—a famous writer with a drinking problem), is common, vulgar, and coarse after they are married. See Gloria T. Hull, ed., *The Works of Alice Dunbar-Nelson* (New York: Oxford University Press, 1988), III, 197–198.

4. Alice recalled this portion of her life in her autobiographical story, "No Sacrifice" (c. 1928–1931), in Hull, *Works of Alice Dunbar-Nelson,* II, 203.

5. Mrs. P. Moore to Paul Laurence Dunbar, November 3, 1897, Paul Laurence Dunbar Collection, Ohio Historical Society, Microfilm Edition, reel 5. Hereafter this source is cited as PLD Collection. The principals are cited as PLD (Paul Laurence Dunbar) and ARM (Alice Ruth Moore). After her marriage, Alice is cited as AMD (Alice Moore Dunbar).

6. The John Brown Watson Collection (John Hay Library, Brown University), has love letters between Watson and his wife. Watson, a 1904 African American graduate of Brown, was president of the Agricultural, Mechanical and Normal College, an African American institution in Pine Bluff, Arkansas. I am indebted to Lloyd B. Monroe, Jr., for bringing the Watson Collection to my attention.

7. The John and Lugenia Burns Hope Papers (Clark Atlanta University Center, Woodruff Library) contain love letters written before and after the Hopes' wedding on December 29, 1897. A microfilm version is available as the Papers of John and Lugenia Burns Hope, ed. Alton Hornsby (Frederick, MD: University Publications, 1984).

8. Karen Lystra, *Searching the Heart: Women, Men and Romantic Love in Nineteenth-Century America* (New York: Oxford University Press, 1989), 12. Her chapter on the love letters of middle-class Euro-Americans is excellent.

9. Loney Butler to Sophronia Collins, September 2, 1889, in Paula L. Woods and Felix H. Liddel, eds., *I Hear a Symphony: African Americans Celebrate Love* (New York: Doubleday, 1993), 131.

10. Marguerite Davenport, *Azalia: The Life of Madame E. Azalia Hackley* (Boston: Chapman and Grimes, 1947), 68. Unfortunately, this valuable cache of love letters appears to be lost.

11. John S. Locke, *The Art of Correspondence . . . Containing Model Business, Social and Love Letters by Distinguished Writers* (Boston: DeWolfe, Fiske, 1883), 140; see also Emily Thornwell, *The Lady's Guide to Complete Etiquette* (Chicago: Belford, Clarke, 1884), 165–169.

12. Locke, *Art of Correspondence,* 143–145.

13. Richard Brodhead, ed., *The Journals of Charles Chesnutt* (Durham, NC: Duke University Press, 1993), 74.

14. Woods and Liddell, *I Hear a Symphony,* 131.

15. Locke, *Art of Correspondence,* 147.

16. PLD to ARM, January 16, 1898, in Metcalf, "The Letters," I, 370.

17. An outstanding study on eleven African American romance novels is Claudia Tate, *Domestic Allegories of Political Desire: The Black Heroine's Text at the Turn-of-the-Century* (New York: Oxford University Press, 1992). For a study of love and marriage among African Americans in twentieth-century fiction, see Ann duCille, *The Coupling Convention: Sex, Text and Tradition in Black Women's Fiction* (New York: Oxford University Press, 1993); Sybille Kamme-Erkel, *Happily Ever After? Marriage and Its Rejection in Afro-American Novels* (Frankfurt am Main: Peter Lang, 1989); Maisha Lois Hazzard Piankhi, "Black Love on Stage: A Profile of Courtship and Marriage Relationships in Selected Broadway Shows by Black Dramatists, 1959–1979, and an Original Play" (Ph.D. diss., Bowling Green State University, 1983).

For turn-of-the-twentieth-century African American advice literature with references to courtship and marriage, see E. M. Woods, *The Negro in Etiquette: A Novelty* (St. Louis: Buxton and Skinner, 1899); William Noel Johnson, *Common Sense in the Home* (Cincinnati: Press of Jennings and Pyle, 1902); Professor and Mrs. J. W. Gibson, *Golden Thoughts on Chastity and Procreation* (Naperville, IL: J. L. Nichols, 1903, 1914); Joseph R. Gay, *Progress and Achievements of the 20th Century Negro* (N.P.: Author, 1913); E. Azalia Hackley, *The Colored Girl Beautiful* (Kansas City: Burton, 1916).

18. ARM to PLD, March 26, 1898, in Metcalf, "The Letters," II, 554; PLD to ARM, October 13, 1895, in Metcalf, "The Letters," I, 68.

19. Ida Husted Harper, "Let Love Be Controlled," *Independent* 53 (June 27, 1901), 1477–1480.

20. Fowler, *Historical Romance of the American Negro,* 195; Alexander

Crummell, "Marriage[,] a Duty," in *Tracts for the Negro Race,* no. 4 (Washington, DC: The Author(?), 1899). See also Katherine Davis Tilman, "The Afro-American Women and Their Work," *A.M.E. Church Review,* 11 (April 1897), 499.

21. "You Will Solve Your Own Problems," Baltimore *Ledger,* December 24, 1898 (unpaged); citing McKinley's speech to African American students at Georgia Agricultural and Mechanical College, December 18, 1898.

22. Giles B. Jackson and D. Webster Davis, *The Industrial History of the Negro Race in the United States* (Richmond: Virginia Press, c. 1908), 369; citing "The Negro in America—An Address," delivered by Andrew Carnegie to the Philosophical Institution of Edinburgh, October 16, 1907.

23. Mrs. N. F. Mossell, *The Work of the Afro-American Woman* (New York: Oxford University Press, 1988), 115, 116.

24. David Levering Lewis, *W. E. B. Du Bois: Biography of a Race, 1868–1919* (New York: Henry Holt, 1993), 435.

25. Anna H. Jones, "The American Colored Woman," *Voice of the Negro* 2 (October 1905), 694.

26. Jones, "American Colored Woman," 694.

27. Quoted in Catherine Clinton, "Southern Dishonor: Flesh, Blood, Race, and Bondage," in *In Joy and in Sorrow: Women, Family, and Marriage in the Victorian South, 1830–1900,* ed. Carol Bleser, (New York: Oxford University Press, 1991), 54–55.

Highly recommended sources on courtship, marriage, and family among slaves are Herbert Gutman, *The Black Family in Slavery and Freedom, 1750–1925* (New York: Vintage, 1976); Deborah Gray White, *Ar'n't I a Woman? Female Slaves in the Plantation South* (New York: Norton, 1985), 142–160; John Blassingame, *The Slave Community: Plantation Life in the Antebellum South* (New York: Oxford University Press, 1972), 77–103; Eugene Genovese, *Roll, Jordan, Roll: The World Slaves Made* (New York: Vintage, 1974), 450–457, 482–534. Of special interest is Brenda Stevenson, "Distress and Discord in Virginia Slave Families, 1830–1860," in *In Joy and In Sorrow,* 103–109.

28. Gibson, *Golden Thoughts on Chastity,* 88.

29. James McCabe, *Household Encyclopedia of Business & Social Forms* (Philadelphia: Standard, 1890?), 462.

30. Woods, *The Negro in Etiquette,* 55.

31. Gay, *Progress and Achievements of the 20th Century Negro,* 244.

32. Walter Griffin, *The Homes of Our Country* (New York: Union Publishing, 1882), 354; also, James H. A. Johnson, "Woman's Exalted Station," *A.M.E. Church Review* 8:4 (April 1892), 402.

33. Tillman, "Afro-American Women and Their Work," 47.

34. See, for example, Mrs. M. E. Lee, "The Home-Maker," *A.M.E. Church Review* 8:1 (July 1891), 63–66.

35. Griffin, *Homes of Our Country,* 348.

36. Gay, *Progress and Achievements,* 240–242.

37. Daniel A. Payne, *Treatise on Domestic Education* (1885) (reprint, Freeport, NY: Books for Libraries, 1971), 71.

38. Lee, "The Home-Maker," 66.

39. Silas X. Floyd, *Floyd's Flowers, or Duty and Beauty for Colored Children* (Atlanta: Hudgins Publishing, 1906), 10.

40. William M. Thayer, *Womanhood: Hints and Helps for Young Women* (New York: Thomas Whittaker, 1895), 173.

41. Gay, *Progress and Achievements,* 243.

42. Mossell, *Work of Afro-American Women,* 117.

43. Fowler, *Historical Romance of the American Negro,* 194.

44. Hattie Rutherford to John Brown Watson, April 27, 1907, Watson Collection, Box 1, Folder 2.

45. Michael Gordon and M. Charles Bernstein, "Mate Choice and Domestic Life in Nineteenth-Century Marriage Manuals," *Journal of Marriage and Family,* November 1970, 667.

46. Gay, *Progress and Achievements,* 250.

47. Gibson, *Golden Thoughts,* 88.

48. McCabe, *Household Encyclopedia,* 400, 401.

49. Gibson, *Golden Thoughts,* 102.

50. PLD to ARM, January 16, 1898, in Metcalf, "The Letters," I, 370.

51. ARM to PLD, February 28, 1898, in Metcalf, "The Letters," II, 484.

52. "A Negro Tragedy," *Alexander's Monthly,* September 15, 1906, 14.

53. PLD to ARM, April 17, 1895, in Metcalf, "The Letters," I, 34.

54. *Century* magazine accepted "A Negro Love Song," "Curtain," and "The Dilettante."

55. "Frederick Douglass" is a memorial poem. Douglass died February 20, 1895. The poem is found in Dunbar, *Complete Poems,* 7–9, and Braxton, Collected Poetry, 6–7. "Phyllis" is in *Complete Poems,* 119, and Braxton, *Collected Poetry,* 74–75.

56. Hull, *Works of Alice Dunbar-Nelson,* III, 203.

57. ARM to PLD, January 29, 1898, in Metcalf, "The Letters," I, 407; AMD to PLD, March 26, 1898, in Metcalf, "The Letters," II, 556; Benjamin Brawley, *Paul Laurence Dunbar: Poet of His People* (1936) (reprint, Port Washington, NY: Kennikat, 1967), 62.

58. PLD to ARM, May 23, 1895, in Metcalf, "The Letters," I, 40.

59. ARM to PLD, May 7, 1895, in Metcalf, "The Letters," I, 37.

60. ARM to PLD, October 1, 1897, PLD Collection, reel 1.

61. ARM to PLD, May 7, 1895, in Metcalf, "The Letters," I, 37–38.

62. ARM to PLD, May 7, 1895, in Metcalf, "The Letters," I, 38.

63. ARM to PLD, May 7, 1895, in Metcalf, "The Letters," I, 38.

64. Du Bois's statement is found in Tony Martin, *Race First* (Dover: Majority Press, 1976), 297.

65. Mrs. A[melia] E. Johnson, *Clarence and Corrine; or God's Way* (1890) (reprint, New York: Oxford University Press, 1988); Mrs. A[melia] E. Johnson, *The Hazeley Family* (1894) (reprint, New York: Oxford University Press, 1988); Emma Kelley-Hawkins, *Medga* (1891) (reprint, New York: Oxford University Press, 1988); Emma Kelley-Hawkins, *Four Girls at Cottage City* (1898) (reprint, New York: Oxford University Press, 1988); Frances Ellen Watkins Harper, *Iola Leroy, or Shadows Uplifted* (1892) (reprint, New York: Oxford University Press, 1988); Katherine D. Tillman, *Beryl Weston'sAmbition: The Story of an Afro-American Girl's Life* (1893), in *The Works of Katherine Davis Chapman Tillman,* ed. Claudia Tate (New York: Oxford University Press, 1991); Katherine Davis Chapman Tillman, *Clancy Street* (1898), in the *Works of Katherine Davis Chapman Tillman.*

66. Tillman, "Afro-American Women and Their Work," 477.

67. Ruby Ora Williams, "An In-Depth Portrait of Alice Dunbar-Nelson" (Ph.D. diss., University of California, Irvine, 1974), 3.

68. Williams, "In-Depth Portrait" 3, 77.

69. PLD to ARM, May 23, 1895, in Metcalf, "The Letters," I, 40.

70. PLD to ARM, May 23, 1895, in Metcalf, "The Letters," I, 40. Alice wrote for her small, hometown African American newspaper, *Journal of the Lodge,* published by the Colored Knights of Pythias.

71. PLD to ARM, May 23, 2895, in Metcalf, "The Letters," I, 40.

72. PLD to Helen Douglass, October 22, 1895, PLD Collection, reel 1.

73. James Weldon Johnson, *Along This Way: The Autobiography of James Weldon Johnson* (New York: Viking, 1938), 169.

74. PLD to ARM, May 23, 1895, in Metcalf, "The Letters," I, 40.

75. Paul moved to Indianapolis temporarily to edit the *World,* from about May to August 1895. See Metcalf, "The Letters," I, 42.

76. PLD to ARM, June 6, 1896, in Metcalf, "The Letters," I, 45.

77. The poem, later entitled "Alice," appeared in Paul's book *Major and Minors* (1895). It is also in *Complete Poems,* 61–62, and Braxton, *Collected Poetry,* 40.

78. PLD to ARM, June 6, 1895, in Metcalf, "The Letters," I, 46. The poem was published as "A Lyric." It is found in Dunbar, *Complete Poems,* 478–479, and Braxton, *Collected Poetry,* 288–289.

79. Dunbar, *Complete Poems,* 477–479; Braxton, *Collected Poetry,* 288–289.

80. Davenport, *Azalia,* 69.

81. Mariam DeCosta-Willis, ed., *The Memphis Diary of Ida B. Wells* (Boston: Beacon, 1995), 26, 31, 44, respectively. When Wells did not use formal names of her suitors in her diary, she identified them by initials.

82. See entries in Broadhead, *Journals of Charles W. Chesnutt.*

83. ARM to PLD, July 6, 1895, in Metcalf, "The Letters," I, 54.

84. Hattie Rutherford to John Brown Watson, April 27, 1907, Watson Collection, Box 1, Folder 2.

85. Virginia Cunningham, *Paul Laurence Dunbar: The Poet and His Song* (New York: Dodd, Mead, 1953), 95. See also Maud Clark to PLD, April 12, 1895, in PLD Collection, reel 1.

86. PLD to ARM, June 25, 1895, in Metcalf, "The Letters," I, 51.

87. Quoted in Ridgely Torrence, *The Story of John Hope* (New York: Macmillan, 1948), 15. An excellent discussion of color as a factor in upper-crust African American society is found in Willard B. Gatewood, *Aristocrats of Color: The Black Elite, 1890–1920* (Bloomington: Indiana University Press, 1990), 149–181.

88. Tate, *The Works of Katherine Davis Chapman Tillman,* 174–175.

89. Brodhead, *Journals of Charles Chesnutt,* 174–175.

90. Gutman, *Black Family in Slavery and Freedom,* 391.

91. Lavinia Hart, "How to Win a Man," *Cosmopolitan,* 35 (September 1903), 548.

92. Brodhead, *Journals of Charles Chesnutt,* 68.

93. PLD to ARM, June 25, 1895, in Metcalf, "The Letters," I, 51. Paul included the poem in *Majors and Minors* (1895). It is found in Dunbar, *Complete Poems,* 131–134; Braxton, *Collected Poetry,* 82–83.

In 1903, in poor health and short of funds, Paul sold "When Malindy Sings" to his publisher for one thousand dollars. See Dodd, Mead and Company to PLD, April 20, 1903, PLD Collection, reel 1.

94. PLD to ARM, July 9, 1895, in Metcalf, "The Letters," I, 58. Later the African American author Charles Chesnutt also became a member.

95. PLD to ARM, August 14, 1895, in Metcalf, "The Letters," I, 63.

96. Lorin Wright to PLD, June 5, 1895, PLD Collection, reel 1.

97. C. W. Dustin to PLD, June 17, 1895, PLD Collection, reel 1.

98. PLD to Matilda Dunbar, September 21, 1895, PLD Collection, reel 1.

99. Maud Clark to PLD, April 12, 1895, PLD Collection, reel 1.

100. PLD to ARM, August 14, 1895, in Metcalf, "The Letters," I, 64.

101. PLD to ARM, June 21, 1895, in Metcalf, "The Letters," I, 66.

102. PLD to ARM, January 27, 1896, in Metcalf, "The Letters," I, 78.

103. PLD to ARM, May 4, 1896, in Metcalf, "The Letters," I, 95.

104. The author's interview with Stephen DiZio, M.D., January 16, 1996, Providence, Rhode Island; the author's telephone interview with James Ralph, M.D., Baltimore, Maryland, January 20, 1996. See also American Psychiatric Association, *Diagnostic Criteria from DSM-IV* (Washington, DC: The Association, 1994), 161–183.

105. PLD to ARM, February 16, 1896, in Metcalf, "The Letters," I, 80; PLD to ARM, March 23, 1896, in Metcalf, "The Letters," I, 85.

106. Metcalf, "The Letters," I, 12; Best, "Crossing the Color Line," 202.

107. Helen M. Chesnutt, *Charles Waddell Chesnutt: Pioneer of the Color Line* (Chapel Hill: University of North Carolina Press, 1952), 31, 41, respectively.

108. Cited in James Horton, *Free People of Color: Inside the African-American Community* (Washington, DC: Smithsonian Institution Press, 1993), 102–103. See also Rosalyn Terborg-Penn, "Black Males Perspective on Nineteenth-Century Women," in Sharon Harley and Rosalyn Terborg-Penn, eds., *The Afro-American Woman: Struggles and Images* (Port Washington, NY: Kennikat, 1978), 28–35; and "How to Keep Women at Home," *Colored American Magazine* 14 (January 1908), 7–8.

109. For Frederick Douglass's comments on Paul's mental health, see Rebekah Baldwin to PLD, September 4, 1894; Rebekah Baldwin to PLD, December 5, 1894, both in PLD Collection, reel 1.

110. The poem was published in Paul's second book, *Majors and Minors.* It is found in Dunbar, *Complete Poems,* 114–115; and Braxton, *Collected Poetry,* 72.

111. PLD to ARM, May 23, 1895, in Metcalf, "The Letters," I, 41.

112. Myrtle Hart to PLD, July 4, 1895, PLD Collection, reel 1.

113. Nettie Maud Christy to PLD, August 18, 1895, PLD Collection, reel 1.

114. MFW to PLD, August 20, 1895, PLD Collection, reel 1.

115. PLD to ARM, October 13, 1895, in Metcalf, "The Letters," I, 68–69.

116. AMD to PLD March 26, 1898, in Metcalf, "The Letters," II, 553; PLD to ARM, January 27, 1896, in Metcalf, "The Letters," I, 78.

117. William Burns to PLD, October 14, 1894, in PLD Collection, reel 1.

118. Quoted in Ellen K. Rothman, *Hands and Hearts: A History of Courtship in America* (New York: Basic Books, 1984), 190.

119. McCabe, *Household Encyclopedia,* 462.

120. PLD to ARM, June 4, 1896, in Metcalf, "The Letters," I, 98.

121. Maud Clark to PLD, March 10, 1895, March 22, 1895, April 2, 1895, April 12, 1895, in PLD Collection, reel 1.

122. Rebekah Baldwin to PLD, September 24, 1893, PLD Collection, reel 1.

123. Only Rebekah Baldwin's letters to Paul survive. Their correspondence, dating from September 24, 1893, to August 21, 1895, consists of twenty-six letters.

124. Best, "Crossing the Color Line," 107; Gossie Hudson, "A Biography of Paul Laurence Dunbar" (Ph.D. diss., Ohio State University, 1970), 67 ff.

125. Rebekah Baldwin to PLD, July 30, 1895, PLD Collection, reel 1.

126. Rebekah Baldwin to PLD, October 27, 1894, PLD Collection, reel 1; Hattie Rutherford to John Brown Watson, Thursday Night (1907), John Brown Watson Collection, Box 1, Folder 2.

127. Rebekah Baldwin to PLD, December 3, 1893, December 13, 1893; PLD to Matilda Dunbar, October 15, 1896, PLD Collection, reel 1.

128. Rebekah Baldwin to PLD, January 19, 1895, PLD Collection, reel 1.

129. Rebekah Baldwin to PLD, July 30, 1895, PLD Collection, reel 1.

130. Rebekah Baldwin to PLD, October 7, 1894, PLD Collection, reel 1.

131. Rebekah Baldwin to PLD, January 19, 1895, PLD Collection, reel 1.

132. Rebekah Baldwin to PLD, February 13, 1895, PLD Collection, reel 1.

133. Rebekah Baldwin to PLD, February 13, 1895, PLD Collection, reel 1.

134. Rebekah Baldwin to PLD, July 1, 1895, PLD Collection, reel 1.

135. PLD to ARM, June 6, 1895, in Metcalf, "The Letters," I, 45–47.

136. Rebekah Baldwin to PLD, July 10, 1895, PLD Collection, reel 1.

137. PLD to ARM, July 25, 1895, in Metcalf, "The Letters," I, 60–61.

138. Rebekah Baldwin to PLD, July 30, 1895, PLD Collection, reel 1.

139. Rebekah Baldwin to PLD, August 21, 1895, PLD Collection, reel 1.

140. PLD to ARM, October 13, 1895, in Metcalf, "The Letters," I, 68–69.

141. PLD to Maud Wilkinson, October 24, 1896; also, James Covington to Jean Blackwell, June 11, 1956, both in the Paul Laurence Dunbar Collection, Arthur A. Schomberg Research Center, New York Public Library.

142. Hull, *Works of Alice Dunbar-Nelson*, III, 197.

143. Rebekah Baldwin to PLD, October 7, 1894, PLD Collection, reel 1.

144. Hattie Rutherford to John Brown Watson, April 27, 1907, John Brown Watson Collection, Box 1, Folder 2.

145. DeCosta-Willis, *Memphis Diary*, 31–32, 35.

146. Rebekah Baldwin to PLD, October 7, 1894, PLD Collection, reel 1. Rebekah married a physician sometime after the turn of the century.

147. PLD to ARM, January 3, 1898, cited in Best, "Crossing the Color Line," 161.

148. Alice Ruth Moore, "Midnight," *A.M.E. Church Review*, October 1896, 226–227; Paul Laurence Dunbar, "Just Whistle a Bit," *A.M.E. Church Review*, October 1896, 228.

149. Mary Church Terrell (1863–1954) was founder and first president of

the National Association of Colored Women (1896). When Alice set up house-keeping with Paul in Washington, D.C., Terrell was their next-door neighbor. For a nontraditional interpretation of the late-nineteenth-century African American women's club movement, see Deborah Gray White's insightful essay, "The Cost of Club Work: The Price of Black Feminism," in *Visible Women: Essays on American Activism,* ed. Nancy Hewitt and Suzanne Lebsock (Urbana: University of Illinois Press, 1993), 247–269.

150. Alice Dunbar-Nelson to Benjamin Brawley, undated, incomplete letter, Benjamin Brawley Collection, Moorland-Spingarn Research Center, Howard University. If Alice applied to Wellesley, there is no extant record.

151. PLD to ARM, October 19, 1896, in Metcalf, "The Letters," I, 108.

152. Metcalf, "The Letters," I, 110.

153. "Here and There," *Colored American Magazine,* September 1900, 258. See also the legend under Sarah Dudley Pettey's photograph and the following pages (which are unpaged), in Daniel Wallace Culp, ed., *Twentieth-Century Negro Literature* (1902) (reprint, New York: Arno, 1969).

154. Hull, *Works of Alice Dunbar-Nelson,* III, 204.

155. PLD to ARM, March 26, 1897, in Metcalf, "The Letters," I, 131.

156. Hull, *Works of Alice Dunbar-Nelson,* III, 204.

157. PLD to Matilda Dunbar, February 10, 1897, PLD Collection, reel 1.

158. PLD to ARM, February 4, 1898, in Metcalf, "The Letters," I, 42.

159. Alice Dunbar-Nelson to Benjamin Brawley, undated, incomplete letter, Benjamin Brawley Collection, Moorland-Spingarn Research Center, Howard University.

160. This custom of a woman giving her fiancé a love token was popular c. 1840–1870.

161. PLD to ARM, August 29, 1897, in Metcalf, "The Letters," I, 92.

162. PLD to Matilda Dunbar, February 10, 1897, PLD Collection, reel 1.

163. Hull, *Works of Alice Dunbar-Nelson,* I, 85, 86, 87.

Notes to Chapter 4

1. Paul Laurence Dunbar to Alice Ruth Moore, December 1, 1897, in Eugene W. Metcalf, "The Letters of Paul and Alice Dunbar: A Private History," 2 vols. (Ph.D. diss., University of California, Irvine, 1973), I, 262. This source is cited hereafter as Metcalf, "The Letters." The principals are cited as PLD (Paul Laurence Dunbar) and ARM (Alice Ruth Moore). After her marriage, Alice is cited as AMD (Alice Moore Dunbar).

2. Mrs. M. E. Lee, "The Home-Maker," *A.M.E. Church Review* 8:1 (July 1891), 63–66.

3. Ellen K. Rothman, *Hands and Hearts: A History of Courtship in America* (New York: Basic Books, 1984), 150–151.

4. Gloria T. Hull, ed., *The Works of Alice Dunbar-Nelson* (New York: Oxford University Press, 1988), I, 25. The essay was published in Alice's first book, *Violets and Other Tales* (1895).

5. Alice Dunbar-Nelson to Benjamin Brawley, undated, incomplete letter, Benjamin Brawley Collection, Moorland-Spingarn Research Center, Howard University. Alice was assigned to Public School 83 in Brooklyn.

6. PLD to ARM, August 2, 1896, in Metcalf, "The Letters," I, 101.

7. On Alice's publication record, see Ora Williams, "Works by and about Alice Ruth (Moore) Dunbar-Nelson: A Bibliography," *CLA Journal* 19:6 (March 1976), 322–326; R. Ora Williams, ed., *An Alice Dunbar-Nelson Reader* (Washington, D.C.: University Press of America, 1979), x; Ruby Ora Williams, "An In-Depth Portrait of Alice Dunbar-Nelson" (Ph.D. diss., University of California, Irvine, 1974), 78–84.

8. Margaret Murray Washington worked as a teacher-administrator at Tuskegee before her marriage to Booker T. Washington, who founded the school in 1881.

9. AMD to PLD, March 16, 1898, in Metcalf, "The Letters," II, 515.

10. PLD to ARM, March 7, 1897, in Metcalf, "The Letters," I, 121. Also PLD to ARM, February 20, 1897, I, 119.

11. PLD to ARM, February 20, 1897, in Metcalf, "The Letters," I, 117.

12. PLD to ARM, February 20, 1897, in Metcalf, "The Letters," I, 119.

13. PLD to ARM, March 7, 1897, in Metcalf, "The Letters," I, 122–123. Also PLD to ARM, March 26, 1897, in Metcalf, "The Letters," I, 133.

14. PLD to ARM, March 7, 1897, in Metcalf, "The Letters," I, 121.

15. ARM to PLD, June 8, 1897, in Metcalf, "The Letters," I, 158.

16. ARM to PLD, June 19, 1897, in Metcalf, "The Letters," I, 163–164.

17. John Hope to Lugenia Burns, June 10, 1896; John Hope to Lugenia Burns, August 19, 1896; John Hope to Lugenia Burns, November 19, 1896, in The Papers of John and Lugenia Burns Hope, ed. Alton Hornsby (Frederick, MD: University Publications of America, 1984), reel 13. This vast collection of love letters (cited hereafter as Papers of John and Lugenia) dates from 1896 to 1913. Mainly they are John's letters to Lugenia. Only a few of her letters to him are included.

On their relationship, see also Jacqueline Anne Rouse, *Lugenia Burns Hope: Black Southern Reformer* (Athens: University of Georgia Press, 1989), 18–40; Ridgely Torrence, The Story of John Hope (New York: Macmillan, 1948), 102–103, 110–112, 116, 118–120.

18. John Hope to Lugenia Burns, June 10, 1896, Papers of John and Lugenia, reel 13.

19. AMD to PLD, March 19, 1898, in Metcalf, "The Letters," II, 531.

20. ARM to PLD, January 15, 1898, in Metcalf, "The Letters," I, 365.

21. ARM to PLD, January 15, 1898, in Metcalf, "The Letters," I, 368.

22. PLD to ARM, November 7, 1897, in Metcalf, "The Letters," I, 236.

23. Mary Church Terrell discussed the "A" list of Washington high society in her article, "Society among the Colored People of Washington," *Voice of the Negro,* April 1904, 150–156. See also Paul Laurence Dunbar, "Negro Society in Washington," *Saturday Evening Post,* December 14, 1901, 9. On how Washington's mainstream population regarded the black elite, see "Color Prejudice in Washington," *Colored American,* February 2, 1902, 8.

24. ARM to PLD, January 1, 1898, in Metcalf, "The Letters," I, 325.

25. PLD to ARM, March 16, 2897, in Metcalf, "The Letters," I, 125. See also PLD to ARM, May 14, 1897, in Metcalf, "The Letters," I, 149.

26. See, for example, Charlotte Perkins Gilman, *Women and Economics* (New York: Harper and Row, 1966); Thorstein Veblen, *The Theory of the Leisure Class* (New York: Modern Library, 1934).

27. Joanne M. Braxton, ed., *The Collected Poetry of Paul Laurence Dunbar* (Charlottesville: University of Virginia Press, 1993), 55–56; Paul Laurence Dunbar, *The Complete Poems of Paul Laurence Dunbar* (New York: Dodd, Mead, 1948), 86–87.

28. Braxton, *Collected Poetry,* 55–56; Dunbar, *Completed Poems,* 86–87.

29. An excellent examination of the debate on traditional marriage is found in Sondra Herman, "Loving Courtship or the Marriage Market? The Ideal and Its Critics, 1871–1911," *American Quarterly* 25:2 (1873), 235–252. See also Michael M. McCall, "Courtship as Social Exchange: Some Historical Comparisons," in *Kinship and Family Organization,* ed. Bernard Farber (New York: John Wiley and Sons, 1966), 190–200.

30. John Hope to Lugenia Burns, December 21, 1896, Papers of John and Lugenia, reel 13.

31. Mrs. N. F. Mossell, *The Work of the Afro-American Woman* (New York: Oxford University Press, 1988), 117, 125.

32. Quoted in White, "Cost of Club Work," 251.

33. PLD TO ARM, March 26, 1897, in Metcalf, "The Letters," I, 132. Before the tragic decline of Paul's health caused by tuberculosis, alcoholism, and mental illness, he had a reputation for writing rapidly and well. He literally composed poems in minutes that were later published.

34. PLD to ARM, March 26, 1897, in Metcalf, "The Letters," I, 131. The

poem was published as "Little Brown Baby" and appeared in Paul's fourth poetry volume, *Lyrics of the Hearthside* (New York: Dodd, Mead, 1899). It is reprinted in Braxton, *Collected Poetry,* 134–135, and Dunbar, *Completed Poems,* 214–215.

35. John Hope to Lugenia Burns, February 17, 1897, Papers of John and Lugenia, reel 13.

36. White, "Cost of Club Work," 256; John Hope to Lugenia Burns, September 30, 1897, Papers of John and Lugenia, reel 13; Amelia Douglass to Matilda Dunbar, October 19, 1900, Paul Laurence Dunbar Collection, Ohio Historical Society, Microfilm Edition, reel 2. This source is cited hereafter as PLD Collection.

37. James H. A. Johnson, "Woman's Exalted Station," *A.M.E. Church Review* 8:4 (April 1892), 402.

38. Johnson, "Woman's Exalted Station," 403–404.

39. PLD to ARM, February 20, 1897, in Metcalf, "The Letters," I, 118.

40. PLD to ARM, May 14, 1897, in Metcalf, "The Letters," I, 148.

41. AMD to PLD, March 29, 1898; AMD to PLD, March 31, 1898; both in Metcalf, "The Letters," II, 568, 573–574, respectively.

42. PLD to ARM, October 10, 1897, in Metcalf, "The Letters," I, 221.

43. AMD to PLD, undated but probably written in 1898, PLD Collection, reel 8.

44. PLD to ARM, December 6, 1897, in Metcalf, "The Letters," I, 272.

45. PLD to ARM, May 11, 1897, in Metcalf, "The Letters," I, 144–145.

46. PLD to AMD, March 28, 1898, in Metcalf, "The Letters," I, 546.

47. PLD to ARM, March 7, 1897, in Metcalf, "The Letters," I, 122–123.

48. Paul Laurence Dunbar, *The Love of Landry* (1900) (reprint, Mnemosyne, 1969), 103.

49. PLD to ARM, February 20, 1897; PLD to ARM, July 20, 1897; PLD to ARM, March 7, 1897; all in Metcalf, "The Letters," I, 118, 181, 121, respectively.

50. PLD to ARM, December 12, 1897, in Metcalf, "The Letters," I, 280.

51. PLD to ARM, February 27, 1898, in Metcalf, "The Letters," II, 479.

52. PLD to ARM, February 3, 1898, in Metcalf, "The Letters," I, 422.

53. ARM to PLD, January 15, 1898, in Metcalf, "The Letters," I, 366.

54. ARM to PLD, January 15, 1898, in Metcalf, "The Letters," I, 366.

55. PLD to ARM, December 19, 1897; PLD to ARM, December 10, 1897; PLD to ARM, January 3, 1897, all in Metcalf, "The Letters," I, 300, 221, 331, respectively.

56. PLD to ARM, December 24, 1897, in Metcalf, "The Letters," I, 222.

57. PLD to ARM, August 2, 1896, in Metcalf, "The Letters," I, 101; Dunbar, *The Love of Landry,* 105.

58. Writer's Literary Bureau to PLD, February 20, 1900, PLD Collection, reel 1. The bureau liked the play's premise, but thought it needed extensive rewriting.

59. Felton O. Best, "Crossing the Color Line: A Biography of Paul Laurence Dunbar, 1872–1906" (Ph.D. diss., Ohio State University, 1992), 155.

60. PLD to Matilda Dunbar, February 18, 1897, PLD Collection, reel 1.

61. PLD to ARM, June 22, 1897, in Metcalf, "The Letters," I, 166.

62. PLD to Matilda Dunbar, October 2, 1897, PLD Collection, reel 1; PLD to ARM, December 29, 1897, in Metcalf, "The Letters," I, 227; Best, "Crossing the Color Line," 157.

63. Sharon Harley, "For the Good of Family and Race: Gender, Work, and Domestic Roles in the Black Community, 1880–1930," *Signs* 15:2 (Winter 1990), 346, n. 26.

64. PLD to ARM, January 18, 1898, in Metcalf, "The Letters," I, 373; Braxton, *Collected Poems,* 102; Dunbar, *Complete Poems,* 162–163; Maya Angelou, *I Know Why the Caged Bird Sings* (New York: Random House, 1969).

65. ARM to PLD, October 6, 1897, in Metcalf, "The Letters," I, 198.

66. ARM to PLD, October 10, 1897, in Metcalf, "The Letters," I, 207.

67. PLD to ARM, October 24, 1897; ARM to PLD, October 10, 1897; both in Metcalf, "The Letters," I, 221, 207, respectively.

68. ARM to PLD, January 12, 1897, in Metcalf, "The Letters," I, 358.

69. PLD to Matilda Dunbar, November 9(?), 1897; PLD to Matilda Dunbar, June 14, 1897; PLD to Matilda Dunbar, July 30, 1897; all in PLD Collection, reel 1.

70. PLD to ARM, January 3, 1898; PLD to AMD, March 9, 1989; both in Metcalf, "The Letters," I, 331, and II, 495, respectively.

71. Robert Burton to Matilda Dunbar, December 3, 1898. See also Lizzie Burton to Matilda Dunbar, March 10, 1898; Lizzie Burton to Matilda Dunbar, June 22, 1898; Elnora McGregor to Matilda Dunbar, March 4, 1898; Elnora McGregor to Matilda Dunbar, July 3, 1898; Elnora McGregor to Matilda Dunbar, August 19, 1898; Elnora McGregor to Matilda Dunbar, September 28, 1898; Rebecca Voss to Matilda Dunbar, May 16, 1989; all in PLD Collection, reel 1.

72. E. G. (?) to Matilda Dunbar, November 28(?), 1897, PLD Collection, reel 1.

73. ARM to PLD, October 24, 1897, in Metcalf, "The Letters," I, 219.

74. PLD to ARM, December 10, 1897, in Metcalf, "The Letters," I, 227.

75. ARM to PLD, October 10, 1897, in Metcalf, "The Letters," I, 208.

76. Rouse, *Lugenia Burns Hope,* 20–23.

77. Rouse, *Lugenia Burns Hope,* 21.

78. John Hope to Lugenia Burns, January 19, 1897, Papers of John and Lugenia.

79. P. Moore to PLD, November 3, 1897, PLD Collection, reel 5.

80. PLD to ARM, November 7, 1897, in Metcalf, "The Letters," I, 236.

81. PLD to ARM, November 16, 1897, in Metcalf, "The Letters," I, 241.

82. PLD to ARM, November 22, 1897, in Metcalf, "The Letters," I, 250–251.

83. PLD to ARM, November 19, 1897, in Metcalf, "The Letters," I, 242.

84. PLD to ARM, November 19, 1897, in Metcalf, "The Letters," I, 242, 244.

85. Patricia L. N. Donat and John D'Emilio, "A Feminist Redefinition of Rape and Sexual Assault: Historical Foundations and Change," *Journal of Social Issues* 48:1 (1992), 11.

86. Sally Gold and Martha Wyatt, "The Rape System: Old Roles and New Times," *Catholic University Law Review* 27 (1978), 695; citing Deuteronomy 22: 23–27. On unchaste nineteenth-century women as damaged goods in the marriage mart, see Keith Thomas, "The Double Standard," *Journal of the History of Ideas* 20 (April 1959), 210.

87. Laura F. Edwards, "Sexual Violence, Gender, Reconstruction, and the Extension of Patriarchy in Granville County, North Carolina," *North Carolina Historical Review* 68:3 (July 1991), 253.

88. PLD to ARM, November 19, 1897, in Metcalf, "The Letters," I, 242.

89. This definition of rape is found in Diana E. H. Russell, *Rape in Marriage* (New York: Macmillan, 1982), 1, 2.

90. Susan Brownmiller, *Against Our Will: Men, Women and Rape* (New York: Simon and Schuster, 1975); Diana E. H. Russell, *The Politics of Rape* (New York: Stein and Day, 1975).

91. Peggy Reeves Sanday, "The Socio-Cultural Context of Rape: A Cross-Cultural Study," *Journal of Social Issues* 37:4 (1981), 19–25.

92. ARM to PLD, December 18, 1897, in Metcalf, "The Letters," I, 297.

93. Alice's niece, Pauline Alice Young, inherited the letters. Ms. Young allowed the Ohio Historical Society to microfilm the documents. They became part of the Society's Paul Laurence Dunbar Collection, a source frequently cited in this manuscript. Alice's original letters are in the archives/ manuscript division of the University of Delaware Library.

94. PLD to ARM, November 22, 1897, in Metcalf, "The Letters," I, 242.

95. PLD to ARM, November 26, 1897; PLD to ARM, December 5, 1897; both in Metcalf, "The Letters," I, 257, 269, respectively.

96. PLD to ARM, December 26, 1897, in Metcalf, "The Letters," I, 288.

97. PLD to ARM, November 25, 1897, in Metcalf, "The Letters," I, 255, 253. See also PLD to ARM, November 22, 1897, in Metcalf, "The Letters," I, 251.

98. John M. Young, *Our Deportment, Or the Manners, Conduct and Dress of the Most Refined Society* (Detroit: F. B. Dickerson, 1883), 423–424.

99. PLD to ARM, November 25, 1897; PLD to ARM, November 26, 1897; both in Metcalf, "The Letters," I, 253, 257, respectively.

100. PLD to ARM, November 26, 1897, in Metcalf, "The Letters," I, 257. See also PLD to ARM, November 20, 1897; PLD to ARM, November 25, 1897; PLD to ARM, December 1, 1897; all in Metcalf, "The Letters," I, 247, 253–255, 262, respectively.

101. PLD to ARM, December 7, 1897, in Metcalf, "The Letters," I, 276.

102. Robin Warshaw, *I Never Called It Rape* (New York: Harper and Row), 1988.

103. Quoted in White, "Cost of Club Work," 255.

104. White, "Cost of Club Work," 255. Black newspapers usually carried unflattering jokes about women of color. See Bess Beatty, "Black Perspectives of American Women: The View from Black Newspapers, 1865–1900," *Maryland Historian* 9 (1978), 40–41.

105. PLD to ARM, December 1, 1897, in Metcalf, "The Letters," I, 262.

106. AMD to PLD, March 28, 1898, in Metcalf, "The Letters," II, 562.

107. E. Azalia Hackley, *The Colored Girl Beautiful* (Kansas: Burton Publishing, 1916), 109–111; E. M. Woods, *The Negro in Etiquette: A Novelty* (St. Louis: Buxton and Skinner, 1899), 62–63; Professor and Mrs. J. W. Gibson, *Golden Thoughts on Chastity and Procreation* (Naperville, IL: J. L. Nichols, 1903), 86–87.

108. Deuteronomy 22: 23–27 (King James), quoted in Gold and Wyatt, "The Rape System," 698–701.

109. Warshaw, *I Never Called It Rape,* 63.

110. Warshaw, *I Never Called It Rape,* 63.

111. Stevi Jackson, "The Social Context of Rape: Sexual Scripts and Motivation," *Women's Studies International Quarterly* 1:1 (1978), cited in Sylvia Walby, *Theorizing Patriarchy* (Oxford: Basil Blackwell, 1990), 115.

112. PLD to ARM, November 25, 1897, in Metcalf, "The Letters," I, 253.

113. ARM to PLD, January 15, 1898, in Metcalf, "The Letters," I, 366–367.

114. Quoted in Rothman, *Hands and Heart,* 166 (footnote).

115. Mary Church Terrell, *A Colored Woman in a White World* (Washington, D.C.: Ransdell, 1940), 103–104; Mae B. Peckham to Hattie Rutherford, August 4, 1907, John Brown Watson Collection, Box 62, John Hay Library, Brown University.

116. Hattie Rutherford to John Brown Watson, September 12, 1907, Watson Collection, Box 1, Folder 2.

117. Alfreda Duster, *Crusade for Justice: The Autobiography of Ida B. Wells* (Chicago: University of Chicago Press, 1970), 239–240.

118. Dorothy Sterling, ed., *The Trouble They Seen: The Story of Reconstruction in the Words of African Americans* (New York: Da Capo, 1994), 222, citing the *New Era,* May 26, 1870.

119. Adelaide M. Cromwell, *The Other Brahmins: Boston's Black Upper Class, 1750–1950* (Fayetteville: University of Arkansas Press, 1994), 56.

120. Hattie Rutherford to John Brown Watson, September 12, 1907, Watson Collection, Box 1, Folder 2. See also the home wedding of Maude Trotter and Charles Gould Stewart in Cromwell, *The Other Brahmins,* 56, and the 1878 home wedding of Senator Blanche K. Bruce and Josephine Willson in Willard B. Gatewood, *Aristocrats of Color: The Black Elite, 1880–1920* (Bloomington: Indiana University Press, 1990), 5–6.

121. Terrell, *A Colored Woman in a White World,* 104.

122. AMD to PLD, March 29, 1898, in Metcalf, "The Letters," II, 566.

123. John H. Young, *Our Deportment or the Manners, Conduct and Dress of the Most Refined Society* (Detroit: F. B. Dickerson, 1883), 183; James McCabe, *Household Encyclopedia of Business & Social Forms* (Philadelphia: Standford Publishing, 1890), 463.

124. PLD to ARM, December 7, 1897, in Metcalf, "The Letters," I, 276.

125. PLD to ARM, December 19, 1897; ARM to PLD, December 31, 1897; PLD to ARM December 27, 1897; PLD to ARM, January 3, 1898; all in Metcalf, "The Letters," I, 291, 293, 299, 322, 310, respectively.

126. PLD to ARM, February 22, 1897, in Metcalf, "The Letters," I, 466.

127. PLD to ARM, December 12, 1897, in Metcalf, "The Letters," I, 279.

128. PLD to ARM, February 19, 1898; PLD to ARM, February 21, 1898; both in Metcalf, "The Letters," I, 459, 463, respectively.

129. ARM to PLD, January 15, 1898, in Metcalf, "The Letters," I, 367.

130. PLD to ARM, February 19, 1898, in Metcalf, "The Letters," I, 459.

131. Brodhead, *Journals of Charles Chesnutt,* 63–64, 68.

132. ARM to PLD, March 1, 1898, in Metcalf, "The Letters," I, 489.

133. John Hope to Lugenia Burns, April 26, 1897, Papers of John and Lugenia, reel 13.

134. John Hope to Lugenia Burns, January 19, 1897, Papers of John and Lugenia, reel 13.

135. Quoted in Lystra, *Searching the Heart,* 114.

136. John Hope to Lugenia Burns, November 20, 1897, Papers of John and Lugenia, reel 13.

Notes to Chapter 5

137. John Hope to Lugenia Burns, May 19, 1897, Papers of John and Lugenia, reel 13.

138. ARM to PLD, December 18, 1897, in Metcalf, "The Letters," I, 297.

139. PLD to ARM, March 2, 1897, in Metcalf, "The Letters," I, 493.

140. PLD to AMD, March 9, 1898, in Metcalf, "The Letters," II, 495.

141. PLD to AMD, March 9, 1898, in Metcalf, "The Letters," II, 495.

142. AMD to PLD, April 6, 1898; AMD to PLD, March 13, 1898, both in Metcalf, "The Letters," II, 578, 500, respectively.

143. Brawley, *Paul Laurence Dunbar: Poet of His People* (Port Washington, NY: Kennikat, 1936), 150. The author states that Alice gave him this information.

144. ARM to PLD, January 15, 1897, in Metcalf, "The Letters," I, 365.

Notes to Chapter 5

1. Alice Dunbar, "Ellen Fenton," in *The Works of Alice Dunbar-Nelson*, vol. III, ed. by Gloria T. Hull (New York: Oxford University Press, 1988), 48, 50.

2. Hull, *Works of Alice Dunbar-Nelson*, III, 230.

3. Alice Dunbar, *The Goodness of St. Rocque and Other Stories* (New York: Dodd, Mead, 1899).

4. Paul Laurence Dunbar, *The Uncalled* (New York: Dodd, Mead, 1899); Paul Laurence Dunbar, *Lyrics of the Hearthside* (New York: Dodd, Mead, 1899).

5. Alice Moore Dunbar to Paul Laurence Dunbar, September 13, 1898, in Eugene W. Metcalf, "The Letters of Paul and Alice Dunbar: A Private History," 2 vols. (Ph.D. diss., University of California, Irvine, 1973), II, 678. This source is cited hereafter as Metcalf, "The Letters." The principals are cited as PLD (Paul Laurence Dunbar), and AMD (Alice Moore Dunbar). Before her marriage, Alice is cited as ARM (Alice Ruth Moore).

6. AMD to PLD, September 13, 1898, in Metcalf, "The Letters," II, 679.

7. Quoted in Robert L. Griswold, "Law, Sex, Cruelty, and Divorce in Victorian America, 1840–1900," *American Quarterly* 38 (1986), 741, note 12.

8. Cited in Griswold, "Law, Sex, Cruelty," 722.

9. C. P. Selden, "Romance after Marriage," *New England Magazine* 13 (c. 1900–1904), 593.

10. Selden, "Romance after Marriage," 594.

11. Selden, "Romance after Marriage," 594.

12. Seldon, "Romance after Marriage," 597.

13. Department of Commerce and Labor, Bureau of the Census, *Marriage and Divorce, 1867–1906* (Washington, DC: Government Printing Office, 1909), II, 608.

14. Griswold, "Law, Sex, Cruelty," 722.

15. Griswold, "Law, Sex, Cruelty," 726.

16. Katherine Davis Tillman, "Afro-American Women and Their Work," *A.M.E. Church Review* 11 (April 189?), 477.

17. Mary Church Terrell, "What Role Is the Educated Negro Woman to Play in the Uplifting of Her Race?" in *Twentieth-Century Negro Literature,* ed. by Daniel Wallace Culp (1902) (New York: Arno, 1969), 175.

18. Elizabeth Pleck, "Wife Beating in Nineteenth-Century America," *Victimology* 4:1 (1979), 66, 65.

19. "Divorce," *A.M.E. Church Review* 8:4 (April 1892), 507.

20. W. E. B. Du Bois, *The Autobiography of W. E. B. Du Bois: A Soliloquy on Viewing My Life from the Last Decade of Its First Century* (N.P.: International Publishers, 1968), 281.

21. Prof. and Mrs. J. W. Gibson, *Golden Thoughts on Chastity and Procreation: Including Heredity, Prenatal Influences, Etc. Etc.* (Naperville, IL: J. L. Nichols, 1914), 162.

22. Gibson, *Golden Thoughts,* 162.

23. Gibson, *Golden Thoughts,* 159.

24. Gibson, *Golden Thoughts,* 159.

25. Dunbar, *Complete Poems,* 392.

26. L. A. Scruggs, "Influence of Negro Women in the Home," in Scruggs, *Women of Distinction: Remarkable Women in Works and Invincible in Character* (Raleigh, NC: L. A. Scruggs, 1893), 380.

27. PLD to AMD, March 7, 1899, in Metcalf, "The Letters," II, 762.

28. Alice Dunbar, "The Decision," in Hull, *The Works of Alice Dunbar-Nelson,* III, 198.

29. Paul Laurence Dunbar, *The Complete Poems of Paul Laurence Dunbar* (New York: Dodd, Mead, 1948), 392. The poem appeared in Dunbar's *Lyrics of Sunshine and Shadow* (New York: Dodd, Mead, 1905).

30. William Noel Johnson, *Common Sense in the Home* (Cincinnati: Press of Jennings and Pye, 1902), 26–31.

31. Johnson, *Common Sense in the Home,* 38.

32. ARM to PLD, October 27, 1897, in Metcalf, "The Letters," I, 217.

33. John Hope to Lugenia Burns, January 4, 1897, The Papers of John and Lugenia Burns Hope, ed. by Alton Hornsby (Frederick, MD: University Publications of America, 1984), reel 13.

34. John Hope to Lugenia Burns, January 4, 1897, Papers of John and Lugenia, reel 13.

35. *Montgomery County Sentinel,* March 20, 1857, quoted in George M. Anderson, S.J., "Premature Matrimony: The Hasty Marriage of Betie Ander-

son and Philemon Cribb Griffith," *Maryland Historical Magazine* 83:4 (Winter 1988), 389.

36. PLD to AMD, March 14, 1898; PLD to AMD, March 24, 1898; AMD to PLD, March 26, 1898, all in Metcalf, "The Letters," II, 509, 549, 555, respectively.

37. J. R. Miller, *The Wedded Life* (Philadelphia: Presbyterian Board of Publication and Sabbath-School Work, 1886), 15–16.

38. Anderson, "Premature Matrimony," 369, 373.

39. AMD to PLD, March 26, 1898; AMD to PLD, March 28, 1898, both in Metcalf, "The Letters," II, 552, 561, respectively.

40. PLD to AMD, March 9, 1898, in Metcalf, "The Letters," II, 495.

41. PLD to AMD, March 13, 1898, in Metcalf, "The Letters," II, 503.

42. PLD to ARM, March 9, 1898; AMD to PLD, c. March 23, 1898, both in Metcalf, "The Letters," II, 495–496, 543, respectively.

43. On Alice's salary, see AMD to PLD, March 22, 1898, in Metcalf, "The Letters," II, 538.

44. Bishop L. J. Coppin, *Unwritten History* (1919) (reprint, New York: Negro Universities Press, 1968), 358.

45. "How to Keep Women at Home," *Colored American Magazine* 14:6 (January 1908), 8.

46. ARM to PLD, October 10, 1897, in Metcalf, "The Letters," I, 208.

47. AMD to PLD, March 31, 1898, in Metcalf, "The Letters," II, 571.

48. AMD to PLD, March 16, 1898, in Metcalf, "The Letters," II, 515.

49. PLD to AMD, March 13, 1898; PLD to AMD, March 19, 1898; PLD to AMD, March 21, 1898, all in Metcalf, "The Letters," II, 505, 533, 536, respectively.

50. John Hope to Lugenia Burns, November 20, 1897, Papers of John and Lugenia, reel 13.

51. Du Bois, *Autobiography of W. E. B. Du Bois,* 281.

52. Nina Gomer Du Bois to W. E. B. Du Bois, November 13, 1910, The Papers of W. E. B. Du Bois, University of Massachusetts at Amherst, Microfilm Edition, reel 1, Frame 792.

53. Allison Davis, "The Intellectual as Leader: The Lonely Warrior, W. E. B. Du Bois," in Davis, *Leadership, Love and Aggression* (New York: Harcourt Brace Jovanovich, 1983), 114–115.

54. Davis, "The Intellectual as Leader," 174, 116–117.

55. John Hope to Lugenia Burns, December 22, 1897, Papers of John and Lugenia, reel 13.

56. Bernard I. Murstein, *Love, Sex, and Marriage through the Ages* (New York: Springer, 1974), 253.

57. AMD to PLD, March 18, 1901; AMD to PLD, March 23, 1901; AMD to PLD, April 22, 1901, all in Metcalf, "The Letters," II, 779, 792, 936, respectively.

58. PLD to AMD, April 11, 1901; PLD to AMD, April 19, 1901, both in Metcalf, "The Letters," II, 884, 924, respectively.

59. Historian Elizabeth Pleck indicates that marital rape was not uncommon in nineteenth-century relationships. See Elizabeth Pleck, "Feminist Responses to 'Crimes against Women,' 1868–1896," *Signs* 8:3 (1983), 456, 459.

60. Quoted in Elizabeth Pleck, *Domestic Tyranny: The Making of Social Policy against Family Violence from Colonial Times to the Present* (New York: Oxford University Press, 1987), 93.

61. Quoted in Diana E. H. Russell, *Rape in Marriage* (New York: Macmillan, 1982), 42.

62. On the general characteristics of husbands who rape wives, see Russell, *Rape in Marriage*, 121, 123.

63. AMD to PLD, March 22, 1898, in Metcalf, "The Letters," II, 539.

64. PLD to ARM, December 5, 1897, in Metcalf, "The Letters," I, 269.

65. PLD to ARM, November 20, 1897, in Metcalf, "The Letters," I, 255.

66. AMD to PLD, March 22, 1898, in Metcalf, "The Letters," II, 539.

67. Quoted in Metcalf, "The Letters," I, 12.

68. AMD to Matilda Dunbar, June 17, 1902, Paul Laurence Dunbar Collection, Ohio Historical Society, Microfilm Edition, reel 2. This source is hereafter referred to as PLD Collection.

69. AMD to Matilda Dunbar, June 17, 1902, PLD Collection, reel 2.

70. AMD to Matilda Dunbar, June 17, 1902, PLD Collection, reel 2.

71. AMD to Matilda Dunbar, June 17, 1902, reel 2.

72. "Dunbar Victim of Fallacy That Whiskey Cured T.B.," Philadelphia *Afro-American*, week of September 28, 1935, 13.

73. Christian A. Fleetwood to Alice Moore Dunbar, February 14, 1906, PLD Collection, reel 8.

74. Christian A. Fleetwood to Alice Moore Dunbar, February 21, 1906, PLD Collection, reel 8.

75. Christian A. Fleetwood to Alice Moore Dunbar, February 21, 1906, PLD Collection, reel 8.

76. Quoted in Metcalf, "The Letters," I, 12.

77. Quoted in Metcalf, "The Letters," I, 12.

78. Jerome Nadelhaft, "Wife Torture: A Known Phenomenon in Nineteenth-Century America," *Journal of American Culture* 10:3 (Fall 1987), 45.

79. Nadelhaft, "Wife Torture," 40–41.

80. Pleck, *Domestic Tyranny*, 109.

81. Pleck, "Wife Beating," 68–71.

82. Quoted in Metcalf, "The Letters," I, 12.

83. Quoted in Metcalf, "The Letters," I, 12.

84. PLD to Matilda Dunbar, February 2, 1902, PLD Collection. reel 2.

85. PLD to AMD, April 12, 1902, in Metcalf, "The Letters," II, 977.

86. Rose to PLD, April 29, 1902, PLD Collection, reel 1.

87. Rose to PLD, August 19, 1902, PLD Collection, reel 1.

88. Bill of W. W. Horlacher, florist, to PLD, July 1905, PLD Collection, reel 2.

89. Felton O. Best, "Crossing the Color Line: A Biography of Paul Laurence Dunbar, 1872–1906" (Ph.D. diss., Ohio State University, 1992), 203.

90. Pearle Henriksen Schultz, *Paul Laurence Dunbar: Black Poet Laureate* (Champaign, IL: Garrard, 1974), 133.

91. Gossie Hudson, "A Biography of Paul Laurence Dunbar" (Ph.D. diss., Ohio State University, 1970), 141–142. This untitled poem does not appear in Braxton, *Collected Poetry*, or Dunbar's *Complete Poems.*

92. Dunbar's poetry volumes published during this time are *Lyrics of Love and Laughter* (New York: Dodd Mead, 1903); *When Malindy Sings* (New York: Dodd, Mead, 1903); *Li'l Gal* (New York: Dodd, Mead, 1904); *Chris'mus Is A-Comin' and Other Poems* (New York: Dodd, Mead, 1905); *Howdy, Honey, Howdy* (New York: Dodd, Mead, 1905); *Lyrics of Sunshine and Shadow* (New York: Dodd, Mead, 1905); *A Plantation Portrait* (New York: Dodd, Mead, 1905).

Paul published two collections of short stories following his separation from Alice: *In Old Plantation Days* (New York: Dodd, Mead, 1903); and *The Heart of Happy Hollow* (New York: Dodd, Mead, 1904).

93. Quoted in Hudson, "A Biography," 140.

94. PLD to Matilda Dunbar, September 9, 1903, PLD Collection, reel 2.

95. Dayton Gas Light and Coke Co. to PLD, August 11, 1904, PLD Collection, reel 2.

96. Statement of the Dayton Breweries Co. to PLD, May 1, 1905, PLD Collection, reel 2.

97. The Fred Kette & Sons Co. to PLD August 1, 1905, PLD Collection, reel 2.

98. Braxton, *Collected Poetry*, xvi.

99. J. H. Finley to AMD, February 17, 1906, PLD Collection, reel 8; Tony Gentry, *Paul Laurence Dunbar* (New York: Chelsea House, 1989), 105.

100. Braxton, *Collected Poetry*, 142; also Benjamin Brawley, *Paul Laurence Dunbar: A Poet of His People* (1936) (reprint, Port Washington, NY: Kennikat, 1979), 110.

101. "Paul Dunbar: The Dead Poet Laureate's Solemn Funeral Service," Cleveland *Gazette,* February 17, 1906, 1.

102. Alice M. Dunbar, "Wordsworth's Use of Milton's Description of Pandemonium," *Modern Language Notes* (1909). Cited in Hull, *The Works of Alice Dunbar-Nelson,* III, lviii.

103. Hull, *Works of Alice Dunbar-Nelson,* III, 33–50, 196–203, 203–231.

104. Hull, *Works of Alice Dunbar-Nelson,* II, 42.

105. Publishing House of Barnes and Company to AMD, February 18, 1903, PLD Collection, reel 8.

106. See, for example, Hull, *Works of Alice Dunbar-Nelson,* III, 166, 176.

107. Alice M. Dunbar, *Masterpieces of Negro Eloquence* (Harrisburg, PA: Douglass Publishing, 1914); Alice Dunbar-Nelson, *The Dunbar Speaker and Entertainer* (Naperville, IL: J. L. Nichols, 1920).

108. Gloria Hull, ed., *Give Us Each Day: The Diary of Alice Dunbar-Nelson* (New York: Norton, 1984), 121, 93.

109. Hull, *Give Us Each Day,* 171.

110. Hull, *Give Us Each Day,* 243.

111. Hull, *Give Us Each Day,* 362.

112. Hull, *Give Us Each Day,* 24.

113. "Body of One-Time Wife of Dunbar Is Cremated," Philadelphia *Afro-American,* week of September 28, 1935, 1; "Body of Mrs. Nelson," Philadelphia *Afro-American,* week of September 28, 1935, 13. See also "One-Time Wife of Paul Laurence Dunbar Is Critically Ill," Philadelphia *Afro-American,* week of September 21, 1935, 1.

114. "Body of Mrs. Nelson," 13.

Notes to the Conclusion

1. Paul Laurence Dunbar to Matilda Dunbar, February 18, 1897, Paul Laurence Dunbar Collection, Ohio Historical Society, Microfilm Edition, reel 1.

2. Paul Laurence Dunbar to Alice Ruth Moore, February 27, 1898, in Eugene W. Metcalf, "The Letters of Paul and Alice Dunbar: A Private History," 2 vols. (Ph.D. diss., University of California, Irvine, 1972), II, 497. This source is cited hereafter as Metcalf, "The Letters." The principals are cited as PLD (Paul Laurence Dunbar) and AMD (Alice Moore Dunbar). Prior to her marriage, Alice is cited as ARM (Alice Ruth Moore).

3. Kathleen Barry, *Susan B. Anthony: A Biography of a Singular Feminist* (New York: New York University Press, 1988), 227.

4. AMD to PLD, September 13, 1898, in Metcalf, "The Letters," II, 675.

5. W. T. B. Williams to John Hope, November 12, 1899, The Papers of John

and Lugenia Burns Hope, ed. Alton Hornsby, (Frederick, MD: University Publications of America, 1984), Microfilm Edition, reel 13. This source is hereafter cited as Papers of John and Lugenia.

6. W. T. B. Williams to John Hope, September 17, 1898; W. T. B. Williams to John Hope, November 12, 1899; W. T. B. Williams to John Hope, December 1899, in Papers of John and Lugenia, reel 13.

BIBLIOGRAPHY

Primary Texts

Manuscript Collections

Benjamin Brawley Collection. Moorland-Spingarn Center, Howard University.

Harlan, Louis, and Raymond W. Smock, eds. *The Booker T. Washington Papers.* Urbana: University of Illinois Press, 1977.

John Brown Watson Collection. Jay Hay Library, Brown University.

Life and Works of Paul Laurence Dunbar. Dayton Public Library, Microfilm Edition.

Papers of John and Lugenia Burns Hope, ed. Alton Hornsby. Frederick, MD: University Publications of America, 1984. Microfilm Edition.

Papers of W. E. B. Du Bois. University of Massachusetts at Amherst. Microfilm Edition.

Paul Laurence Dunbar Collection. Ohio Historical Society. Microfilm Edition.

Paul Laurence Dunbar Collection. Schomburg Center for Research on Black Culture, New York Public Library.

Newspapers

Afro-American

Baltimore *Ledger*

Boston *Daily Standard*

Cleveland *Gazette*

Denver *Colorado Statesman*

Dunbar News

New York *Age*

New York *Sun*

Philadelphia *Afro-American*

San Francisco *Western Outlook*

Texas Freeman

Woman's Era

Public Documents

Birth Certificate of Alice Moore. Recorder of Births, Marriages and Deaths, in and for the Parish and City of New Orleans (1875). No. 974.

Birth Certificate of Mary Moore. Recorder of Births, Marriages and Deaths, in and for the Parish and City of New Orleans (1869). No. 389.

Soards' New Orleans City Directory for 1874. New Orleans: L. Soards Co., 1874.

Soards' New Orleans City Directory for 1876. New Orleans: L. Soards, n. d.

Soards' New Orleans City Directory for 1877. New Orleans: L. Soards, n. d.

Soards' New Orleans City Directory for 1880. New Orleans: L. Soards, n. d.

Soards' New Orleans City Directory for 1883. New Orleans: L. Soards, n. d.

Soards' New Orleans City Directory for 1887. New Orleans: L. Soards, n. d.

Soards' New Orleans City Directory for 1892. New Orleans: L. Soards, n. d.

Soards' New Orleans City Directory for 1895. New Orleans: L. Soards, n. d.

United States Bureau of the Census. *Historical Statistics of the United States: Colonial Times to 1970*. Washington, DC: U.S. Department of Commerce, 1975.

United States Department of Commerce. Bureau of the Census. *10ᵗʰ Census (1880)*. Vol. 8, Enumeration District 9. 2nd Ward, Orleans Parish.

United States Department of Commerce and Labor. Bureau of the Census. *Marriage and Divorce, 1867–1906*. 2 vols. Washington, DC: U.S. Government Printing Office, 1909.

Articles and Essays

"Body of Mrs. Nelson." Philadelphia *Afro-American*, week of September 28, 1935, 13.

"Body of One-Time Wife of Dunbar Is Cremated." Philadelphia *Afro-American*, week of September 28, 1935, 1.

"Color Prejudice in Washington." *Colored American*, February 2, 1902, 8.

Crummell, Alexander. "The Care of Daughters." *Tracts for the Negro Race*. Washington, DC: N. p., 1899.

———. "Marriage a Duty." *Tracts for the Negro Race*. Washington, D.C.: N.p., 1899.

"Divorce." *A.M.E. Church Review* 8:4 (April 1892): 504–508.

Dunbar, Paul Laurence. "Just Whistle a Bit." *A.M.E. Church Review* (October 1896): 228.

———. "Negro Society in Washington." *Saturday Evening Post* 174 (December 14, 1901): 9.

Dunbar-Nelson, Alice. "People of Color in Louisiana. Part 1." *Journal of Negro History* 1:4 (October 1916): 361–376.

"Dunbar Victim of Fallacy That Whiskey Cured T.B." Philadelphia *Afro-American*, week of September 28, 1935, 13.

Harper, Ida Husted. "Let Love Be Controlled." *Independent* 53 (June 27, 1901): 1477–1480.

Hart, Lavinia. "How to Win a Man." *Cosmopolitan* 35 (Sept. 1903): 548–553.

"Here and There." *Colored American Magazine*, September 1900, 258.

"How to Keep Women at Home." *Colored American Magazine,* January 1908, 7–8.

Johns, Jasper. "Body of One-Time Wife of Dunbar Is Cremated." Philadelphia *Afro-American,* week of September 28, 1935, 2.

Johnson, James H. A. "Woman's Exalted Station." *A.M.E. Church Review* 8:4 (April 1892): 402–406.

Johnson, Wiletta. "A Southern City." *A.M.E. Church Review* (July 1893): 163–171.

Jones, Anna H. "The American Colored Woman." *Voice of the Negro* 2 (October 1905): 692–694.

Lee, M. E. Mrs. "The Home-Maker." *A.M.E. Church Review* 8:1 (July 1891): 63–66.

Moore, Alice Ruth. "Midnight." *A.M.E. Church Review* (October 1896): 226–227.

"A Negro Tragedy." *Alexander's Monthly,* September 15, 1906, 14.

"One-Time Wife of Paul Laurence Dunbar Is Critically Ill." Philadelphia *Afro-American,* week of September 21, 1935.

"Paul Dunbar. The Dead Poet Laureate's Solemn Funeral Services." Cleveland *Gazette,* February 17, 1906, 1.

Pearson, Paul M. "Paul Laurence Dunbar." *Talent* 16 (March 1906): 12–13, 26.

Petty, C. C. Mrs. "What Role Is the Educated Negro Woman to Play in the Uplifting of Her Race?" In *Twentieth-Century Negro Literature,* ed. Daniel Wallace Culp (1902). Reprint, New York: Arno, 1969.

Scruggs, L. A. "Influence of Negro Women in the Home." In *Women of Distinction: Remarkable Women in Works and Invincible in Character.* Raleigh, N.C.: The Author, 1893.

"A Southern Authoress." Undated news article. 1895(?) Paul Laurence Dunbar Collection, Ohio Historical Society. Microfilm Edition, reel 7.

"The Story of Paul Laurence Dunbar by a Southerner." Installment VI. Undated news article. Benjamin Brawley Collection, Moorland-Spingarn Research Center.

Taylor, E. B. "When Dunbar Came to Baltimore." *Afro-American,* October 7, 1933.

Terrell, Mary Church. "What Role Is the Educated Negro Woman to Play in the Uplifting of Her Race?" In *Twentieth-Century Negro Literature,* ed. Daniel Wallace Culp (1902). Reprint. New York: Arno, 1969.

———. "Society among the Colored People of Washington." *Voice of the Negro,* April 1904, 150–156.

Tillman, Katherine Davis. "Afro-American Women and Their Work." *A.M.E. Church Review* 11 (April 189?): 477–499.

Whittle, Gilberta S. "Paul Dunbar." *A.M.E. Church Review* 18 (April 1902): 327.

"You Will Solve Your Own Problems." Baltimore *Ledger,* December 24, 1898, unpaged.

Books, Diaries, and Dissertations

Anthony, Arthe A. "The Negro Creole Community in New Orleans, 1880–1920." Ph.D. diss., University of California, Irvine, 1978.

Best, Felton O. "Crossing the Color Line: A Biography of Paul Laurence Dunbar, 1872–1906." Ph.D. diss., Ohio State University, 1992.

Boyd, Rubie. "An Appreciation of Paul Laurence Dunbar." Unpublished manuscript. The Life and Works of Paul Laurence Dunbar, Dayton Public Library. Microfilm Edition.

Brodhead, Richard, ed. *The Journals of Charles Chesnutt.* Durham, N.C.: Duke University Press, 1993.

Cable, George Washington. *Madame Delphine.* New York: Charles Scribner's Sons, 1881.

Catalogue of Straight University, New Orleans, LA., 1894–95. New Orleans: University Press, 1895.

Catalogue of Straight University, New Orleans, LA., 1897–98. New Orleans: University Press, 1898.

Conover, Charlotte Reeve. *Some Dayton Saints and Prophets.* N.p.: N.p., 1907.

Cooper, Anna Julia. *A Voice from the South* (1892). Reprint, New York: Negro Universities Press, 1969.

Coppin, L. J. Bishop. *Unwritten History* (1919). Reprint, New York: Negro Universities Press, 1968.

Corrothers, James D. *In Spite of the Handicap: An Autobiography* (1916). Reprint, Freeport, NY: Books for Libraries, 1971.

Culp, Daniel Wallace, ed. *Twentieth-Century Negro Literature* (1902). Reprint, New York: Arno, 1969.

DeCosta-Willis, Miriam, ed. *The Memphis Diary of Ida B. Wells.* Boston: Beacon, 1995.

Dunbar, Alice. *The Goodness of St. Rocque and Other Stories.* New York: Dodd, Mead, 1899.

———. *Masterpieces of Negro Eloquence.* Harrisburg, PA: Douglass Publishing, 1914.

Dunbar, Paul Laurence. *Oak and Ivy.* Dayton, OH: Press of the United Brethren Publishing House, 1893.